WHERE TWO
OR THREE
ARE
GATHERED

D0254953

WHERE TWO OR THREE ARE GATHERED

CHRISTIAN FAMILIES AS DOMESTIC CHURCHES

Florence Caffrey Bourg

University of Notre Dame Press
Notre Dame, Indiana

Manufactured in the United States of America

Library of Congress Cataloging-in-Publication Data
Bourg, Florence Caffrey.
Where two or three are gathered : Christian families as domestic
churches / Florence Caffrey Bourg.
p.   cm.
Includes bibliographical references (p.   ) and index.
ISBN 0-268-04405-8 (cloth)
ISBN 0-268-02179-1 (pbk.)
1. Family—Religious aspects—Catholic Church.   2. Marriage—Religious
aspects—Catholic Church.   3. Pastoral theology—Catholic Church.
4. Catholic Church—Doctrines.   I. Title.
BX2351.B66   2004
261.8'3585—dc22
2003024969

∞ *This book is printed on acid-free paper.*

To my grandmothers

May Isabella Russell

and

Florence Rita Caffrey

who shared their faith with my parents, Robert and Joanne,
and thus laid the foundation for my own domestic church.

CONTENTS

CONTENTS

ACKNOWLEDGMENTS

This book began as my doctoral dissertation at Boston College. Professors in many areas of expertise guided me in both the book-learning and the practical wisdom needed to write on a subject which cuts across disciplines. I am grateful for a doctoral committee—Lisa Sowle Cahill, Stephen Pope, and Rev. Michael Himes—who were open to an interdisciplinary project such as this, who worked together well, provided useful criticism, and steered me through my writing (and rewriting) in a timely manner. Lisa Cahill, my director, was especially attuned to my need for emotional support and practical advice as I negotiated a dissertation and job search with two preschool children in tow. Other faculty who provided feedback on pieces of this project during its formative stages include Thomas Groome, James Keenan, S.J., and Francis Sullivan, S.J. My thanks as well to Bill Roberts and Joann Heaney-Hunter, who reviewed a preliminary book manuscript and graciously offered advice and encouragement to this young scholar.

I am grateful for moral support from many Boston College faculty who encouraged me to stick with this project even when the light at the end of the tunnel seemed very dim, but special mention goes to Thomas Wangler, Rev. Matthew Lamb, and Francis Clooney, S.J. I am indebted to several friends who repeatedly lent their time and expertise to help my outdated computer (and its technically challenged owner) make it through the dissertation. They are Bob Barry, Tom Kelly, Ann-Marie Gorman, and Chris Rossano.

This project materialized out of my interest in the ecclesial context of moral formation, but equally out of need to strike out a relatively peaceful coexistence between my academic vocation and my other vocation as "Mommy." My two older children, Seth and Molly, were as patient and encouraging as little children could be for the years that Mommy needed to complete her dissertation. Through the additional years that passed as the dissertation was revised into a book, two more daughters, Cecilia and Elise, have joined our little house church. With these four wonderful children in my life, I have been challenged to consistently practice the faith that I profess, and I am (I hope better able to assess whether my ideas about domestic church are true to life. My friend and colleague, Julie Hanlon Rubio, shared insight on the validity of a "dual vocation" among Christian parents, and helped me sort through the mixture of positive and negative emotions shared by so many working mothers.

I am grateful for friends, babysitters, and preschool and elementary-school teachers who have cared for my children when I needed to work alone. In particular, I thank my sister Mary Caffrey, who took Seth and Molly off my hands (during her own maternity leave) for a critical week that I needed to finish the dissertation, and my sister-in-law, Kathy Bourg, who traveled from New York to Cincinnati to provide childcare during a critical week that I needed to complete the book manuscript. My employer, the College of Mount Saint Joseph, provided a summer research grant in 2002, which helped pay for childcare I needed in order to make final revisions to the manuscript. I am grateful for my parents, my in-laws, and my grandmothers (who did not live to see this project through to completion). They have cheered me on in my academic pursuits, and they have given me rich and diverse examples of domestic churches living through good times and bad.

It would be impossible to enumerate the gifts of emotional and practical support that have been given by my husband, Michael. A household with four young children and two parents working full-time is a lot to manage. I can't count the number of times a professional colleague or student has told me, "I don't know how you do it!" My usual reply is that my husband's cooperation makes it all possible. Still very hectic, but possible. Michael is also a model—for our family and for many who know him—of a Christian whose faith informs his life on a full-time basis. He has taught me much about the virtues of fidelity, patience, generosity, faith, hope, and charity.

Some of the material in this book has been adapted from previously published articles, listed in the bibliography. In particular, chapter 11 is a revised and expanded version of my "The Family Home as the Place of Religious Formation," and chapter 12 is a revised and expanded version of my "Family as a 'Missing Link' in Bernardin's Consistent Life Ethic."

Introduction

The family is, so to speak, the domestic church.[1]

Catholicism has begun talking about Christian families in a distinctive way—as *domestic churches*. The trend has grown, slowly but steadily, since the term was retrieved by the Second Vatican Council and inserted into the *Dogmatic Constitution on the Church*. What does this expression mean? As the U.S. bishops put it in their 1994 pastoral, *Follow the Way of Love,* "The point of the teaching is simple, yet profound. As Christian families, you not only belong to the Church, but your daily life is a true expression of the Church."[2] Christian families are "two or three gathered in Christ's name." In them, Christ is present. They become his body, his Church: they make Christ present in the world. In the words of John Paul II's *Familiaris Consortio,* each Christian family is a "living image and historical representation of the mystery of the Church. . . . they not only *receive* the love of Christ and become a *saved* community; but they are also called upon to *communicate* Christ's love to their brethren, thus becoming a *saving* community."[3] By any estimation, this is pretty provocative language.

1

Particularly remarkable is the fact that this distinctive way of thinking and talking about Christian families is not confined to official Church documents, or to academic theology, or to resources for pastoral ministers, or to popular reading for believers. References to domestic church are found in all these genres. Moreover, authors who invoke the idea of domestic church come from many countries and continents, and from everywhere on the ideological spectrum. It is true that many authors who allude to the idea of domestic church do not make it the central focus of their writing, but this need not reflect poorly on the idea itself. Indeed, the idea of domestic church gains credibility or significance when we consider the range of authors and writings that have used the expression, however briefly. Their fields of interest include biblical studies, ecumenism, religious education, canon law, spirituality, ecclesiology and inculturation of the church, sacramental theology, feminist theology, and social justice.

There are probably several reasons why such diverse constituencies have taken up the idea of domestic church. In keeping with the twin postconciliar principles of *ressourcement* and *aggiornamento,* it has both a good pedigree and a trendy quality. The idea has scriptural and patristic roots, and it has precedent in Orthodox theology and among some Protestant authors. Thus, it has timely ecumenical value among Christians of East and West. But perhaps the most important reason the expression has been so widely received is that it lends an important measure of affirmation to many people's most treasured and formative experiences. It seems to articulate and honor the unrecognized efforts of Christians amongst their families as they try to discern and obey God's will, and to provide Christian witness in their particular neighborhood and walk of life.

Increasing, widespread interest in domestic church presents a consensus-building opportunity that cannot be taken for granted and should not be wasted. Domestic church presently lacks much of the richness of similar symbolic concepts, for Christians have not lived with it long enough or critically enough. The time is ripe to explore the nascent idea with the full array of theological resources at our disposal. This is one reason this book was undertaken. On the other hand, it would be an overstatement to say that authors who invoke the idea of domestic church are of one mind as to the significance of this term or its practical implications. Before consensus can be built, lack of consensus needs to be clarified. This is a second, perhaps more compelling, reason for the book.

This study accomplishes two goals: to assemble and analyze literature on domestic church from Vatican II to the present, and to redress what one author has aptly referred to as a "doctrinal vacuum" surrounding the term in Catholicism.[4] My reflections have been steered by two concerns: first, the need to articulate ordinary family life as a sphere of grace and a medium of encounter between humans and God; second, my long-standing interest in the relationship of family and larger Church in moral and spiritual formation. This book formulates the role of the family as the basic cell of society and of Church in character education, formation of religious identity and vision, and creation of just social structures. It provides a foundational treatment of Christian family life—which has all too often been relegated, somewhat disparagingly, to the practical or pastoral divisions of theology—as a proper concern of systematic theology, especially ecclesiology. Finally, it makes a conscious effort to concentrate attention on *family* as a distinct entity—related to, but not synonymous with, marriage.

Besides addressing a recognized need of the Catholic Church *ad intra*, this book will provide a Catholic perspective on a broader contemporary conversation on the family. In the American context there is great interest—secular and religious, popular and academic—in promoting the fullest possible human flourishing through strategic intervention at the level of family life.[5] I do not intend this investigation to be a commentary on any single theory of family. However, I will contrast my perspective on family as domestic church with viewpoints that I believe suffer from impoverished understanding of human nature, inflexibly hierarchical vision of the relationship of spouses, lack of appreciation for the sanctity of ordinary family activities or for the lay vocation, absence of moral norms, or failure to present families as morally obliged to protect and promote the common good.

The book begins by recounting how the idea of domestic church was revived in Catholic thought and then addresses the question of sources—whom should we consult for insight into domestic church? Chapter 2 treats the question, "What kind of term is domestic church?" Is it a juridical term, or a symbolic expression, or both? Chapters 3 through 8 will survey existing literature that treats domestic church, as well as selected literature on Christian family life that does not mention the term explicitly. My goal will be to identify points of consensus regarding domestic church as well as unsettled or disputed issues surrounding the concept. Thus a framework will exist onto which new insights will be added in succeeding chapters. Issues to be covered include the relationship between individual domestic churches and the larger church, the religious significance of ordinary life, the dynamic between ideal images of family life and actual life; identifying features of domestic churches; theologies of baptism and marriage as sources of insight into domestic church; and the mission of domestic churches in view of God's plan for humanity. One area of consensus regarding domestic church is that it has a crucial *educational* role. Although education is not the only lens through which domestic church may be seen, it is the one of most ongoing interest to me. Attention to this role will influence all chapters of this volume.

Following analysis of existing literature, I offer several chapters of what I consider more creative, constructive theology. Because my overall aim is to redress the doctrinal vacuum surrounding domestic church, I will articulate the meaning of domestic church by bringing this idea into conversation with several established, potent, and distinctive concepts of Roman Catholic theological tradition: sacramentality, virtue, and the consistent ethic of life. Most educated observers would recognize these as integral themes of Roman Catholic theology. As yet, though, there is very little scholarship available that explores any of these core concepts in conjunction with the specific term domestic church. Fortunately, however, it is fairly common for contemporary theologians writing on sacramentality, virtue, and life issues to mention family life in connection with their primary terms of focus. My approach will be the opposite—to make the lives of Christian families, understood as domestic churches, the primary focal point, and then to organize and creatively connect insights that sacramental, virtue, and life-ethic theologies yield for Christian living in the context of family. These constructive chapters demonstrate Catholicism's appreciation for the potentially sacred significance of ordinary activity—which is seen with the eyes of faith—and insistence that this potential not be taken lightly. Mature members of Christian families should make it their mission to bring new initiates to embrace this faith-based vision. I propose that these core concepts, brought to bear on the emerging concept of domestic church, provide a rich, and perhaps unique, appreciation of the religious importance of family life.

ONE

Why Do We Need Theology of Domestic Church?

This marvelous teaching was underemphasized for centuries but reintroduced by the Second Vatican Council. Today we are still uncovering its rich treasure.[1]

Have you ever had the experience of meeting with someone you had last seen as a child or young adult, perhaps ten or fifteen years ago? You can recognize a familiar face, perhaps a familiar voice or other traits—it is still the same person you knew before. And yet, a metamorphosis has occurred: "You're so grown up! I can hardly believe it!" Perhaps the girl you remember as an aimless, self-conscious preteen has turned out to be a confident adult, engaged in responsible work in her profession, family, and neighborhood, and able to see that there is more to life than the narrow range of concerns that absorbed her attention before. Perhaps the boy who never seemed to accomplish anything has finally found his niche in life, with the combination of ingenuity and support from a few trusted friends who stuck by him when no one else saw much potential. When someone you had not paid attention to for years, or someone you thought would never accomplish anything special, or someone you had put in a certain category surprises you in this way, it is a wonderful thing.

Over the past generation or two, something similar has been happening in Catholic discourse on family life. It is beginning to mature to its full potential. The metamorphosis has been slow, and it is hardly complete, but it is striking and hopeful. Thoughtful Christians are realizing and voicing the fact that ordinary family life need not be a distraction from God—in fact, it can be the setting where God's presence is made real and concrete. They are recognizing the untapped potential of family life as an outlet for their Christian vocation. Speaking of Christian families as domestic churches is one way of naming these discoveries. Unless you know how Catholicism has depicted family life through history, it is hard to appreciate the significance of the label "domestic church."[2]

To provide a before-and-after demonstration, I begin my college course on theology of marriage by distributing photocopies of a lesson on "vocations" from the 1962 illustrated edition of the *Baltimore Catechism*.[3] The text and the visual images are startling. Three pairs of pictures, meant to contrast secular life with religious life based on the evangelical counsels, are grouped under two headings—on the left, "This is Good"; on the right, "This is Better." The pictures on the right show priests and vowed religious sisters and brothers; those on the left show the secular life. For the pair of pictures depicting chastity, a sister dressed in a habit kneels before a glowing crucifix and says, "I choose Christ as my spouse." The accompanying picture on the left shows a couple at their wedding: "I want to marry the person of my choice." On the right, illustrating the vow of obedience, two men in cassocks read a list of assignments on a bulletin board, commenting, "I want to spend the day the way God prefers." On the left, a picture of a family at the breakfast table (with mother pouring the milk for father) is captioned, "I want to spend the day the way I think best." For poverty—on the left, a group of children look in a store window: "I want an air rifle. I want a car. I want jewels. I want pretty clothes." On the right, St. Francis kneels before an appearance of Jesus floating in a cloud: "You can have all that: I want Christ."

Although the catechism lesson states that "[t]he comparison between religious and secular life is not a comparison between good and evil, but between good and better," my students are convinced otherwise. They cannot read the lesson as anything other than an insult to people who do not become celibate priests, brothers, or sisters. Basically, the catechism tells them that secular life is for people who are selfish, people who don't put God first in their lives. My older students, many of whom were teens or young adults in 1962, were taught that celibate religious vocations were far holier than marriage, and that marriage was not a vocation. "You got married if you *didn't* have a vocation," they say. Unfortunately, most of my younger students have absorbed the same understanding of religious vocations, Vatican II reforms notwithstanding. Few students, of any age, apply the label of vocation to marriage when they begin the course. This tends to be true even for students who are married and have been through Catholic marriage preparation. Few have ever thought of marriage and family life as equally holy to the lifestyle of celibate priests, brothers, and sisters. And few, whether single or married or parents, have ever thought of family life as a way to spend their days doing what God prefers. One of my goals for the course is to provoke my students to consider, and perhaps embrace, a different way of thinking—about family life, about what it means to have a religious vocation, about what it means to love the God you don't see by loving the people you do see, and about what it means to be a Christian on a full-time basis.

Ironically, the *Baltimore Catechism* lesson is valuable in provoking my students to think in this direction. Because of the airtight categories in their inherited religious vocabulary, few have thought about marriage and family life in religious terms before. But because they perceive the catechism as so insulting, and so negative in its assessment of their chosen or intended path in life, many feel compelled to come to the defense of the so-called secular lifestyle. Many, especially those who are parents, insist that people like themselves cannot be categorized as selfish. "I can't remember the last time I bought jewelry or new clothes. There's never a day when I can just do whatever I want to do. From morning till night, I'm constantly meeting other people's needs." Nor is it always true that family responsibilities crowd out attention to God. "I pray every day. I need God to help me get through the day. If I didn't have a family, I wouldn't have nearly as much to pray about!" "I believe God brought me and my fianceé together. And if it weren't for her, I would have never set foot in a church." "I used to tune out my parents when they said, 'You should thank God every day for what you have—don't you know there are children starving to death in Africa?' Now I find myself saying the same thing when my kids try to waste food, or complain about what they don't have. Being a parent has really opened my eyes."

My hope is that over the semester students in my marriage course will arrive at the conclusion that their inherited distinction of religious and secular life, based largely on family demographics, is a misnomer. More importantly, I hope that their eyes will be opened fully, and their ability to find God in everyday life will be expanded once their religious categories are less restrictive. It has been the idea of domestic church that has most helped my students to rethink the religious categories they had when they entered the course.

A History of the Concept's Evolution and Revival

Domestic church is a concept that directs our attention to the ecclesial character of Christian families and, conversely, the familial character of the Church.[4] Alternate expressions are "church in miniature," "church of the home," "house church," or "little church." What do these expressions mean? Broadly speaking—and in many ways, this broad perspective is most significant—the notion of domestic church is a recognition of Jesus' promise to be present wherever two or three are gathered in his name.[5] The idea of domestic church presupposes that religious activity is not confined to a sanctuary or a particular day of the week; rather, it incorporates the Pauline principle "Whatever you eat or drink—whatever you do—you should do all for the glory of God." (1 Corinthians 10:31; cf. Colossians 3:17)

Recent magisterial documents make some provocative claims about the ecclesial character of Christian families. As the U.S. Catholic bishops put it in their 1994 pastoral statement, *Follow the Way of Love*, "The point of the teaching [i.e., domestic church] is simple, yet profound. As Christian families, you not only belong to the Church, but your daily life is a true expression of the Church."[6] To suggest what they mean by "daily life as a true expression of Church," the bishops remark, "The profound and the ordinary moments of daily life—mealtimes, workdays, vacations, expressions of love and intimacy, household chores, caring for a sick child or elderly parent, and even conflicts over things like how to celebrate holidays, discipline children, or spend money—all are the threads from which you can weave a pattern of holiness."[7] Turning to Pope John Paul II's *Familiaris Consortio,* we read that each Christian family "is in its own way a living image and historical representation of the mystery of Church. . . . they not only *receive* the love of Christ and become a *saved* community; but they are also called upon to *communicate* Christ's love to their brethren, thus becoming a *saving* community."[8] Looking further back to Pope Paul VI's comments on domestic church in *Evangelii Nuntiandi,* we find, "[T]here should be found in every Christian family the various aspects of the entire Church."[9] For those who have trouble shaking the habit of thinking about Church as an ornate building, or an elite group of ordained clergy, or a spiritual sanctuary one visits on Sundays as a retreat from worldly affairs, such statements about domestic church will appear new indeed.

But the idea of domestic church is not new, even if it may appear so. Where did the concept originate? Many authors trace its scriptural roots to the Pauline Epistles (Romans 16:3–5 and 23, 1 Corinthians 16:15–20, Colossians 4:15, 2 Timothy 4:19, Philemon 1–2),[10] and by extension to the Jewish tradition of family-based religious education and worship.[11] St. Paul's letters give evidence that early communities of Christians identified themselves with particular households: "Give my greetings to Prisca and Aquila; they were my fellow workers in the service of Christ Jesus and even risked their lives for the sake of mine. Not only I but all the churches of the Gentiles are grateful to them. Remember me also to the congregation that meets in their house" (Romans 16:3–5). "You know that the household of Stephanus is the first fruits of Achaia and is devoted to the service of the saints. I urge you to serve under such men and under everyone who cooperates and toils with them" (1 Corinthians 16:15–16). A number of authors, especially in the patristic period and the present day Orthodox tradition, discuss domestic church in connection with the ecclesial significance attached to marriage in Ephesians 5:21–33. This passage reflects a pattern of marital and family imagery used throughout the Bible to describe the covenant between God and God's people, and among fellow Christians.

We know that households of the New Testament and patristic periods differed in many respects from the modern nuclear family,[12] which tends to be the focus in recent magisterial statements on domestic church.

Contemporary theologians concerned with marriage and family are still undoing the damaging gender stereotypes associated with literalist and selective readings of Ephesians 5. The modern Western mind, with its strong sense of individual autonomy, particularly in matters religious, may balk at the idea of household conversions, such as those mentioned at 1 Corinthians 1:16 and Acts 16: 25–34. With facts like these in mind, we must be nuanced in using biblical proof texts to construct a theology of domestic church. However, these texts do provide useful springboards for our discussion. They provide a healthy balance to other texts (such as Matthew 10:35–36 and 1 Corinthians 7:32–35) that have been used to instill the presumption that religious vocations necessarily draw individuals away from family, rather than incorporating family bonds and everyday lifestyle choices. They also challenge Christians to scrutinize the cultural gospel, which steers us to compartmentalize, privatize, and individualize religious life, such that it need not be a communal experience, even among members of a family.[13]

The notion of domestic church has patristic precedent among figures such as John Chrysostom, Augustine, Clement of Alexandria, and Gregory of Nazianzus.[14] For instance, in a homily on Ephesians, John Chrysostom states, "If we regulate our households [properly], . . . we will also be fit to oversee the Church, for indeed the household is a little Church. Therefore, it is possible for us to surpass all others in virtue by becoming good husbands and wives."[15] In a homily on the book of Acts, Chrysostom writes, "Let the house be a Church, consisting of men and women. . . . 'For where the two,' He saith, 'are gathered together in My Name, there am I in the midst of them.'"[16] Augustine describes Christian heads of households as having an episcopal function similar to his own: "Take my place in your families. Everyone who is head of a house must exercise the episcopal office and see to the faith of his people. . . . Take care with all watchfulness for the salvation of the members of the household entrusted to you."[17] Though we must strive for a positive theology of domestic church that matures beyond mere proof-texting, we must gratefully acknowledge that the existence of such patristic proof texts has allowed the idea of domestic church to gain a hearing among some audiences who otherwise might have dismissed the concept.[18]

Domestic church is a prominent theme in Orthodox marriage liturgy and theology; here it is typical to invoke the ecclesial symbolism attached to marriage in Ephesians 5:21–32.[19] As one of the highlights of an Ortho-dox wedding, the bride and groom are adorned with crowns. There are several symbolic meanings attached to these crowns; one is that the crowns remind the spouses of their role as rulers or leaders of their own house church.[20] In another ancient ritual, the "churching" of new mothers (forty days after childbirth), we see a vestige of ritual purification, but also a ceremonial acknowledgement of the fact that a Christian mother intro-duces her child, even before his or her baptism, into the liturgical assembly of the Church.[21] Alexander Schmemann comments, "The Christian family *belongs* to the Church, finds in the Church the source, the content, and the transcendent goal of its existence as a family. Therefore the child who belongs to the family, and in a most concrete biological sense to the mother, *thereby* belongs to the Church, is truly *her* child, already offered, already committed to God in the rite of churching."[22]

Following the patristic period, domestic church was all but forgotten in Roman Catholic theology. However, titles like "little church," or even "seminary of the church," have enjoyed favor among some Protestants. Perhaps the best-known exemplar is the American Congregationalist Horace Bushnell (1802–1876), whose book *Christian Nurture* has become a classic in the field of religious education.[23] Bushnell critiqued the domi-nant assumption of Protestant revivalism that a dramatic emotional ex-perience of conversion is the necessary mark of a true Christian. Instead, Bushnell contended that "the child is to grow up a Christian, and never know himself as being otherwise."[24] Bushnell considered Christian fami-lies as little churches and thought that family, not the larger institutional church, was the most effective medium of contact with God. He insisted, "Religion never thoroughly penetrates life until it becomes domestic."[25]

Lisa Sowle Cahill's book *Family: A Christian Social Perspective* provides analysis of Reformation-era references to domestic church, not simply as proof texts, but set in their broader theological and cultural context.[26] A few examples Cahill uncovers are these: in his commentary on one of St. Paul's "house church" texts (1 Corinthians 16:19), John Calvin remarks enthusiastically, "What a wonderful thing to put on record, that the name 'church' is applied to a single family, and yet it is fitting that all the fami-lies of believers should be organized in such a way as to be so many little churches."[27] Thomas Taylor, a seventeenth-century English Puritan, ad-vises, "Let every master of his family see to what is called, namely, to make his house a little church, to instruct every one of his family in the fear of God, to contain every one of them under his holy discipline, to pray with them and for them."[28] Thomas Martin describes the Old Order Amish as an example of a denomination that still organizes itself via house churches. For them, the basic unit of church organization is the Church district, which is defined by "the number of people who can meet for the preaching service in one dwelling house."[29]

Both Cahill and Martin clarify that these examples of domestic church were not as social-minded as current Catholic magisterial teaching encourages Christian families to be. For instance, the Amish have maintained themselves as pure communities by segregating themselves from the world, as well as by shunning those members who fall into sin after adult baptism, even members of one's own family.[30] The English Puritans made the father responsible for teaching the faith to his own family, but chastised him for reaching out to a more public audience.[31] By comparison, Cahill says, the African-American churches—both Protestant and Catholic—seem to have maintained a more consistent pattern of family-centered social outreach.[32] In *Roots of a Black Future: Family and Church,* J. Deotis Roberts concurs: "Traditionally the black church has been an extended family and the family has been a 'domestic church.' At the center of this affirmation is the Biblical image of the church as the family of God. . . . Throughout the African-American tradition the family system has been central to understanding the church—its purpose and mission. At the same time religion has been the core of fulfilled family life. Because of severe racist oppression, there have been times when the church has been a family for the homeless and times when the family altar has been a domestic church."[33]

After a very long hiatus, the expression "domestic church" found its way into Vatican II's *Dogmatic Constitution on the Church* through the persistent efforts of Bishop Pietro Fiordelli, who had been involved with the Christian Family Movement.[34] Fiordelli knew of patristic texts referring to the Christian family as "little church" or "church of the home," and to heads of households exercising an "episcopal" role; he used these texts to substantiate his proposal to include some treatment of marriage and family in the Council's statement on the Church. In the end, Fiordelli's efforts yielded only a single reference to domestic church in *Lumen Gentium.*[35]

A seed had been planted. The germination process was slow, but the soil stirred up by the Council was conducive to growth. The Council's renewed vision of Church as the "People of God," its reminder that all believers share responsibility for the Church's mission by virtue of their baptism, its recovery of the concept of "local church," its revolutionary description of marriage as a vocation, its commissioning of the Church to immerse itself in the world as a leaven and servant—these were to become the support system for a developing theology of the Christian family as domestic church.

Immediately following Vatican II, appeals to the notion of domestic church remained relatively uncommon. Besides Paul VI's brief reference to the term in *Evangelii Nuntiandi* in 1975, and John Paul II's citation in *Catechesi Tradendae* in 1979,[36] a few pamphlets and articles devoted to the subject of domestic church can be found from the period between Vatican II and Pope John Paul II's *Familiaris Consortio* in 1981. Of these, most of the more extensive and scholarly pieces come from Europe.[37] The 1980 Synod of Bishops[38] and release of *Familiaris Consortio* in 1981 marked a turning point in the theological revival of domestic church. The idea, which had often appeared in John Paul II's speeches and weekly general audiences, now became a more prominent feature in his writings.[39] The U.S. bishops followed by exploring the idea of domestic church in *A Family Perspective in Church and Society* in 1988 and in *Follow the Way of Love* in 1994. The term appeared a few times in the 1994 *Catechism of the Catholic Church*.[40] Also in 1994, the Special Assembly of the Synod of Bishops for Africa chose "Church as family" as its guiding ecclesiological model, particularly for efforts at evangelization through small Christian communities. This event prompted a number of thoughtful essays from the African continent that examine pastoral and ecclesiological implications of the idea of domestic church.[41] Through the 1980s and 1990s remarks concerning domestic church became more common in Catholic literature from the fields of family spirituality and pastoral theology. Contributions of academic theology toward a deeper understanding of domestic church emerged more slowly, but interest has grown dramatically in recent years.[42]

The character of these various contributions is mixed. Some authors devote an entire essay to domestic church; many others only a few sentences. Some sources are creative and theologically sophisticated; others simply acknowledge magisterial recognition of domestic churches without adding much new insight. Judging by their citations, it seems many of these authors are largely unaware of other scholars' writings on the theme of domestic church. While this is unfortunate, the fact that so many authors have discovered and embraced the idea of domestic church relatively independently of each other reveals something very positive about the concept. Somehow it seems to speak to a shared religious experience.

Regrettably, there is still some recent theology of the Christian family that gives little or no consideration to domestic church. For instance, Carlo Caffara's 1985 essay, "The Ecclesial Identity and Mission of the Family," never uses the term.[43] Almost as disappointing is Angelo Scola's 1997 essay, "Formation of Priests in Pastoral Care of the Family," which in twenty-five pages intends "to ensure that marriage and family become an integral dimension of pastoral and intellectual formation" of seminarians but mentions domestic church only once.[44]

Perhaps more regrettably, longstanding theological disputes concerning sexuality, divorce, and gender roles seem to stifle the imagination when it comes to theology of family and domestic church, confining it to a narrow range of topics. [45] One example is William E. May's chapter on domestic church in his *Marriage: The Rock on Which the Family is Built*— it is preoccupied with defending natural forms of birth control, which in his mind seem to be the crucial identifying feature of domestic churches.[46]

On the other end of the ideological spectrum, a constrained understanding of domestic church is seen in the summary report of a 1992 NCCB colloquium. Here, some participants did not find the expression meaningful because it appeared to them as judgmental of "nontraditional" family structures.[47] However, African and Hispanic Americans in attendance at the meeting "found the concept and the teaching considerably less problematic." Why? "If the symbol of domestic church appears to be exclusive and to absolutize the nuclear family, they suggested, it is not because the concept itself is limiting, but rather because Anglo culture has too restricted an appreciation of family. When faith and culture are more intertwined, and when family is understood to have more extended, flexible boundaries, the church and the home need not be antithetical."[48] It would be unfortunate if we allowed conservative and progressive camps to constrict nascent theology of domestic church along the lines of their pre-existing turf battles.

In sum, the Church as a whole has barely begun to articulate the significance of domestic church. As recently as 1995, Michael Fahey remarked, "Despite the theological correctness of Catholicism's reappropriation of the family as 'domestic church,' the teaching is formulated in a doctrinal vacuum that fails to address serious issues that need to be articulated in dialogue with sociologists, psychologists, and demographers, to name only a few."[49] The increasingly popular expression is intuitively recognized as important, but remains lacking in precision and depth of meaning. Whatever usefulness this concept might have, either descriptive or prescriptive, thus remains largely untapped, and there is risk that the term may be invoked to validate anything and everything, without discretion. A systematic analysis of domestic church in relationship to core concepts of Catholicism is needed.

For instance, "Church" is a concept on which vast quantities of theological reflection have been done. But it is not immediately clear how expositions of models of the Church, marks of the Church, or the nature and mission of the Church are transferable to Christian families considered as domestic churches. Mitch and Kathy Finley lament,

> An important insight in the teachings of the Second Vatican Council has been neglected by virtually every major theologian whose subject has been theology of the church. Little if any awareness is found in their writings of the value of the conciliar teaching that the family constitutes "the domestic church." Theologians tend to ignore this idea, or mention it only in passing with a very limited understanding of its implications for both families and the church as a whole. . . . Christian tradition clearly teaches that the family—in its various forms—is an authentic and indispensable form of church. Yet the notion that the family is the most basic cell of ecclesial life has had little impact on the life of the average Catholic. It has had almost no effect on most parishes. . . . Now and then a diocese has latched onto the idea of calling the church a "family" at fund-raising time. But only recently have there been efforts to benefit from the ancient teaching that the family is *ecclesia*, the foundational church.[50]

How Might Theology Contribute to Our Understanding of Domestic Church?

The slow pace at which theology of domestic church has emerged may well be due to neglect, as suggested by Mitch and Kathy Finley. Because the term is associated with marriage and family, and thus with the practical or pastoral divisions of theology, many scholars who focus their work on other branches of theology may not be adequately exposed to it.

On the other hand, the time lag could be viewed as appropriate. If an expression such as domestic church is truly rich, as many authors who employ it agree, we can expect it will take experience, time, and critical, self-conscious reflection for its significance to become fully apparent and to be explained systematically. In his preparatory paper for the 1992 NCCB colloquium on domestic church, Ennio Mastrioianni regards statements on marriage and family in *Lumen Gentium* #11 as a "seed text"— a "cluster of sentences laden with meaning and potential for ongoing theological reflection."[51] Re-emergence of the idea of domestic church might be compared to the development of ideas of the Trinity, the incarnation, or the real presence of Christ in the Eucharist. These originated in religious experiences that were intuitively recognized as giving insight for peoples' lives. People searched for words to convey their experiences and the insights revealed in them, and over time certain theological concepts have emerged as especially adequate to make sense of shared experiences. Future reflection on domestic church might fruitfully take up theological themes such as incarnation, communion, sacrament, *sensus fidei, imago dei,* nature/grace, secular/sacred, vocation, discipleship, ministry, and evangelization.

Theology does more than simply describe patterns of belief; it also evaluates a faith community's articulated beliefs for consistency with each other and with lived experience. History has shown us the evaluative or prescriptive benefits of theology on many occasions. For instance, appreciation of Jesus (and, by extension, the Church) as truly human has led to increased willingness to incorporate the human sciences in Christian theology and pastoral practice, and indigenous cultural customs in worship. We can expect that as Christians experiment in living deliberately as domestic churches, and as theologians critically connect this concept with others in the tradition, new directives will emerge and be tested. Already, suggestions include:

- family impact studies of all parish and diocesan programs[52]
- more involvement of families in official Church discernment, teaching, and governance[53]
- refashioning of marriage preparation along the model of the RCIA (Rite of Christian Initiation of Adults) formation process[54]
- revised attitudes toward interdenominational Christian marriages and shared Eucharist among interchurch families[55]
- alternate styles of worship[56]
- reformulation of catechesis to be more adult-centered or adult-and-child-centered.[57]

SOURCES OF EXPERTISE REGARDING DOMESTIC CHURCH— FROM THE TOP DOWN OR THE BOTTOM UP?

Who is the most reliable source of knowledge concerning domestic church—bishops and popes who have reintroduced the term through their official statements? Theologians, pastoral ministers, and spiritual authors? Or average Christian families, most of whom have never heard the expression?[58] If we opt to bring testimony of these groups together, how do we do justice to both the collected wisdom of tradition and continuing experience of Christian living? What conclusions can be reached at points where these groups seem to be carrying on separate conversations or confronting each other in clear disagreement? I employ testimony of all these groups in my reflections on domestic church. Given the sensitive methodological questions involved, the validity of this investigation requires that I give extra attention to justifying my choices.

Roman Catholic theological and magisterial tradition has several qualities that may appear to compromise its expertise on contemporary family life. Its natural-law commitments, along with principles of catholicism and apostolicity, amount to an assertion that, underlying everything unique in humans of various times and places, the most important human values are timeless. These convictions, along with the deductive reasoning style characteristic of much Roman Catholic thought, present at first glance an uneasy fit with the awareness of historical and cultural diversity so prominent in contemporary discussion of family life.

Even more peculiar is that Roman Catholicism has a history of separation (both perceived and real) between celibate male clergy in positions of theological and hierarchical leadership, and the laity whom they lead. There is an easy temptation to assume that lifestyles of Roman Catholic leaders and their flocks are so different that clergy have little or no expertise to offer where family matters are concerned. In this line of reasoning, knowledge is regarded as the product of direct experience, and experiential knowledge is regarded as the basis of teaching authority. Therefore, Roman Catholic clergy without firsthand experiences of marriage and parenthood lack the most important resource needed to make knowledgeable and authoritative judgments concerning family life. Thus, some people might say it is presumptuous, or even manipulative, for celibate men with all their material needs met by others to assume any expertise in directing the lives of average families struggling to get by in the real world, let alone assert universal principles or goals of family life. Re-emergence of the notion of domestic church has coincided with development of feminist and other experience-based critiques of historically and culturally blind generalizations regarding human nature, especially roles within families. However, in existing literature on domestic church, the question of how to make historically conscious generalizations regarding family life is not often dealt with in detail. The U.S. bishops show awareness of the issue in their 1992 colloquium statement, but in that forum gave it only limited attention:

> [T]he church's teaching about domestic church is historically and culturally rooted in an understanding of family different from our own (at least in Western society) today. In earlier ages, the family was less an affective and interpersonal domain and much more a unit for broad social and economic purposes. In the early church, the "family" which was viewed as domestic church was actually a household consisting of related and unrelated family members. Our challenge today is to find new life in a theological concept which originated against a different horizon of experience.

But, just as we cannot be constrained by family models of an earlier historical period, neither can we allow today's experience and expectations of family life to exhaust the possible meaning of domestic church. . . . In general, it is important to maintain a "critical edge" or "hermeneutic of suspicion" when constructing a theology of the domestic church. There must be an ongoing and critical reflection between the data of our experience and the data of our Christian tradition and scriptures.[59]

The U.S. bishops also recognize the assumption that their unusual station in life makes expertise in family matters completely out of their reach. They aim to correct this distortion in *Follow the Way of Love* by describing their experiences as brothers, sons, and uncles who have known both the joys and hardships of family life.[60]

When celibate male theologians and bishops teach or give advice, they inevitably draw upon their life experiences. Their experiences will include some things shared in common with the average member of their audience (growing up in a family, experiencing themselves as moral agents both limited and free) and others more unusual (reading lots of theological books, adopting the evangelical counsels as a way of life). Of course, they will not have shared every life experience of persons they address. But this fact, in itself, need not render them incompetent to provide guidance. Like other leaders and populations they serve, they share a general knowledge of themselves as human beings. Like leaders in other fields, they can study experiences and histories of populations they serve, so as to gain deeper knowledge of their circumstances. For instance, not every pediatrician is a parent; not every obstetrician has given birth; not every special-education teacher has a physical handicap or learning disability; no doctor has suffered all the illnesses he treats; no politician knows all the constituents she represents; few judges or juries will have firsthand experience of all the issues they must consider in their decisions. Recent history of Roman Catholicism has witnessed a growing (albeit uneven) effort by leaders to consult with traditionally neglected groups, to allow for more accurate discernment.

Still, much remains to be done to bring Catholic clerical/religious and lay lifestyles into conversation. I have already mentioned that my students

usually begin my marriage course assuming that they do not have a religious vocation, and that their lifestyles are not as holy as that of a priest
or nun. Wendy Wright illustrates how deeply the religious lifestyle has
colored—and limited—Christians' spiritual imaginations. She points to
a wealth of Christian literature employing metaphors of journey, pil-
grimage, or battle to describe the spiritual life. Wright notes that such
metaphors "reflect the experience of those who are not bound by particular cares and responsibilities of family and who may literally journey into the wilderness." She says that Christians who *are* bound by such
loves and responsibilities must search the rich Christian tradition to
find new ways to depict Christian life. Wright suggests the metaphor
of "dwelling": "What we lack as a spiritual community is a language for
the spiritual life that also speaks in terms of settled habitation. We need
the freedom to imagine ourselves not only as 'journeying' but also as
'dwelling.' We need to see that we need not always enter new landscapes
in order to grow in God, that we can also cultivate a settled space and
make it richer and more inhabited with meaning."[61]

On a general level, then, there are limits in trusting any particular individual's or group's faith experience as authoritative; on the other hand,
there is no getting around experience as a source of theological reflection.
Feminist, deconstructionist, and postmodern types will persistently remind
us of grave errors in judgement made by experts, notably male Christian
theologians, claiming to speak on behalf of all humans. A hermeneutic of
suspicion leads some to disregard anything this suspect group has to say.
But such an attitude amounts to throwing the baby out with the bath
water. In fact, many critics of traditional power structures retain, seemingly instinctively, the urge to assert universal human rights or values, and
thus implicitly some universalizable human experiences. Cristina Traina
and Lisa Sowle Cahill argue that multinational efforts to articulate crimes
against humanity and to redress violence against women, often spearheaded by feminists, evidence broad consensus, grounded in the truth
of practical experience, that there are absolute and universalizable human
values. It may be difficult to articulate these values without undue cultural bias, but this challenge does not remove the need to do so.[62]

Thus, I do not intend to minimize whatever limits there may be in
relying on persons like Karl Rahner, Thomas Aquinas, John Paul II, and

Joseph Bernardin to construct a theology of domestic church. I am convinced their writings contain many insights that can be brought to bear on my subject matter. This investigation will rely equally on works of married theologians, family spirituality specialists, how-to guides of family-based peace and justice activists, and diaries of everyday moms and dads. I will take some guidance from social scientists and religious educators. I share the attitude of Rosemary Haughton: "Neither the measured words of the professional theologian, nor the inarticulate need of the couples who struggle and suffer and do not understand, nor the passionate statement of the layman who bears witness to what he knows, are sufficient by themselves. All of them are needed, together with similarly mixed witness of past centuries of effort and study and failure and hope. . . . [T]he modern theologian of marriage needs all possible resources, old and new."[63]

Within these resources, perspectives on issues relevant to domestic churches are not always in agreement, as we shall see. On the other hand, as this book unfolds there will be many occasions where truths concerning domestic church that might be deduced from theological principles can be discovered just as readily in the common experiences of family life recounted by less technical authors. To give but one example, one might logically deduce that if the Church Universal has the nature of a sacrament (as claimed by *Lumen Gentium* #1), and a sacrament is a visible sign of Christ's invisible presence (traditional definition), then if the family is a domestic church (as magisterial documents attest), it must likewise have a sacramental character that makes Christ present. By an opposite inductive or experiential sort of reasoning, many spiritual authors and autobiographical accounts of Christian families display a conviction that Christ becomes really present to them through ordinary and extraordinary family activities. Therefore, these experiences are fittingly called sacramental, based on a traditional description of sacraments.

To recapitulate, my analysis will presume (1) some generalizable family values grounded in a shared human nature, and (2) a cooperative effort of multiple sources of expertise in discerning these values, and means to attain them. Persons of different cultural settings may need to adapt my reflections in order to apply what is timelessly true in them to their environments. While I am aware of potential limits of my premises, I believe they must be retained, for without them all possibility of conversation regarding anything important to humans collapses. At the level of emotional engagement, cooperation degenerates into partisan competition; from an intellectual point of view, the task of discerning what is true for humans is abandoned in the name of relativity. Mitch Finley and Kathy Finley strike a good balance in explaining what is particular and what is universal among domestic churches: "[E]very family is unique in its spirituality as every family has a personality of its own. In a very real sense, the Smith family will have a Smith spirituality, the Atkinsons an Atkinson spirituality, and the Wilsons a Wilson spirituality. Of course, each of these unique family spiritualities will also share a common spirit through a shared faith in the real presence of Christ who dwells in each."[64]

TWO

What Sort of Term Is "Domestic Church"?

The symbol of domestic church helps us concretize
two basic teachings of Vatican II, namely, that the church
is a community of people, and that the church is in the world.[1]

Within documents produced under Catholic auspices, different sorts of language are employed for distinct purposes. There is a difference between symbolic or analogical language (God as Father, Kingdom of God, Body of Christ) and juridical language, which is used to define aspects of Church, and is often the focus of discussion of so-called family issues (in/valid, il/licit, annulment, dispensation, diocese, etc.). Juridical language is used to mark boundaries and to establish disciplinary clarity and fairness. Symbolic language is more fluid, it functions primarily to stimulate our religious imaginations, though not without implications for institutional structure. Various authors attach both symbolic and juridical meaning to domestic church. This is legitimate to do, but if the two sorts of language are not distinguished, it will be easy for domestic church to be understood as an elitist and exclusive category. Wendy Wright describes how symbolic or ideal models of family life work upon our imaginations.[2] Distinguishing various ideal models of family life, which evaluate by criteria such as "functional," "pious," "moral," "intact," or "socially conscious," Wright asserts—correctly, I think—that for Catholics ideal models have a particularly strong behavioral influence:

> Our Catholic spiritual tradition is full of models. We look to the saints, to priests and religious, to monastic communities, to the "ideal" family, to papal and episcopal authority, to canon law, to doctrine, creed and moral codes to lead us toward the fullness of life. We theologize from universal principles and develop moral theory that is normative rather than descriptive. This provides us with idealized visions of marriage and family into which we strive to grow. There is, I would venture to say, something essentially Catholic about this propensity to look to and live into models. It has to do with our preference for the ideal, our penchant for perfection, our persistent intuition that we really can get it right.[3]

How do religious ideals function for Catholics? As Wright puts it, ideals "simultaneously encourage and inhibit genuine encounter with God."[4] Wright considers the idealism of the Catholic imagination valuable because it allows believers "to live more passionately, more intentionally, and with more daring spiritual freedom in our familied lives."[5] But she warns against the temptation to use an ideal model, legitimate in itself, as a weapon against those different from ourselves. In addition, Wright alerts us to the possibility that focusing on a single interpretation of an ideal may blind us to unexpected ways God is present in our families, with the result that families forever find themselves falling short of what seems "right." Wright says, "I have seen familied people be as thwarted in their spiritual aspirations as the 'perfect' family or the 'Christian' family as they have been by an unattainable monastic vision of the holy life."[6]

The possibility of symbolic images or ideal models contributing to the Catholic's sense of falling short seems especially likely when matters under consideration concern family life. Many Catholics are probably unaccustomed to thinking of the relationship between religion and family life in imaginative or symbolic terms, for, in considerations of marriage and family, the Catholic Church's interests are often juridical. Or, at least, the Church's interests may be perceived as such by people not regularly engaged (on the giving or receiving side) with its social service efforts on behalf of families. Whether or not Catholic leaders intend it, when it comes to issues that impact upon families most immediately, the Church's preoccupation often seems to be posing definitions or criteria—of validity, of being in good standing, of eligibility, of completing requirements— to which families are asked to measure up. Does your family come to mass every week? Is your marriage valid? Are you using the correct form of birth control? Are you registered in the parish at least six months before seeking to be married here? Have you and/or your children attended the religion classes necessary for reception of their next sacrament? Do your child's prospective godparents have a letter of reference from their pastor— stamped with the parish seal? Can you produce an annulment certificate so as to have a clean record before completing our RCIA program? Have you correctly monitored your family's eating habits during Lent? Can you get your teenage children to accept the standards of dress and personal grooming necessary to attend Catholic school? Have you documented your mandatory service hours and met the school's family fund-raising requirement? Do you use the parish's donation envelopes consistently enough to qualify for the in-parish tuition rate?

Standards or expectations such as these can have a legitimate purpose, but their existence creates an environment in which it is easy to feel inadequate or guilty for falling short. In this environment, it is not surprising that participants in the 1992 NCCB colloquium on domestic church expressed concern that the term could "discourage those who fall short of where they would like to be." Some "thought the teaching on domestic church can seem to be judgmental and to communicate a message that the church of the home can be embodied only in a certain kind of family structure," and others "question the value of the concept because they suspect it might be a means of the official church extending its control into family life."[7]

In my opinion, domestic church is primarily a symbolic expression. It should function first and foremost to stimulate imaginations to a deeper appreciation of the mystery of the Church and of how family life figures into God's plan of gracious presence in history. We shall see it is very similar in function to two other symbolic expressions used to explain the mystery of the Church: "Body of Christ" and "sacrament." Each formula renders both the Church's corporate, bodily element and its spiritual significance, which can be appreciated with the eyes of faith. In the case of domestic church, we can say that without simplistically claiming that families are exactly the same thing as "the Church" or vice versa, the expression alerts us to the fact that there is an essential relationship between the two. We should consider the essential relationship between family and Church with the same level of seriousness we give to the bond between Christ's body and Church, or sacrament and Church. And like those potent symbols, domestic church should guide formation and ongoing evaluation of institutional structures.

Domestic church can sometimes be understood in a more juridical sense, as a demographic or geographic subdivision of the Church Universal, like a diocese or parish. I consider this juridical meaning of the term secondary or derivative, for reasons to be discussed shortly. Still, one must be aware of instances where the term has been employed this way, because theologically speaking they are important. Notably, such connotations of domestic church were in the forefront of the minds of bishops who included it in *Lumen Gentium* because of the way Bishop Fiordelli framed his interventions. As popular as the term has become in recent years, it was not accepted at Vatican II without debate, and the issue at stake was whether family-based Christian communities should receive any consideration in ecclesiology. Michael Fahey summarizes the first conciliar interventions of Bishop Pietro Fiordelli:

> At the Thirty-Fourth General Congregation (5 December 1962), four days after the introduction by Cardinal Ottaviani to the council fathers of the first draft of "On the Church," Bishop Pietro Fiordelli was given permission to speak. . . . Bishop Fiordelli addressed the council fathers, arguing that a substantial section on the sacrament of marriage and the Christian family was needed. [Cardinal] Alfrink interrupted the bishop's speech, claiming that the issue of marriage did not seem germane to the discussion at hand. Fiordelli retorted that marriage and the Christian family were indeed at the heart of church life, but agreed to summarize his written text in only a few words. In the written text, subsequently published in *Acta*, we read for the first time the family described in these discussions as the domestic church. In his ecclesiological remarks

Fiordelli argued that the universal church comprised a vast number of local churches or dioceses, but the the diocese was not the last sub-division of the church. Christian families should be conceived of as *minisculae ecclesiae* (mini-churches). As proof for the antiquity of this teaching, he cited texts from St. John Chrysostom and St. Augustine that described the family as a small church or as a domestic church.[8]

Fahey notes that an early draft of *Lumen Gentium* claimed, citing Augustine, that parents "exercise a sort of episcopal function," but this phrase was dropped from later versions. In the final text of *Lumen Gentium,* domestic church appeared in a section on the sacrament of marriage, having been moved from its place in an earlier draft in a section on "the universal priesthood, the *sensus fidei,* and the charisms of the faithful," which would suggest a more integral relationship with baptism and membership in the Church. In the final text, the link between domestic church and local/particular church that Bishop Fiordelli seemed to have in mind was not emphasized.[9] Instead, domestic church is presented alongside a traditional reminder for married parents to be the first preachers of the faith to their children and to encourage them in vocations, with special care given to religious vocations.

However, Fiordelli's sense of domestic church has been largely recovered in subsequent magisterial statements. Paul VI's statements on domestic church in *Evangelii Nuntiandi* #71, though brief, represent development beyond *Lumen Gentium*'s presentation. Notable in his remarks was that

- "[t]here should be found in every Christian family the various aspects of the entire Church"—suggesting an ecclesial mission beyond raising up faith and vocations among one's own children;
- in a family conscious of its mission of domestic church "all members evangelize and are evangelized";
- a domestic church should be "an evangelizer of other families and of the neighborhood of which it forms a part";
- in a "mixed marriage" of two baptized Christians this mission remains the same because it is a consequence of their "common baptism." Such families "have the difficult task of becoming builders of unity."

John Paul II's treatment of domestic church in *Familiaris Consortio* includes several potent statements concerning Christian families as ecclesial entities. Building upon Paul VI, John Paul II says the Christian family is "a specific revelation and realization of ecclesial communion" and "a living image and historical representation of the Church." He continues, "The Christian family is grafted into the mystery of the Church in such a way as to become a sharer, in its own way, of the saving mission proper to the Church."[10] Though he does not explicitly link the idea of domestic church to diocese, parish, or local church, John Paul II here retrieves something of the sense of domestic church that Bishop Fiordelli seemed to have in mind but that *Lumen Gentium* #11 did not really capture.[11]

In *Follow the Way of Love* the U.S. bishops propose a mission statement that really covers "the various aspects of the entire church"—it runs on for two pages! Following the mission statement, the bishops take the significant step of comparing domestic church to parish or diocesan church communities, as Fiordelli did: "No domestic church does all this perfectly. But neither does any parish or diocesan church."[12] Ennio Mastroianni observes that in post-conciliar statements on domestic church two key insights are "[t]he Christian family is the smallest unit of Church," and "Christian parents have their own proper office or task (*munus*) as overseers of the Christian family."[13]

All this being said, I should explain my hesitation to consider the juridical meaning of domestic church dominant over the symbolic. There is potential for distortion in a juridical understanding of domestic church because it suggests there are clearly observable features that might be used to mark some families as domestic churches and categorize other families as something "other" or inferior.[14] As we shall see, Christian writers assert that many types of families can be domestic churches.

Further, as I shall argue throughout this book, the most essential feature of domestic churches is not some easily observable activity or demographic configuration. Rather, it is the way members see and interpret the world and their lives. It is an interpretation formed by *shared faith* in Christian revelation—for which observable marks such as shared baptism, a sacramental wedding celebration, or regular Eucharistic worship are important visible signs. At some level, with varying degrees of maturity, intensity, and explicitness, members of domestic churches come to "see" ordinary life as God's instrument for relating to them and as their medium for embodying love of God. Evaluating the living, growing faith of Christian families is far more complex than drawing parish boundaries, and so it is misleading to consider domestic church to be primarily a juridical category. Juridical implications of domestic church should be important to future ecclesiology and institutional policy, but these should be derived from the concept's symbolic meaning.[15] At present, domestic church lacks much of the richness of similar symbolic concepts because Christians have not lived with it long enough or critically enough. As I see it, domestic church has—potentially—the same sort of symbolic power, which waits to be uncovered.

With a sense of both the symbolic and juridical significance implicated in the idea of domestic church, we will continue in the next few chapters to examine assumptions that seem operative where the term has been employed in recent literature of various types.

Areas of consensus to be examined are:

- There is both continuity and contrast between "domestic church" and "the Church";
- domestic churches are particularly concerned with the ordinary, worldly, practical, and actual, rather than simply the theoretical and ideal; but,
- domestic churches are characteristically caught up in tension between ideal and actual, between goals and progress toward them;
- domestic churches are called to the same mission as the larger church; domestic churches translate a general mission into specific embodiment. Often the task is described in terms of *education,* understood as socialization by word and example.

Several issues surrounding the idea of domestic church that remain unsettled are:

- The relationship of domestic churches to the Church's hierarchy, particularly concerning evangelical discernment, leadership and governance, authoritative teaching, and ecumenical relations;
- whether domestic churches are grounded primarily in the sacrament of baptism or marriage;

- whether the nuclear family model is the only ideal for domestic churches to emulate;
- whether the romantic model of family is an appropriate guide for domestic churches;
- whether hierarchy of some sort is intrinsic to domestic churches;
- whether there are certain characteristic beliefs or activities that families who strive to be domestic churches share, or ought to share.

THREE

A Small Church Community

At different moments in the Church's history . . . the family has well deserved the beautiful name of "domestic church." This means that there should be found in every Christian family the various aspects of the entire Church. Furthermore, the family, like the Church, ought to be a place where the Gospel is transmitted and from which the Gospel radiates.[1]

Christian families are nothing new. What is new about the idea of domestic church is the way the term has come to be used to stress that a Christian family is a small community or manifestation of the Church. Here we have an important point of consensus. We have seen already that magisterial references to domestic church use rather strong language—"living image," "historical representation," "church in miniature"—to describe the function of domestic churches as a specification of the Church Universal. In various sources we find domestic church called the basic, foundational, or fundamental church, the smallest individual church, the smallest unit of church, the smallest of local churches, or a living cell in communion with other cells. Sometimes qualifiers are also used, such as "in its own way" in *Familiaris Consortio* #49, but other texts use quite unequivocal language, such as "the family 'is' Church."[2] However, based on the developing consensus in magisterial and theological sources, this formulation may be considered potentially misleading, for it may not convey an essential ecclesial element—communion among Christians of all times and places.[3]

Ennio Mastroianni provides particularly helpful comments on this matter by explaining the Latin word *velut*, which appears in the original reference to domestic church in *Lumen Gentium* #11: "In hac velut Ecclesia domestica parentes verbo et exemplo sint pro filiis suis primi fidei praecones, et vocationem unicuique propriam, sacram vero peculiari cura, foveant oportet."[4] He translates *velut* as "sort of" or "kind of," comparing the reference in *Lumen Gentium* #11 to article #1, which describes the Church Universal as a "'kind of' sacrament."[5] Mastroianni says the bishops of Vatican II used *velut* in both instances in order to be precise. In both cases the comparison they are drawing is analogical—the relationship between Church and sacrament, or between family and Church, is something less than complete equivalence but more than mere metaphor.[6] The subject expresses an essential truth, but not the fullness of that truth:

> What has been said about the analogical meaning of the word "sacrament" as applied to the Church can help one to understand the true force and meaning of the term "domestic church" which the conciliar Fathers apply to the Christian family. First, the meaning of the Christian family as "domestic Church" is not weakened because of the analogical nature of the word "Church." Because the Christian family is a mystery, one must use analogical terms which are rich in several layers of meaning to express the Christian family's nature. Second, the term "domestic Church" is not a mere metaphor; it discloses an essential truth about the Christian family. For while the Christian family is not in itself the fullness of the Church (a communion of local eucharistic communities under the leadership of their bishops in communion with the bishop of Rome); nevertheless, the Christian family by its very origin in the sacrament of marriage is both a true participation in the Church and a realization and embodiment of the Church. For in and through the Christian family the union between Christ and the Church and the unity of humankind are deepened and furthered.[7]

Although formulations vary, there is developing agreement among varied authors that household, local, and universal embodiments of Church are inextricably related and should be regarded as such in terms of their mission and responsibilities. The ecclesial status of the domestic church is, I think, best explained by the NCCB colloquium and *Follow the Way of Love* cited previously, for, unlike Mastroianni, the bishops do not confine the foundation of domestic church to sacramental marriage. I also like Bernard Boelen's explanation: "Each Christian family presents 'in a unique way' the all-encompassing reality of the *same* Spirit, the *same* Mystical Body, the *same* ministry of Christ, the *same* sacrament of the Church. Each family *is* the Church, but in a particular way, namely, as the 'domestic' Church. Each Christian family is essentially more than it is by participation in the entire Church. . . . Building a Christian home and building the Church are not two separate activities."[8]

RELATIONSHIP OF DOMESTIC CHURCHES TO THE CHURCH'S HIERARCHY

We now move from an area of consensus to a more unsettled issue. As the saying goes, "The devil is in the details," and so it is when one asks what specific implications follow from recognition of Christian families as ecclesial entities. In the Catholic context, the most provocative questions surrounding domestic church concern its relationship to institutional church structures. Already the NCCB colloquium indicates that "domestic church" connotes to some people simply the lowest rung on Catholicism's hierarchical ladder; to them it appears as a device to promote clerical control, obedience, and uniformity.[9] Meanwhile, many authors interpret revival of the expression as a creative work of the Holy Spirit; in their writings it appears as a device that musters Catholic theological tradition (or, certain neglected strands of it) to legitimate a dramatic reconfiguration of Catholic patterns of leadership. Speaking for many, Bernard Boelen writes,

The shift from the preconciliar understanding of the Christian family in terms of "functions" and "subjects" to the renewed understanding in terms of the "domestic church" is so profound, so overwhelming and far-reaching, that its full realization will be long in coming. . . . It goes without saying that the Christian Family encounters many obstacles to its attempts to renew itself. To elaborate on just one example, the habit of looking upon itself as "laity" in the preconciliar sense is hard to break. . . . With Vatican II, however, leadership and ministry were rooted not in the hierarchy, but *in the total Church,* in "the people of God." The ministry and leadership of the Church now become "shared" leadership and ministry of *all* the people of God, including the laity (Gr. *laos*—people). Yet, many laypersons and their families still want "to be told" what to do; they hold only the hierarchy responsible for all decisions in the Church, and feel guilty or even sinful when they themselves take the initiative or accept responsibility. . . .

The habit on the part of some Church officials of looking upon themselves as "hierarchy" in the preconciliar sense is understandably hard to break too. . . . When these Church "officials" fail to listen to what the Holy Spirit is revealing to the domestic Church, *they fail to listen to the Church itself. . . .*

The Church cannot become an integral part of the Christian family's self-understanding unless this domestic Church becomes an integral part of the Church's self-understanding. The hierarchy and the family will make it through the present crisis if they can free themselves from being prisoners of the old static and dualistic categories of thought, if they "together" share *the same hierarchy* in the postconciliar sense (Gr. *hieros*—holy and *archein*—to rule), if they have the willingness to be ruled by the same sacramental holiness of the people of God.[10]

The underlying issues at stake are at the heart of all contemporary debates in ecclesiology—principles of hierarchy and apostolic succession weighed against recently articulated or revived principles of *sensus fidei,* reception of teaching, collegiality, subsidiarity and the autonomy of local churches, as well as traditional principles of unity and universality juxtaposed with the Church's relatively new awareness and acceptance of historical development and plurality within itself. No contemporary Catholic thinker I have encountered disputes the validity of any of these principles taken individually, but interpretations of what they mean in relationship with each other vary considerably. I will not try to settle these matters here.

However, a few observations pertinent to domestic church should be introduced. We have already reviewed many strong magisterial statements concerning the domestic church's ecclesial status; perhaps the most significant is the U.S. bishops' brief comparison of domestic church to parish and diocesan church. Later we shall see that Karl Rahner also spoke of domestic church as "the smallest of local churches"—an especially potent expression. In his mind, and since Vatican II, "local church" refers not to an incomplete piece of the church, but rather to the fullness of Church in a particular locale and, so long as it maintains communion with its bishop, an authentic source of religious knowledge. Mary Ann Foley explores this approach to domestic church, citing the characteristically Orthodox premises that "the larger church must be conceived as a communion of churches" and that "each local manifestation of church is truly church," with the proviso that "no local church can be 'catholic' in isolation."[11]

Normand Provencher, the only other author whom I have found to consider the concepts of "local church" and "domestic church" together, says the family is *not* a local or particular church as Vatican II defines it; its proclamation of the Word is not officially authorized and it does not celebrate Eucharist in union with a bishop.[12] Nevertheless, he says, the Christian family is a true cell of the Church, because we recognize in it many realities essential to the constitution of the entire Church—Christ's presence, the mission of evangelization, the life of prayer and charity. It represents in some manner a unity fundamental to the Church and realizes her presence concretely in a determinate milieu.[13]

Bearing in mind Rahner's notion of Church as basic sacrament that "realizes" Christ's presence in history, Provencher, Foley, and Rahner appear in close agreement as to domestic churches' ecclesial *function*. Their recognition of domestic church as a community that manifests, realizes, or communicates Christ's presence converges with John Paul II's conviction that "future evangelization depends on the domestic church."[14] One might just as well say that they continued embodiment or incarnation of Christ in the world, in each family's particular neighborhood and walk of life, depends on each domestic church.

With regard to ecumenism, many scholars and pastoral ministers view as highly significant the domestic church's status as a localized embodiment of the Church Universal. There was a time, not long ago, when the Catholic partner in a "mixed" marriage[15] was expected to pray for the conversion of the non-Catholic spouse to Catholicism. That expectation is becoming a thing of the past. *Familiaris Consortio* #78 encourages both spouses in these marriages to remain faithful to the duties of their respective traditions, while at the same time witnessing the unity symbolized by their common baptism. Timothy Lincoln reminds us that interdenominational domestic churches are true ecclesial entities founded upon shared sacraments of baptism and marriage, no less so than a domestic church comprised entirely of Catholics. These "little churches" must be taken seriously in any discussion of ecclesiology. He says, "[B]ecause of the existence of interdenominational families, the Catholic Church and various Protestant Churches are already in a closer degree of communion with one another than official documents on both sides indicate."[16]

What would the Catholic Church look like if the idea of domestic church were truly integrated at the grass-roots and hierarchical levels? Rosemary Haughton offers a detailed vision of what the Church might look like if Christian families understood themselves as household churches.[17] The most fundamental point she makes is that whereas in the past individuals physically or emotionally separated themselves from their families in order to live a truly spiritual life and serve the Lord without distraction, in the future we will assume that God will be encountered and served most readily in ordinary life, among members of one's household. Haughton envisions home masses becoming "part, but not the whole, of normal liturgical fare." Such a setting would best encourage natural, rather than forced, influence of Christian faith in practical life. "One reason is the obvious practical one that at this kind of gathering it is natural to stay on, and talk over anything that arises over coffee or even a communal meal. Projects can arise from this, but also there is a continuing process of education in Christian awareness, and this is probably more important." Likewise Haughton sees natural friendships and gatherings of children within a household as the setting for religious education and whatever issues are timely in their situation as the subject matter.

Though home gatherings may seem elitist, Haughton argues that any parish or other Church organization is bound to have an elite group, but at least in the smaller home setting it would be less likely that the "vaguely committed" would feel neglected. "A gathering centered on the family home makes it hard for people to be shy or standoffish." Haughton expects that household gatherings would keep themselves from becoming narrow-minded by including visitors. Members would visit each others' households, and so exchange ideas and cross-fertilize. In such a future church, the parish would become "a place for occasional celebration and large meetings . . . this might strengthen, rather than weaken, the *reality* of the local parish church, since the people who gathered for the occasional big celebration would be people normally and seriously engaged in liturgical and other activity at the smaller household level." Haughton says the diocese and parish would assist cooperative efforts of household communities and suggest ways they might get started and grow. She sees a similar role for smaller religious community houses, allowing for large community houses as sites for (re)training, retreats, and tasks unmanageable for small groups.

Two issues that would have to be dealt with in such a future church would be a shortage of ordained clergy and denominational divisions that extend to the household level. With regard to the first issue, Haughton argues that natural leaders (celibate or not, male or female) who emerged within household communities could be approached by diocesan leaders and asked if they would be willing to be prepared for ordination "with the clear prospect of continuing the same functions in the same place, but with the added impetus of ecclesial recognition." Dioceses and religious orders would still provide for training and ordination of the "comparatively mobile type of apostle" (probably celibate) who would plan for a life of ordained ministry and who would be available to fulfill needs beyond the reach or resources of the household church. With regard to denominational divisions and the thorny issue of intercommunion, Haughton says that practical approaches within the home church and the parish church could legitimately differ:

> [A] household of the open kind will often include people with different denominational origins. But even if older members of the family are aware of this as a problem, it must always be more natural to include these people in all that goes on, including the liturgy, rather than exclude them. Exactly how the mixing goes on is bound to vary, but mixing there is and will be. But where the present younger generation is concerned there is very little awareness of

divisions, at least as a problem. The young Christians who take their faith most seriously are the ones least likely to see any sense in denominational divisions. If they find themselves in a group of other Christians they will normally worship together if they worship at all, and that includes taking communion, if a Eucharist is celebrated. This is not an act of defiance, it is simply that the arguments against it, and the prohibitions, make so little sense to them that they set them aside without noticing it, and without any sense of rebellion. But whereas in a "proper" church building this must seem to others an act of aggressive defiance, in a home it is scarcely noticeable.

This is simply the way things are, and this tendency is likely to increase, whatever anyone thinks about it, but the experience of house-centered churches should make it easier and less controversial. . . . For [the new generation of Christians], the enclosing of liturgy in a particular building and time seems artificial, so here, also, the household, of some kind, is the place where Christianity is lived, if it is lived at all.

Whether or not one accepts all her practical suggestions, Haughton deserves credit for her attempt to flesh out, in concrete detail, what domestic churches might look like in the future. No one should suppose that the period since Vatican II has provided enough time for the Church (as a whole) to work out all the details of its recognition of Christian families as domestic churches. Surely Catholicism has come a long way in encouraging laity to assume new ecclesial responsibilities. Still, there is certainly need for further experimentation and improvement. The fact that most Catholic families have never heard the expression "domestic church" is evidence that much remains to be done at the grass-roots level. Perhaps someday domestic church might be part of our common theological vocabulary, as familiar to the typical believer as sacrament, minister, salvation, conscience, or the golden rule.

What can we conclude about the ecclesiological significance of domestic churches? Without doubt, one inference to be drawn from renewed attention to domestic church is that various constituencies of the Church, even those with significant differences in lifestyle, can learn from each other in discerning the nature and mission of the Church at every level.

Conjunction of the words "domestic" and "church" correctly indicates that lay and clerical/religious constituencies have more in common than we may usually think. We must never forget that clergy and members of vowed religious orders are also members of families, and thus may consider themselves participants in domestic church, with ensuing insight as to the meaning of this idea.[18]

But there is more. If the status of Christian families as domestic churches is taken seriously, their contribution to the *sensus fidelium* must also be taken very seriously. Structures and personnel must be in place to assist a broad range of families to become knowledgeable, thoughtful, and active contributors to the Church's leadership on *all* matters, not just those usually categorized as "family issues." As the NCCB colloquium on domestic church puts it, "A major responsibility of parish ministers is to be the 'ministry of intersection' between family and the larger church community."[19]

Like any religious truth, the idea that families are to be domestic churches will be apprehended gradually, in a process of trial, error, and occasional flashes of insight. If nothing else, the expression should prompt us to exercise our imaginations, to take a periodic respite from telescopic vision in order to reflect upon Church at the microlevel. Meanwhile, we should expect governing, liturgical, teaching, and cultural institutions of the Catholic Church to gradually develop a different look and feel when and if the idea of domestic church takes hold, at both a popular level and among the Church's leadership. We can expect that if this insight is treated thoughtfully and carefully by diverse peoples, the Church will retain essential elements such as unity, sacramental spirituality, reverence for tradition, and even hierarchy—while nevertheless presenting itself differently from the way it does now.

FOUR

A Sense of Mission

*The Christian family, in fact, is the first community called to
announce the Gospel to the human person during growth and to
bring him or her, through a progressive education and catechesis,
to full human and Christian maturity.*[1]

It is common for institutions such as universities, social service organizations, special interest groups, or religious communities to have "mission statements." A mission statement is a summary of what the group
sees as its purposes or goals. It is a tool by which a group determines what
they should be doing on a daily basis, and why. It is also a tool by which
the group introduces itself to new members, benefactors, and the community at large. Often these statements seem idealistic, but it is important for the institution to articulate them. Otherwise, leaders won't know
how to prioritize projects the group will work on, and they won't be able
to "sell" the group to potential supporters. Without a sense of how she
or he contributes to the group's mission, and a belief that the mission is
truly important, the average member's enthusiasm for their work with
the group will be dampened.

Our families are not so different from other institutions. Perhaps we do not need a mission statement printed on our stationery. But still, we need a *sense* of mission. We need to *believe* what we are doing is important, in order to remain enthusiastic about the hard work of maintaining relationships and running a household, let alone be motivated to reach out to others beyond our own household. We must be able to *articulate* our family's goals in order to budget our finite resources of money and time, or teach and discipline children. One weakness in the lesson on vocations from the 1962 *Baltimore Catechism*, discussed in chapter 1, was that persons who pursued the "secular" lifestyle were portrayed as lacking a positive mission. In rejecting the negative tone of the catechism lesson, my students instinctively knew that their family life had an important purpose. But many lacked the imagination or the vocabulary to describe the purpose of family life in relation to their professed Christian faith.

Ernest Boyer describes the lack of a sense of purpose, and the lack of a sense of accomplishment, that many people experience in their family lives as they complete daily tasks such as diaper changes, washing dishes, waiting in line at the checkout counter, settling arguments, or searching through an entire drawer to find a match for a child's favorite sock:

> All of these never-ending, everyday tasks can seem far from what is most important in life and that probably more than anything else makes them hard to endure. It is not easy to see how each of these acts, so fleeting in itself, adds up to much more collectively. How hard it is to give yourself to something that seems to have so little significance! A scientist may work year after year in the most painstaking and meticulous accumulation of data. There is nothing at all exciting about the task itself, but his resolve never falters, his interest never fades, because he is convinced of the ultimate importance of what he does. . . . Some tasks are grueling, demanding, and repetitious but are done with enthusiasm. Others are varied and complex but viewed with scorn. It is seldom the nature of the work itself that determines our attitude toward it. That comes instead from our assessment of its ultimate value.[2]

Boyer believes the Christian tradition can provide families what they crave—a sense of the ultimate value of the work they are doing.[3] Yet, he insists that this sense of purpose will not be internalized easily—hence his use of the expression "spiritual discipline." We will return to this theme in later chapters. For now, bear in mind that the first step of discipline is having a goal in mind. This, in turn, requires having the imagination to envision that goal and the words to describe it. So, when we describe the mission of domestic churches, the goals will be high and the language will be idealistic, but they have a practical usefulness.

The mission of domestic churches can be described as moving persons toward those ideals, goals, or ends God has designed for them, so that they reach the fullness of their potential as humans. Christian tradition teaches that the end, or *telos,* to which humans are oriented is a *sharing in divine life,* which is a life of love. In the language of the sources to be explored in later chapters, this sharing in divine life is described as encounter/communion with God, partaking in supernatural virtue, or establishing life worthy of humans created in God's image.

This mission is not exclusive to the Christian family as domestic church, but given to the entire Christian Church and to each individual member, as symbolically captured in their baptism. Still, it is fair to say that for the average believer it is not primarily in the setting of the Church Universal, or even the parish church, that this mission is adopted and fulfilled. More often than not, it is within the setting of one's family (of origin or of marriage) that the general call is addressed to individuals, accepted, and acted upon.[4] If the purpose of human history is to bring the human race (and each individual) consciously and freely to fullness of potential as images of God, then John Paul II is absolutely correct in asserting that "the future of humanity passes by way of the family."[5] Indeed, John Paul II has been the clearest and most detailed voice speaking to the role of the Christian family, understood as domestic church, as an indispensable instrument in God's grand plan for the human race. This plan, he says, is to "guard, reveal, and communicate love."[6] Love protected and shared within the family, and with those it encounters, is none other than God's own love.[7] By engendering the ability to give and receive love, families bring humans incrementally to their *telos* as *imago dei.*[8]

Having adopted this teleological understanding of domestic church, a most helpful way of specifying details of this mission is in terms of *religious education.* Tasks of religious education entrusted to the Church and, by extension, to domestic churches, include

- evangelization of new disciples
- cultivation of virtues
- ongoing catechesis
- prophetic witness to fellow Christians and others alike.

An advantage of using educational language to discuss the domestic church's mission is that it indicates a willingness to view Christian conversion and perfection as an incremental, lifelong process. This view of conversion is a distinctive attribute of Catholic theological anthropology (as we shall see in the upcoming chapter on virtue), though it may be shrouded by equally traditional language of ideals and universal norms. It is easy to incorporate educational imagery within an eschatological perspective that sees humanity as moving (individually and collectively) toward ideals present in a true, if rudimentary, way here and now. Using educational images and language, the ideal life of families as domestic churches can be discussed in a manner that can give hope, motivation, and direction, rather than discouragement, to all of us who fall short of perfection. It becomes possible to give positive meaning to errors and deficiencies inherent in growth while affirming ideals and universal moral norms—indeed, showing their pedagogical usefulness. In the Church as a whole, and in any family functioning as a domestic church, attention to similarities and differences between actual lives and ideals presented via religious education can give motivation and direction to individuals and communities as they mature toward their potential.

A survey of magisterial references to the Christian family or domestic church reveals its role to be frequently described as educational, and often specifically as an education in being human. Theologians and spiritual authors who write about family life agree that the family is, by God's design, the primary agent of education, both religious and social.[9] This understanding of family derives from natural law tradition, which posits nurture of children and intellectual life as basic human needs,[10] and from Scripture, which depicts human history as a great unfolding of revelation (or education) of God's love for us as children.[11] A sampling follows.

- "In what might be regarded as the domestic Church, the parents, by word and example, are the first heralds of the faith with regard to their children" (*Lumen Gentium* #11).

- "Inspired by the example and family prayer of their parents, children, and in fact everyone living under the family roof, will more easily set out upon the path of a truly human training, of salvation, and holiness. As for the spouses, when they are given the dignity and role of fatherhood and motherhood, they will eagerly carry out their duties of education, particularly religious education, which primarily devolves upon them" (*Gaudium et Spes* #48).
- "The family is a kind of school of deeper humanity" (*Gaudium et Spes* #52).
- "At different moments in the Church's history and also in the Second Vatican Council, the family has well deserved the beautiful name of 'domestic church.' . . . The family, like the Church, ought to be a place where the Gospel is transmitted and from which the Gospel radiates. In a family which is conscious of this mission, all members evangelize and are evangelized. The parents not only communicate the Gospel to their children, but from their children they can themselves receive the same Gospel as deeply lived by them. And such a family becomes the evangelizer of many other families, and of the neighborhood of which it forms part" (*Evangelii Nuntiandii* #71).
- "Family catechesis therefore precedes, accompanies and enriches all other forms of catechesis. Furthermore, in places where anti-religious legislation endeavors even to prevent education in the faith, and in places where widespread unbelief or invasive secularism makes real religious growth practically impossible, the 'church of the home' remains the one place where children and young people can receive an authentic catechesis" (*Catechesi Tradendae* #62).
- "[T]he Christian family, in fact, is the first community called to announce the Gospel to the human person during growth and to bring him or her, through a progressive education and catechesis, to full human and Christian maturity" (*Familiaris Consortio* #2).
- "[I]n the family the human person is not only brought into being and progressively introduced by means of education into the human community, but by means of the rebirth of baptism and education in the faith the child is also introduced into God's family, which is the Church" (*Familiaris Consortio* #15).
- "[I]t is from the family that citizens come to birth and it is within the family that they find the first school of the social virtues that are the

animating principle of existence and development of society itself" (*Familiaris Consortio* #42).[12]

- "Insofar as it is a 'small-scale Church,' the Christian family is called upon, like the 'large-scale Church,' to be a sign of unity for the world and in this way to exercise its prophetic role by bearing witness to the Kingdom and peace of Christ, towards which the whole world is journeying" (*Familiaris Consortio* #48).
- "Future evangelization depends largely on the domestic church" (*Familiaris Consortio* ## 52, 65).
- "Certainly one area in which the family has an irreplaceable role is that of religious education, which enables the family to grow as a 'domestic church'. Religious education and the catechesis of children make the family a true subject of evangelization and the apostolate within the Church" (*Letter to Families*, #16).

Given this broad consensus, continuing analysis of domestic church must give consideration to Christian families' role in education *ad intra* and *ad extra*. Our exploration of this theme will continue in chapters 11 and 12.

ARE THERE CHARACTERISTIC BELIEFS AND ACTIVITIES OF DOMESTIC CHURCHES?

A chapter on the mission of domestic church is a good a place to ask this question: can we identify certain beliefs or activities that all families who strive to be domestic churches share, or ought to share? Given the Catholic penchant for universalizing and for classifying behaviors, there is an instinctive urge to do so, though demographic researchers and historians would advise us to proceed with caution here. It will be as difficult to identify shared traits of domestic churches as it is to identify shared traits of Catholics or Christians in general.

Consider relations between parents and children. There is consensus among both lay and magisterial authors that in Christian families parents should treat their children with love, while still maintaining authority over them. But practical interpretations of "love" and "authority" vary considerably. For instance, some envision regular family meetings where children and adults set agenda items and decide issues ranging from discipline to menus to vacation destinations to charitable contributions.[13] But routines such as these are by and large a recent evolution in parenting technique, and certainly not a cross-cultural norm; most faithful Christian adults have matured in the distinct absence of them. It seems an empirical fallacy to say democratic family meetings are necessary for domestic churches.

Or consider family worship. Pope John Paul II recommends group recitation of the rosary for all family members and regular celebration of the sacraments of Eucharist and reconciliation.[14] Certainly these are not to be discouraged. Yet, lay writers often lament the difficulty they encounter when attempting to participate in traditional worship services with children of any age. While admitting that in Latin American cultures the rosary seems to engage many age groups, Dolores Leckey says that for her this prayer was empty until she reached middle age.[15] Leckey describes the dilemma of parents who must decide whether to abandon their "home parish" in search of a more family-oriented one, seek out some alternative Christian community, or simply persevere in a worship environment that does not capture the interest of their children. She recalls her difficulty finding words to answer her teenage son when he requested his parents not force him to go to mass, which he found boring.[16] Wendy Wright describes the humiliation of being asked to leave mass when her baby would not keep quiet.[17] James and Kathleen McGinnis recount how most of the service and worship events that engaged their children as youngsters were found unappealing as soon as they hit puberty.[18]

What is said about authority or worship within Christian families could be said about any other generalized criteria of domestic church activity. We are faced with a gap between ideals and reality. As we shall see in the next chapter, a good many authors dwell on this theme in their reflections on domestic spirituality. Rarely does any Christian family succeed at everything it ideally should. Some families, perhaps because of diverse personality types, interdenominational marriages, scheduling conflicts, or restless toddlers who will not sit still for even ten minutes, may find it hard to worship together; they may nevertheless be deeply involved in working for social justice, or aware of daily life as the embodiment of love for God. In some families, formal education in doctrines of the faith is simplistic or not readily available, but celebrations, welcoming of neighbors, and basic trust in God's love may be rich and unshakeable traditions. While it would be wrong to water down Christian family ideals to their least common denominator, we must pay due respect to whatever successes families achieve. Spiritual discipline means maturing to the potential for which God created us, and this is a lifelong process comprising many small steps. Moreover, the path to spiritual maturity is not always linear and predictable.

For example, I know one family wherein the parents' marriage, though on paper sacramental, underwent years of infidelity, anger, and depression. Financial resources were lost to gambling and consumption of tobacco and alcohol. Often the children felt that important emotional and material needs were neglected. Though the father was not the church-going type, he worked as many as four jobs simultaneously to send his children to Catholic schools, while the mother assumed more direct responsibility for the children's religious formation. One son, whose teenage years coincided with some of the most difficult years of his parents' marriage, drifted away from Catholicism in his teens and twenties. Imitating his father, he developed a habit of alcohol and drug abuse. Years later, he became a "born-again" Christian through encounter with both Alcoholics Anonymous and his wife's Baptist Church. Today this young man and his wife, along with their children, worship alternately at the Baptist Church or at the parish where the husband grew up, where his children now attend school and his daughter is an altar server. The young man isn't quite sure what his denomination is, but he is certain Jesus Christ is his Lord and Savior. He and his father, too, have moved beyond their substance abuse, and both have found a sense of peace. Ironically, in recent years the elder father of this family has ventured to attend mass with his wife—not regularly, but more often than just for weddings and funerals. In a strange twist of events, he was spurred to re-explore the Catholic faith by witness of the son who found in Christ and in his wife's Baptist community the strength to overcome years of substance abuse learned from his father. Somehow, mysteriously, God has been present and working in this family. Though hardly perfect, it embodies many of the ideals of a domestic church.

I believe the best explanation of specific beliefs and practices that befit domestic churches is provided by the U.S. bishops in *Follow the Way of Love*. In describing the mission of the domestic church, a whole array of faith commitments and activities is listed. Some will be shared by Christian families everywhere (for example, belief in God, forgiving and seeking reconciliation; praying together; welcoming strangers, acting justly), but others have a more distinctively Catholic edge (e.g., an across-the-board commitment to respect human life; the raising up of vocations to priesthood and religious life, fostered in part by "the way you speak of priests, sisters, brothers, and permanent deacons").[19] A family's immediate reaction to this list might be, "How could we ever do all that?" The bishops, in anticipation of this response, continue, "No domestic church does all this perfectly. But neither does any parish or diocesan church. All members of the Church struggle daily to become more faithful disciples of Christ."[20]

Catholicism tends to seek observable, definable characteristics or boundaries. Though this desire for objectivity has its value, it also has its limitations. Because the many demands of Christian life are difficult to attend to simultaneously, because of the variety of ways Christian beliefs can legitimately be embodied, and because of the gap between ideals and reality that characterizes life in this world, we cannot easily observe uniformly shared activities of domestic churches.

But perhaps instead of focusing on specific observable behaviors, it would be better to focus on the shared spirit underlying behavior. This is Rosemary Haughton's approach. In *The Knife Edge of Experience,* she reviews historically changing patterns of Christian family life and concludes that the "Christian" element of family life cannot be found in easily observable customs of child rearing, choice of marriage partners, or work routines. The purpose of a Christian family is "to create people who are able to love,"[21] specifically, to instill the sense of personal security and community identity prerequisite for loving one's neighbor.[22]

To complement Haughton's conclusions, areas of consensus in literature reviewed throughout this book can help us identify distinctive goals for domestic churches. These small communities should come to recognize that their family life makes Christ and his Church present in the world, but only if nourished by communion with the larger Church community. Through faith in Christ, they should see God's presence in the ordinary, secular world and be strengthened to make their ordinary lives an embodiment of ideals they confess and celebrate with the Church at large. Members of domestic churches will inevitably discover that they are inadequate to perfectly embody Christian ideals. Thus, part of their spirituality will be cultivating humility, hope, a desire to grow, and receptivity to guidance and comfort that God may offer them in their weak moments, often through each other as human instruments. Reciprocally, they will be open to the possibility of being used as God's instruments to help others in need. More mature members should try to be patient role models for others. Members of Christian domestic churches should come to sense, in greater or lesser degrees of explicitness, that in their ordinary efforts to love their families and neighbors they are participating in something of ultimate value—nurturing children of God.

FIVE

The Significance of Ordinary, Imperfect Family Life

The recognizing and naming of the "sacred in the ordinary" is the necessary substratum for an awareness of domestic church. Something must first be called holy before it can be identified as a work of the domestic church.[1]

It is not hard to find, both in Christian tradition and in the attitudes of many people today, an implicit or explicit difficulty linking ordinary domestic matters with Church or religious matters.[2] Historically the difficulty has been exaggerated by Catholicism's separation of lay and clerical/religious lifestyles via a vow of celibacy, but it is not unique to Catholicism. Ernest Boyer convincingly argues that the struggle to achieve a truly balanced spirituality is a very basic human phenomenon, and that separation of domestic and religious affairs finds parallels in many of the world's religions.[3]

If nothing else, the idea of domestic church challenges much of our cultural common sense by affirming the potential holiness of everyday activity. It can serve as a tool for overcoming false and dangerous separation between sacred and secular life, the "dichotomy between our professed faith and practice of our daily lives," which Vatican II called "one of the most serious errors of our age."[4] The expression likewise affirms the irreplaceably important role of the laity, the religious/moral significance of the material and bodily along with the spiritual, and the potential of everyday activity to be a source of religious and ethical insight. Bridging the perceived gulf between "religious" and "secular" life seems to be the self-chosen task of nearly every author in the field of family spirituality. In their reflections on spirituality for domestic churches, Mitch Finley and Kathy Finley capture the general sentiments of family spirituality authors.

> "Spirituality" is one of those time-worn terms which tends to suggest more—and less—than it should. Even today it summons up a split between body and soul, between spirit and flesh, between religious and secular life. Another understanding of "spirituality" is taken for granted here. For the spiritual life takes human nature as a cohesive whole and relates it to Divine Mystery. That is, a spirituality for families refers as much to family conflict as it does to family prayer. It has as much to do with the day in, day out, relationships between family members as it does with the relationship between the family and God.[5]

Three core concepts to be investigated in subsequent chapters (sacramentality, virtue, and consistent life ethic) can be employed to address domestic churches' need to discover ultimate value in the tedious and unglamorous routines of family life. They articulate the ultimate goal humans are designed to pursue and illuminate the manner in which seemingly insignificant acts do, in fact, add up to much more. These themes can be appropriated to show that God's great plan of self-revelation and perfection of creation requires human participation, not simply through endeavors that survive in history books, but through everyday routines of family living.

Tension between Ideal and Actual Family Life

Once one assumes ordinary family life—with its successes and imperfections—as religiously significant, composing a theology of domestic
church becomes a delicate task indeed. This brings us to another area of
consensus evident in literature on domestic church: domestic churches
are characteristically caught up in the tension between ideal and actual,
between the attractiveness of their life's goals and the mediocrity of their
journey toward those goals.

When we speak of domestic church, we speak of family as a central
part of God's great plan for the fulfillment of the human race. For those
who take the idea seriously, it is an awesome prospect indeed. One is
intrigued and inspired by the possibility that one's life can make some
ultimate difference and, at the same time, humbled by limitations both
personal and in one's surroundings. William Everett says that when symbols or purposes of marriage and family are discussed, we quickly center
on a "central theological problematic—namely, how to relate life as it is
with how it can or ought to be."[6]

This central theological problematic is an experience many of us are
quite familiar with, even if we don't use that phrase to describe it. For me,
it is embodied in the most challenging time of my day: the time when I
have to make the transition from my office to home. I have a rather uncommon career as a theology professor. It's pretty easy for me to feel I'm
acting like a Christian at work. I spend much of my day discussing the
credibility of Christian teachings—about human life in keeping with
God's plans, about life "as it can or ought to be." When I enter my home,
these lofty goals often seem to crumble to pieces. Once a friend I knew
through my parish, an attorney at her day job, told me that she thought
I was "such a holy person." I remember feeling awkward when she said
it. If only she really knew me, I thought. I suppose that, looking at my
public life, one might assume that I am a very pious Christian, that I find
it easy to pray and to be generous, that I rarely get angry or hold a grudge,
that I always practice what I preach, and so on. Well, that just isn't true.

On a typical day, my four kids and I tumble in the door, scattering
book bags, lunch bags, the diaper bag, and the day's mail. Within a minute,
Seth asks for a snack and wonders if I know where he put his Gameboy.
Molly wants to play with the neighborhood kids who have followed us in

the door, but needs help getting her school uniform unbuttoned and find-ing a clean pair of shorts to change into. Cecilia is climbing up my legs and whining that she wants a bottle (something she "should" have given up around her first birthday, according to my parenting advice book). Elise is crying because she needs to breastfeed. What I want to do most is use the bathroom, change out of my work clothes, and eat something. There is no way to please everyone at once. The more unmet needs I am confronted with, the more difficult it is not to lose my temper. Instead of the pleasant voice I use at work, I find myself snapping at the kids. After about half an hour, there are a few minutes of calm—I have managed to get Molly out the door and a round of snacks for the rest of us. Then the cycle starts again—Molly has returned with the neighborhood kids, and now they're ready for the snacks I just finished putting away. Elise spits up all over me, and I'll need to change clothes again. I forgot to close the bathroom door; I discover Cecilia has unrolled half the toilet paper and is splashing in the toilet. Seth rummages through his backpack and pro-duces two items for me—instructions for a social studies project, due by the end of the week (this means a trip to the library and an evening de-voted to assembling his display) and an invitation to a birthday party (this means a trip to the toy store and helping Seth wrap a present and make a card). And so on.

Although I know the value of education, I have little enthusiasm for overseeing the social studies project, or for cleaning up after Cecilia's exploring. Although I believe it is wrong to cultivate habits of indulging kids with things they don't really need, I haven't mustered the resolve to break Cecilia of her bottle. Although I know that hospitality and friend-ship are among the things that really matter in life, I find it hard not to depersonalize my children's friends by thinking of them in terms of the chores they create for me. Although I love my children, and I know in principle that love entails a "gift of self," in practice I find it hard not to be resentful when their bodily and emotional needs compete with my own. Reflecting on my afternoon ritual from the relative tranquility of my office, I am reminded of my need for a merciful and compassionate God.

What help can Christianity give us in addressing such tension between ideal and actual life? It is to be resolved? Is it part of our lives for a rea-son? An interesting distinction among writings on the Christian family is worth noting here. In considering goals and ideals of family life vis-à-vis

actual existence, Pope John Paul II focuses proportionately more attention on "ideal" (interchangeably called "real" or "true") exercise of family
life, marriage, love, procreation, education of children, and so forth. The
very phrase "*the* Christian family" bespeaks this pattern. Language is very
lofty, and much effort is spent in a sort of theoretical pep talk, which aims
to inspire families to muster their strengths, conquer temptations and
enemies, and go out to save their local communities and the world from
error. Where family difficulties are discussed, they are generally described
as conquerable, so long as families recognize true priorities and stick to
them, praying for God's grace to guide and strengthen them. "Ideals"
function as "norms," and on the basis of these norms many types of families are labeled as being in "difficult or irregular situations."[7]

John Paul II is not in a category by himself. Examples can be found
of both lay and clerical authors describing the Christian family more on
the basis of its ideal form than its actual life.[8] This approach should not
be considered out of bounds. From earlier examination of symbolic language we know that ideals have a valuable motivating function for humans
in general and Catholics in particular. However, results of this sort of reasoning about "the Christian family" must still be subject to the critique
of firsthand, lived experience of Christian families. In the absence of such
evaluation, skewed generalizations about family life may be the result.
One striking case appears in *Covenant of Love,* a commentary on John
Paul II's writings on the family by Richard Hogan and John Levoir:

> *Children desire to love and they cannot. Love is a mutual self-
> donation of at least two persons to one another.* Each possesses the
> other through the other's self-gift. Often children try to satisfy their
> longing to love by possessing things. The almost universal phe-
> nomenon of a child clinging to a favorite blanket, doll, teddy bear,
> or some other object he claims as belonging exclusively to him tes-
> tifies to the child's need to love. *Unable to love in the true sense,* the
> child substitutes the possession of an object in the (unconscious)
> hope that this will alleviate the loneliness. Of course, the ownership
> of an object never quite satisfies the child's longing for a true
> loving relationship. Other children solve their need by fabricating
> mythical friends who are their constant companions. They know
> these "friends" intimately because they have created them from

their own experiences. They can possess these "friends" completely. Of course, this is also a *poor counterfeit for true love*. Both these recurring phenomena point to the loneliness of childhood, to the solitude which Adam felt and which children feel. Still, it must be emphasized that this loneliness is only clearly understood from the vantage point of an adult. The child does feel a certain loneliness, but he does not understand it and could not identify it. It is only as adults that we can fully appreciate the tribulations of childhood.[9]

Armed with their definition of "true" love, Hogan and Levoir have written off childhood as a time for humans to express the love of God in whose image they are created.[10] They are so narrowly focused on a particular interpretation of the ideal that they are blind both to other ways of defining love and to whatever goodness the child's expressions of love may have. Hogan and Levoir do not explain when and how transformation from false, counterfeit love to true, mutual love takes place in the process of human maturation. Childhood seems to be a big waste of time.[11] One wonders how they would explain Jesus" admonition that "[u]nless you become like little children, you shall not enter the Kingdom of God."

A very different approach is found in most lay authors writing on Christian family life. Rather than centering their attention on inherited ideals concerning marriage and family, this second group is more attentive to, and one could say preoccupied with, the limitations, disappointments, conflicts, and tensions inevitable in family life. As I see it, the difference stems from their preference for inductive, rather than deductive, reasoning. Although they do not make such distinctions themselves, one can distinguish in these two sets of texts a difference between "norm" as "morally normative" (synonymous with "ideal") and "norm" as "normal" (synonymous with "real"). For this second group, the normal is certainly not perfect or ideal, but it is no less true or real.

Like John Paul II and similar idealistic theologians, this second group of authors aims to draw readers' attention to the beauties of family life, and to unleash the untapped potential of families as agents of full human development. But more than the first group, the second wants to address families' need to deal with deficiencies, mistakes, temptations, and enemies that change form but never completely go away. They want to find some fresh approach to traditional ideals that they accept as "true" in some sense, but find incredibly difficult to incorporate in their lives, as they have been handed down.

Statements of the U.S. bishops on families as domestic churches, in my estimation, fall between the other two groups of writings. They are more perceptive (or perhaps simply more frank) than others in attending to different reasoning styles that underlie the respective characters of the two groups of authors I have distinguished:

> Our prevailing theology of domestic church has arisen historically from a reflection on the sacramentality of marriage. The method is a deductive one. However, within our contemporary culture, we tend to reason inductively. We would start with the "givenness" of family by examining the many ways in which people consider themselves to be families. We would look for patterns within the total phenomenon that disclose an ecclesial meaning. There is clearly an unresolved tension between the two approaches and, consequently, within our theologizing about family and domestic church.[12]

The U.S. bishops, along with the second group of typical lay authors, seem to be trying to find a way to present the norms, or truth, of family life as coexisting with limitations they find inherent in the human condition generally, and in family life specifically. Their efforts do not appear as a simplistic strategy of interpreting whatever is statistically normal as morally normative—something that John Paul II specifically criticizes in his writings.[13] Rather, the Christian tradition is re-examined for stories, symbols, and theological concepts that incorporate tension between ideal/ normative and actual/statistically normal in considerations of what is "true." At least three sorts of responses can be detected, using images of *eschatology, growth,* or *God's continual presence* to address the relationship of ideal existence to actual existence.

LIVING THE ALREADY-BUT-NOT-YET

The field of *eschatology* is an obvious source of the theological resources needed to explain tension between ideal and actual life. The idea of God's kingdom being "already but not yet" is invoked by several sources on the

Christian family.[14] Some authors remind us that, like the Church Universal, the domestic church in this life is the "Church militant" or "pilgrim Church," that is, a work in progress.[15]

John Paul II alludes to Augustine's image of two "cities" or "civilizations" in his 1994 *Letter to Families,* but, characteristic for him, the focus is not so much on the Christian family experiencing tension *ad intra* as on the Christian family as guardian of truth and love in a world often dominated by error and evil.[16] Those invoking ideas of "pilgrim Church" or "already but not yet" appear convinced that being "unfinished" is inherent in a Christian domestic church, and thus some degree of anxiety is the norm, even before relations *ad extra* are considered.

A CONTINUOUS, PERMANENT CONVERSION

A different set of theological metaphors used to explain distance between ideals and realities of life in a domestic church includes *conversion, growth, progressive integration, education,* and *maturation.* When this sort of language is used to interpret the distance between ideals and actuality, closing that gap is regarded as a family project that lasts a long time, if not a lifetime. In this mindset, "real" and "ideal" are understood as orienting points on a journey of human maturation, rather than logical or metaphysical antitheses. Imperfections and mistakes are not ignored, but, at the same time, they are not the center of attention. Rather, hints of ideal behaviors and attitudes, and efforts to expand upon them, become the focal point.

Such an approach is characteristic of Mary Perkins's reflections on her son, Thomas Edmund, age one and a half, in her book *Mind the Baby.*[17] Her insights provide a background for issues that will be taken up again in the upcoming chapter on families as schools of virtue. Perkins says that if Thomas were a kitten, taking care of him would be much easier. It is not so much his physical needs that exhaust her, but the things he needs in order to mature as a human: "[N]eeds to find out about things and master them; to find out about his own growing powers and master them; needs to do things for himself and yet to be protected and helped and loved at the same time." She says the task of helping Thomas to use his human powers is complicated by the effects of original sin in him *and* in herself. "No wonder that it takes a whole lifetime of God's grace, and one's own efforts and those of one's parents and teachers and friends and unknown benefactors to grow up to the fullness of Christian living."

In an approach very different from that of Hogan and Levoir, Perkins describes Thomas's efforts as "true, if rudimentary," human actions. For instance, she says, he has rudiments of a conscience. "He knows he should not grab match boxes. He feels guilty even before I find him with one, and even guiltier when I do. He is sorry and hurt when I scold him, and wants to make everything all right with me right away." Likewise, his "true, if rudimentary," human reason understands universals and particulars, such as "cookie in general" and "favorite kind of cookie." When Thomas raids the cabinet for his favorite cookies, he is exercising his intellect and will, "seeing a general good embodied in an actual object, making a plan, choosing the means and finally taking the action necessary to achieve that good." Perkins poetically concludes,

> In all his funny and infuriating and pathetic activities he is discovering and exercising and beginning to coordinate his powers of body and mind and soul toward the time when he will be capable of a fully human action, of choosing to do something or not to do it according to right reason, and of acting on that choice—his senses and muscles and emotions and tendencies all subordinate in act to his mind and his will. And, thank God, while he is discovering the strength of the disintegration and perversity in himself caused by original sin—"the evil that I will not, that I do"—at the same time he will be discovering the power of grace to help him overcome it. Now he is sorry for having offended Mummy, but in time he will be sorry for having offended God. Now he wants Mummy to love him and be pleased with him, but in time, with God's help, he will seek only God's good pleasure.

For there are further powers wrapped up in that small human person swinging so sedately over there on the swing, supernatural powers which are waiting for the ordinary human development of his mind and will to be ready for exercise and growth. Because of his Baptism, this little boy will be capable not only of human action, but of Christian action. He will be able to make choices not only in light of right reason, but in light of faith. He will be able to act on his choices not only by the power of his own will, but with the power of God's Own Love, Charity. He will be able not only to know himself and his capabilities and weaknesses, but to know himself in light of God's mercy and to hope in it. And, with God's help, the grace given him at Baptism and its wonderful powers will prove the fruitful seed of life everlasting, of sharing God's Own Happiness, of seeing and loving God himself for all eternity. All this present existence of playing with toys, getting in and out of boxes, falling down and crying, eating cookies and swinging, learning not to do what Mummy says not to do and to do what she says to do—all the unimportant attempts and achievements and tragedies which make up a small boy's life—are the first steps toward future actions which can affect the whole world, the actions of a Christian, a member of the Mystical Body of Christ, whose every work and deed and suffering and joy can be intelligently and lovingly and willingly united to Christ's and so help to save his own soul and those of his fellowmen for the glorious life of eternity.

And Mummy, who feels so sorry for herself so often, is really in the amazing position of assistant coach, helping the future athlete of Christ in his first exercises—assistant to the Holy Spirit, the Trainer and Sanctifier of Christians! Mummy has the job of helping little Thomas to develop human habits of right and loving action which the Holy Spirit will transform with those supernatural habits of faith, hope, and charity, of prudence, justice, fortitude, and temperance, already rooted in Thomas' faculties by Baptism, flowing forth from divine life given to his soul.... Surely, then, even in this seemingly endless and wearing and humble job of helping a little boy to gain the simple physical habits and skills of ordinary human living, the light and grace of the Holy Spirit will not be lacking to his imperfect and unskilled assistants, Thomas Edmund's parents.

Language of maturation is not confined to the writings of lay authors. John Paul II often speaks of family life in terms of growth; an example is found in *Familiaris Consortio* #9.

What is needed is a continuous, permanent conversion which, while requiring an inner detachment from every evil and an adherence to good in its fullness, is brought about concretely in steps which lead us ever forward. Thus a dynamic process develops, one which advances gradually with the progressive integration of gifts of God and the demands of His absolute love in the entire personal and social life of man. Therefore an educational growth process is necessary, in order that individual believers, families, and peoples, even civilization itself, by beginning from what they have already received of the mystery of Christ, may patiently be led forward, arriving at a richer understanding and fuller integration of this mystery in their lives.[18]

Within this citation are hints of an unresolved tension in John Paul II's writings on the family. Perfection (signified by "detachment from every evil" and "adherence to good in its fullness") is "required" of families even while they are still growing in terms of understanding and integration. Elsewhere the pope's rhetoric is even stronger:

Married people too are called upon to progress unceasingly in their moral life. . . . They cannot however look on the law as merely an ideal to be achieved in the future: they must consider it as a command of Christ the Lord to overcome difficulties with constancy. And so what is known as "the law of gradualness" or step-by-step advance cannot be identified with "gradualness of the law," as if there were different degrees or forms of precept in God's law for different individuals and situations.[19]

It is theoretically challenging to come up with an explanation of growth that incorporates ideas of both unceasing progress and absolute requirements of perfection; it is even more difficult to craft a pastoral approach that respects both concerns. John Paul II's bias in his writings on family life is to stress the latter concern, somewhat at the expense of the former.[20] I find Perkins's explanation of human deficiency and growth more balanced and compelling while still being well rooted in traditional Catholic theology. Obviously there is a difference in their subject matter— John Paul II is focused on adults, who, it is to be hoped, are more mature than Thomas Edmund Perkins. However, it is my opinion that moral development is lifelong, and that the two age groups have a lot in common in terms of how they progress, or stagnate, or backslide.

REMEMBER, I AM WITH YOU ALWAYS

A third response to the frustration families feel when they fall short of ideals centers on the truth that *God will never forsake us and is continually present, even at the ugliest times in our lives.* This insight rescued Willie Teague from despair when his "ideal" family was apparently corrupted by his separation from his wife after eight years of marriage. Teague describes his sense of failure and his feelings of isolation within his Church: "Few families reflect the kind of family life which the church seems to insist upon as reality. This disparity is the source of much grief and pain. We all know that we live in imperfect families, yet we cannot share our imperfection in the place where truth is supposed to be most valued: the church."[21]

Teague found solace when he "looked beyond the church's romantic and unrealistic image of family to the reality of family rooted in the gospels. They give rise to new hope that every family, however broken, can be filled with God's gracious presence."[22] Specifically, Teague finds reassurance in stories of the Holy Family. With a perspective that perhaps comes most readily to those whose family life is weak or broken, Teague reminds us that the family in which God chose to become incarnate was in many respects far from ideal, but nonetheless a true family in which God was surely present and at work, and which was clearly used as God's instrument. Through incarnation in the Holy Family, Teague contends, God has experienced "unexpected teenage pregnancies, shaky marriages, questions of divorce, parent-child conflicts, single-parent families, sickness and weakness, aging parents, and death."[23]

With an approach akin to Teague's, Dolores Leckey finds another resource for putting family ideals in perspective—the witness of Saint Catherine of Genoa, which she discusses in her chapter on the monastic principle of *stability*.[24] Like Teague, Leckey is convinced that "God and grace are indeed present in all kinds of families, in those with compatible spouses, orderly children, and neat dinner tables, and in those we might call marginal."[25] Catherine experienced the trauma of an unfaithful husband who squandered family wealth and fathered a child with his mistress. She slumped into severe depression, as might be expected. But somehow, in the midst of this ugliness, God's love became strikingly present to Catherine. Catherine's story ends happily, with her husband reforming his ways and converting to Christianity, and Catherine taking on an active public life in hospital ministry. But the great lesson of Catherine's life, says Leckey, is not so much the happy ending as the truth that God can be encountered *in* the failures of personal and family life.

Leckey argues convincingly that the monastic principle of stability can serve as a theoretical tool for making sense of situations such as Catherine's. The principle of stability, one of the most striking elements of monasticism, is explained by Thomas Merton as follows: "The real secret of monastic stability is the total acceptance of God's plan by which the monk realizes himself to be inserted into the mystery of Christ through this particular family and no other."[26] Leckey adds that the vow of stability, by which one binds oneself permanently to a particular family, for better or worse, presupposes that family life is almost never ideal: "In fact, imperfection is normal; and it is precisely there, in reality rather than in idealized fantasies, that God will be found. . . . God is there as all the sharp edges of our personalities are worn smooth in our encounters with one another. And God is there as defenses and false self-images are given up in the daily routines of living and working and praying together. God is there in our neuroses as well as in our health."[27] Insertion into the mystery of Christ may take place via divorce, poor health, poverty, scandal or tactless gossip concerning members of one's family, the drudgery of household chores, or the recurrent annoyances of a family member's neuroses or bad habits. In *Follow the Way of Love*, the U.S. bishops pick up this theme at several points. As they put it, "In a family, you don't have to look far to find your cross."[28]

It is this third perspective on family ideals that is least represented in John Paul II's best-known writings on the family. His understanding of truth, ideals, norms, and of humans being made in the image of God, does not easily accommodate imperfection or ambiguity.[29] At one point he suggests that families with serious problems are not really families at all, in the "true" sense:

There exist in the world countless people who unfortunately cannot in any sense claim membership in what could be called in the proper sense a family. Large sections of humanity live in conditions of extreme poverty, in which promiscuity, lack of housing, the irregular nature and instability of relationships, and the extreme lack of education make it *impossible in practice to speak of a true family.* There are others who, for various reasons, have been left alone in the world. And yet for all of these people there exists a "good news of the family."[30]

John Paul II's scope here is quite broad and might include the Holy Family, which by his own admission was poor and, as we all know, sometimes lacked proper housing.[31] The pope is attempting to show compassion for distressed families, but my guess is that many families who need to hear good news of compassion will not easily gain it in this sort of writing. The section of *Familiaris Consortio* devoted to "Pastoral Care of the Family in Difficult Cases," from which this citation is drawn, devotes more attention to dissecting problems than to providing encouragement.[32] The "good news of the family," which John Paul II says exists even for families in difficulty, remains vague. A more thorough attempt to articulate good news comes in the pope's *Letter to Families* in a chapter entitled "The Bridegroom Is with You." Readers are reminded that Christ is with us whenever we face challenges that require great fortitude; he is the Good Shepherd who watches over us and is prepared to sacrifice on our behalf.

Conspicuously lacking, however, is proportionate attention to Jesus' personally experiencing the sorts of hardships that accompany family life. In fairness, it should be noted that the U.S. bishops and many lay writers are weak in this regard as well—but, their efforts to present weakness and imperfection as a normal part of family life help compensate. In a theological system such as the present pope's, in which the concept of *imago dei* is so pivotal, much could be made of the fact that Jesus' family life was, in many respects, as troubled as our own.

Some background information is in order here: beginning in John Paul II's early writings and continuing in his most recent ones, *imago dei* has developed as the concept that connects doctrines of creation/

anthropology, sin, incarnation, redemption, church, and morality.[33] The redemption accomplished by Jesus is directed precisely to the image of God, which each human being is created to embody.[34] The image of God implicated in creation and redemption pertains not simply to our souls, but also to our bodies and, by extension, our work and all our activities.[35] Because it is the basis for human dignity and standard for human perfection, the *imago dei* is the foundation of moral formation and social justice.[36]

If morality is a matter of perfecting God's image in ourselves and others by imitating the perfect image provided in Jesus, it makes sense to look to his family life to guide domestic churches today. What good news does Jesus' family life bring for troubled families? In *Familiaris Consortio* and *Letter to Families* John Paul II does advise his audience that "crosses" cannot be removed completely from this life, and particularly from family life.[37] But he misses opportunities to portray the God we know through Jesus as one who is present and genuinely suffers with us in our family struggles, as compassion requires. God's gift of compassion is distinct from gifts of courage and endurance. God's compassion is understood uniquely in Christianity, and it is crucial that this piece of "good news" be conveyed clearly. There is often a difference, in effect, from a sufferer's point of view between sympathy offered, however sincerely, by someone who hasn't "been in his shoes" compared to someone who has been. In Jesus we have a God who has walked in our shoes.

What I wish for in *Familiaris Consortio* and *Letter to Families* is more attention to the Jesus who, like so many parents, is continually asked to give more when he seemingly has nothing left to give, and only one in ten times gets a "thank you" for his efforts. Could Jesus not empathize with desperate parents who have no resort but trust in God and prayer for miracles when faced with crowds of hungry mouths to feed and scant resources? Surely he knew the anguish of parents and surrogate parent figures who do all they can to prepare their charges for life in the real world, and then must trust them to go out on their own "like sheep in the midst of wolves," praying for the best. From stories of events surrounding his birth and the birth of his cousin John, Jesus may have known something of the emotional strain and social stigma that stem from infertility, unexpected pregnancy, suspected promiscuity, poverty, homelessness, and political exile (some of which continued in his adult life). As for many of us, Jesus' work as an adult meant life constantly on the road, with seemingly little downtime. Most likely he saw what little family he had only on rare occasions. And even then, encounters do not appear to have been especially happy. As a young adult, Jesus had run-ins with his parents on several occasions as he tried to discern his vocation and assert his independence. In his visits at his "home away from home"—the family of Martha, Mary, and Lazarus—Jesus found himself having to referee arguments and defend himself against attacks on his judgment. His cousin John—apparently loved and respected, despite his strange personal habits—ended up in jail and was eventually beheaded. Jesus seems to have gone through adulthood without his earthly father figure, Joseph. He had to worry about who would take care of his mother after his own death. Most likely he had a lot of soul-searching to do as he lived a single adult life in a predominately married world.[38] Though the Gospels recount a relatively small percentage of the events of Jesus' life, they show that he walked in our shoes more often than we may think. He participated fully not only in some generic or abstract humanity, but in the concrete experience of a specific family that was fully human.[39]

John Paul II is absolutely correct in placing the concept of *imago dei* at the center of his theology, and in adopting Vatican II's premise that Jesus Christ, the God-man, "fully reveals man to himself." But our similarity to God does not lie only in traits and experiences we consider good, and this is especially true in matters pertaining to family life. If we want to include *imago dei* in a theology of domestic church, we must check inherited images of God the Father, Jesus the Son, the human family of God, and the Holy Family for balance. Too often we overemphasize the squeaky-clean image of "one big happy family." We may forget that two of the most prominent and poignant biblical images of God and God's people are that of a faithful, but frustrated, husband brooding over an unfaithful wife, and that of a stern, but patient, father trying to raise a disobedient, stubborn, selfish, and foolish son. Less well known but no less moving is the maternal image of God in Isaiah 42:14—"I have looked away, and kept silence, I have said nothing, holding myself in; but now I cry out as a woman in labor, gasping and panting." If the New Testament tells us that Jesus, the perfect image of God, was "like us in all things but sin," we need not interpret this to mean that he never made mistakes, or that he had no need to grow in maturity, integrity, and conviction. Immaturity, deficiency, and error are intrinsic to the human growth process, and they do not necessarily amount to sin (which, in its subjective element, requires distancing oneself from God with full knowledge and full consent). In fact, such deficiencies, even when sinful, can serve as raw material to be transformed into imitation of God. When they are overly idealistic, inherited images of God and God's human family can prompt some people to reject the symbol of domestic church as a source of discouragement rather than hope and growth.

John Paul II could do more to explain human growth toward perfection as images of God, from where we are now to where we ideally ought to be, from the "already" to the "not yet." His best-known writings on family life, *Familiaris Consortio* and *Letter to Families,* contain eloquent descriptions of virtues and values that family life ought to embody, and mention growth, progress, education, maturation, and conversion toward these goals. What is needed is a more productive explanation of deficiencies that accompany a lifetime of Christian maturation.[40] Authors exploring the idea of domestic church must search the tradition to find ways to give positive meaning to the halting steps and falls that families make while they grow as Christian communities. Otherwise, theological discussion of domestic church will provide discouragement, rather than hope, to all of us who fall short of perfection.[41]

Such efforts are found in the writings of many lay authors and the U.S. bishops. *Follow the Way of Love* sees less-than-ideal family situations as opportunities for faith, peacemaking, and recognition of the universality of God's love. The bishops remind us that holiness does not lie in perfection, and that even broken families can be used for God's purposes. In her enlightening article on the "forgotten ministry" of pastoral care to incomplete families in Africa, Prisca Wagua insists that "members of these families are loved by Christ as much as any other, by virtue of being among those who need him the most."[42] In an essay on African family patterns and inculturative evangelization, Kris Owan remarks that polygamists who are refused baptism and marriage in the Church and yet remain associated with the Church as fully as is feasible can provide, in a lifelong catechumenate, a special sort of witness of faith and life both to non-catechumenate polygamists and Christian monogamists.[43]

Both Wright and Leckey cite forgiveness as the "central spiritual dynamic of family life."[44] With specific reference to family life helping us grow into the image of God, Wright lists unconditional love, patience, compassion, humility, and self-knowledge (including knowledge of limitations and the "need to rely on a source of strength greater than ourselves") as character traits acquired in the lessons of family life.[45] None of these can be learned without experience of deficiency and error. Frank O'Loughlin, William Roberts, and Patricia McDonough find Eucharistic and paschal overtones in the seemingly universal family experiences of "dying" to oneself or an outgrown pattern of life; of breaking or sacrificing oneself, giving one's body energy to sustain another; of commending or giving oneself or one's children over to God's trust.[46] Wright concludes, "Whatever the particulars of the formation, parenting [or, family life] breaks us open, cracks our smooth veneers and offers us the opportunity to grow. The direction of growth, if we let our lives become a prayer, is toward God."[47]

It should be clear by now that deficiency, limitation, error, and sin are inherent in domestic churches *ad extra* and *ad intra*. An "interplay of light and darkness" is not only characteristic of "the historical situation in which the family lives," as John Paul II asserts,[48] but equally so within family life, even for families who appreciate themselves as Christian domestic churches.[49] Thus, a theologian's or pastoral minister's task in exploring or working with domestic churches is not to concentrate solely on ideals, nor to give up on them as unrealistic, but to attend to the dynamic and often tense relationship between the two which is at the heart of the families' growth as humans and as Christians. In connection with this theme, I find the following comments from Wendy Wright helpful:

> Only a small percentage of you will be able to construct an accurate picture of your life-situation by appealing to what I might call the myth of the American family: a working father (smiling), a stay-at-home mother (smiling), two children (smiling), perhaps a dog, a single-family dwelling surrounded by a neat lawn. . . .
>
> At the same time that we usher in these almost archetypal images of home, we also recognize the current reality of our homes and families. There may be considerable disjuncture between these sets of data. But this gap need not be uncreative. Nor, I think, should we be deterred from looking at our unidealized life situations as

potential windows through which to touch and be touched by God's presence. *While our "real" homes may not always conform to our "ideal" homes, there is a profound relationship between the two.*

By this I do not mean to suggest that we image ourselves as other than we are. This is not a book that will attempt to articulate a spirituality exclusively out of the experience of the "perfect" or even the clinically "functional" family. After all, an authentic spiritual life assumes that we start exactly where we are, not in some unattained ideal realm. God cannot find us in any place other than the one in which we find ourselves. But neither is this a book that ignores the profound spiritual yearning in each of us to "come home," to realize the "more," both the "more" of what we would want our families to be and the desire for "more" that spurs our religious seeking.

Within this lived tension our spiritual lives are cultivated: the tension between the *factuality* of our daily lives with their monotony, opaqueness, limitations, and sorrows with occasional moments of insight and beauty, and the *equally factual but less realized* soarings of our hearts. "Home" for each of us is at the lived center of this creative tension.[50]

SIX

Domestic Churches Formed
by Baptism and Marriage

---

*Baptism brings all Christians into union with God. Your family life
is sacred because family relationships confirm and deepen this union
and allow the Lord to work through you.*[1]

When I give a lecture on the theme of domestic church, the first question
I usually get from my audience is, "What counts as a domestic church?"
Most people who pose this question to me seem concerned that "domestic church" not be used in a way that ranks some families as more "Christian" than others, based on quantifiable characteristics such as a certain
number of children, a particular division of labor among spouses, or a
canonically valid marriage.

The ranking of marriages (or lack thereof) is an especially delicate
issue, one that often creates obstacles for families trying to worship
together. For instance, celebration of a child's first Communion becomes
awkward when parents in canonically invalid marriages are asked to
refrain from receiving the Eucharist.[2] Prisca Wagua reports that in Africa

most local churches refuse to baptize children of unwed mothers.[3] Similar obstacles can be experienced in interchurch Christian families, even though Catholicism teaches that any valid marriage of two baptized Christians is sacramental. The web-site of the Association of Interchurch Families is replete with stories of families who wish for more opportunities for the Eucharistic sharing.[4] Some testimonials report that teenagers raised in interchurch families find themselves torn when the time for confirmation approaches. Sarah Mayles in England wishes that an ecumenical confirmation service could be developed. In the meantime, she says, "I am an interchurch child; my father is an Anglican and my mother a Roman Catholic. I have grown up as an active member of both denominations and have attended confirmation classes both in the Anglican and the Roman Catholic traditions. I feel an equal member of both churches, and I have decided not to be confirmed to this date. I do not want to affirm publicly my allegiance within one particular church if in so doing I have to discard my commitment to the other."[5]

In a global context, where such sensitive cases are increasingly common, we are faced with a theological question: what is the sacramental foundation of a Christian family or domestic church? Is it shared baptism and/or confirmation, shared Eucharist, sacramental marriage, all of the above, some of the above, or none of the above? Because I am still sorting out my thoughts on issues of shared Eucharist and confirmation for interdenominational families, I will confine this chapter to an examination of how domestic churches are formed by the sacraments of baptism and marriage. The topic of this chapter is closely linked with the theme of our next chapter, which explores whether the nuclear family model is the only one, or the most appropriate one, to have in mind when describing domestic church.

Even before I began lecturing on domestic church, I was sensitized to these questions by my own family history. On the one hand, I am the product of what might be considered the ideal model of a domestic church. Both my parents are Catholic; they were married in the Catholic Church and have been married for forty years. I am one of five siblings, all of whom went through Catholic schools and through the usual childhood sacraments. My mother, a math teacher, quit her profession when her first child was born and didn't resume it till the youngest started kindergarten. On the other hand, I knew from the beginning of my research on domestic church that not all Christian families look like my immediate family. I knew this because neither of my parents had grown up in a family that fit the so-called traditional demographic model. My parents were both raised, for the better part of their childhood, by single mothers. I have never known either of my grandfathers. My paternal grandmother was widowed at a young age. She was left to care for six children ranging from two to thirteen years old. She had only an eighth grade education. She was blessed with my grandfather's brothers, who helped her keep my grandfather's pub in business and acted as surrogate fathers until five of the six the children were on their own. (Sadly, one of the children died in a car accident when he was twenty-one years old.) My grandmother never remarried. For her last few years, when she was no longer able to live alone, her children took turns taking her into their homes for a few months at a time. She died at my Uncle Jack and Aunt Betsy's house when she was ninety-four years old.

My maternal grandmother has an equally remarkable story. When she was four years old, she sailed from Ireland to America with an aunt, leaving her parents behind. Eventually her mother and brother joined her. Because my great-grandmother Katherine supported herself as a nanny for another family's children, my grandmother grew up in a "blended" family, with surrogate sisters and brothers along with her blood brother. My grandmother eventually married and had three children. However, her marriage was not happy. Her husband was often away on military duty. When he was home, he drank too much. Eventually my grandmother packed up the three kids and left, a daring thing to do in her day. She sought an annulment, but it was denied, and she never remarried. She raised my mother, aunt, and uncle with the help of my great-grandmother Katherine. She managed to send her children to Catholic school by working at the school as a gym teacher. She never earned enough money to buy a home or a car. My aunt, as it turned out, developed mental illness as a teenager and was never able to live independently, so she and my grandmother lived together until my grandmother died, also at the age of ninety-four.

Although on paper both my grandmothers had a sacramental marriage, in practice neither could draw upon a sacramental marriage for the strength needed to raise their children to adulthood. Neither had an easy life, but despite these hardships both kept their faith. This faith was passed on to my parents, and from them to me and my siblings, and now to our own children. Because it was so clear to me that my faith derived from Christian families that did not fit the so-called traditional model, I knew when I began work on the theme of domestic church that I'd need to give careful thought to the "marriage or baptism" question and the "nuclear family" question.

THE STATE OF THE QUESTION

The "marriage or baptism" issue is one on which we find significant differences of perspective, sometimes within a single text. At times the lack of clarity is not so much in the authors' intention as in their consistency of presentation. For example, in *Christian Families in the Real World*, Mitch Finley and Kathy Finley define domestic church in their introduction as "a community of baptized Christians." Chapter 4, somewhat misleadingly titled "Marriage: Foundation for the Domestic Church," attempts to clarify that the most basic of all sacraments is baptism and that marriage, a specification of baptism, is the smallest authentic form of church. But, later, chapter 7, titled "Spirituality and the Single Parent," states, "The single-parent family is a true family and a legitimate form of domestic church." Here it appears that baptism, not marriage, is the sacramental foundation of domestic churches.[6]

Beginning with the documents of Vatican II and continuing in the writings of John Paul II, most magisterial reflections on the domestic church's sacramental basis or its practical duties are derived primarily from theology of marriage. (Recent statements of the U.S. bishops are a significant exception, to be discussed shortly.) Marriage theology tends to be based on natural law rather than on Scripture—it revolves around marriage as God's institution for the procreation and education of children and the perpetuation of human society. Baptism is mentioned in connection with domestic church, but not as often as marriage. Sometimes sacraments of marriage and baptism are cited in close proximity with each other as grounding for domestic church, without much clarification of their relationship—*Lumen Gentium* #11 is one example; another is the *Catechism of the Catholic Church*, which includes discussion of domestic church within its treatise on the sacrament of marriage, but comments that "members of the family exercise the priesthood of the baptised in a privileged way" (#1657).

Paul VI takes the opposite approach, introducing the idea of domestic church in a section of *Evangelii Nuntiandi* describing the family's share in the evangelizing apostolate of the laity. Evangelization is not construed solely as the parents' duty flowing from the natural and sacramental purposes of marriage. Rather, "[i]n a family which is conscious of this mission [as domestic church], all members evangelize and are evangelized." Indeed, in families resulting from a "mixed marriage" the duty remains because it is a consequence of common baptism. These families have "the difficult task of becoming builders of unity" (#71).

Familiaris Consortio gives varying explanations of the sacramental grounding of the domestic church's mission. In section #49, which begins formal reflection on the Christian family as sharing in the life and mission of the Church, the pope states that he will "examine the many profound bonds linking the Church and the Christian family and establishing the family as a 'Church in miniature' (*Ecclesia domestica*)." Surprisingly, baptism is not included as one of these bonds. (The closest is an explanation of the Church as Mother.) The sacrament of marriage, however, does get attention as a point of entry in the Church's saving mission:

> [T]he Christian family is grafted into the mystery of the Church to such a degree as to become a sharer, in its own way, in the saving mission proper to the Church: by virtue of the sacrament, Christian married couples and parents "in their state and way of life have their own special gift among the People of God." For this reason they not only receive the love of Christ and become a saved community, but they are also called upon to communicate Christ's love to their bretheren, thus becoming a saving community.

The quote in this passage comes from *Lumen Gentium* #11; the "sacrament" referred to is marriage, not baptism. It is difficult to understand why baptism is not cited as the sacrament by virtue of which Christian families become a saving community, since it is this sacrament, not marriage, that all Christians share and which is most directly indicative of new life in Christ. It appears as if only sacramentally married members of a Christian family are full-fledged members of a domestic church.

The puzzle becomes more perplexing when we consider other sections of *Familiaris Consortio*. Section #52 describes the Christian family's mission as an evangelizing community. We read, "This apostolic mission of the family is rooted in Baptism and receives from the grace of the sacrament of marriage new strength to transmit the faith, to sanctify and transform our present society to God's plan."[7] But an earlier section, #36, entitled "The Right and Duty of Parents Regarding Education," asserts that "[t]he task of giving education is rooted in the primary vocation of married couples to participate in God's creative activity." Are evangelization and education so different as to be rooted in different sacramental vocations? Perhaps one could argue that evangelization is a specifically Christian activity rooted in baptism, while education is a separate, secular, or natural activity rooted in marriage, understood in natural law terms. But this view seems at odds with the Church's post-Vatican II agenda of removing the dichotomy between sacred and secular life, and with some of the pope's statements elsewhere regarding education.[8] Section #38 of *Familiaris Consortio*, entitled "The Mission to Educate and the Sacrament of Marriage," continues the argument begun in section #36 and goes to great lengths to ground Christian parents' educational ministry in the sacrament of marriage:

> The sacrament of marriage gives to the educational role the dignity and vocation of being really and truly a "ministry" of the Church at the service of the building up of her members. So great and splendid is the educational ministry of Christian parents that Saint Thomas has no hesitation comparing it with the ministry of priests: "Some only propagate and guard spiritual life by a spiritual ministry: this is the role of the sacrament of Orders; others do this for both corporal and spiritual life, and this is brought about by the sacrament of marriage, by which a man and a woman join in order to beget offspring and bring them up to worship God."[9]

While no one would question that married parents have a solemn duty to educate their children, or that education is a creative activity, it is not clear why the sacrament of marriage, rather than baptism, gives parental education its character as a "true ministry of the Church." In my mind, any Christian education should be considered, first and foremost, a reflection of the general baptismal vocation to "preach the gospel to all nations, teaching them everything I have commanded you" (Matthew 28:18–20). This passage in *Familiaris Consortio* leaves us wondering whether single, divorced, widowed, or foster parents can consider their education of children a Christian ministry. It would seem much simpler and more theologically consistent to link all Christian education with the apostolic mission of evangelization, rooted in baptism.

Turning to the gift of evangelical discernment, which surely must be a crucial task of any domestic church, the "marriage or baptism" muddle becomes even muddier. We are told in *Familiaris Consortio* #5 that "[t]his discernment is accomplished through the sense of faith, which is a gift that the Spirit gives to all the faithful." One might assume the charism for evangelical discernment is given by the Holy Spirit in baptism, and perhaps in other common experiences shared by the faithful, such as hearing the Word of God and using it to interpret everyday experiences. But neither is mentioned as a source of evangelical discernment; instead, we are told that "Christian spouses and parents . . . are qualified for this role by their charism or specific gift, the gift of the sacrament of matrimony." The pope does not convincingly explain how people like my two grandmothers (let alone the countless Christian single parents who have never married) might have the capacity for evangelical discernment in raising their children to be mature Christian adults.

One may ask whether the sacraments of baptism and marriage, singly or in combination, are the sole or sufficient source of a domestic church's discernment of its nature and mission, or its capacity to fulfill them. Even for domestic churches that do arise from sacramental marriage, a more complex explanation of the capacity for evangelical discernment seems demanded by common sense. Isn't the capacity for discernment a growing thing, linked not only to experiences of sacrament ritual, but also to broader life experience? It seems odd to think that a lifetime supply of discernment skills is given all at once to a young bride and groom or to a person being baptised. Most any parent will acknowledge that wisdom in raising a Christian family comes from trial and error, and also from the borrowed wisdom of persons who have had similar experiences. A simplistic, deductive explanation of sacraments as the source of a domestic church's evangelical discernment capacities would eliminate the need for permanent catechesis, which John Paul II promotes.[10] Two options present themselves: either sacraments of marriage and baptism must be understood as including some element of continual process, or some experiential foundation for domestic churches' evangelical discernment must be added.[11]

John Paul II's writings do not completely settle the question of how baptism and marriage are related in forming domestic churches or in indicating their mission. He gives no argument for the domestic church's existence in anything other than a traditional nuclear family—a happily and, most importantly, sacramentally married husband and wife raising young children. He does not satisfactorily explain how members of a family whose relationship is not marital or parent-child participate as agents of the domestic church's ministry.[12]

The U.S. bishops present a significantly different picture. Beginning in their 1992 colloquium on domestic church and continuing in *Follow the Way of Love*, the U.S. bishops regard the sacrament of baptism as the most important source of insight into the nature and mission of domestic churches. *Follow the Way of Love*'s introductory discourse on the meaning of domestic church focuses on gifts and missionary tasks given in baptism. In this pivotal section of the document, the sacrament of marriage is not mentioned at all in the first few pages (8–10) as the foundation of either family or domestic church. Instead, we are told, "Baptism brings all Christians into union with God. Your family life is sacred because family relationships confirm and deepen this union and allow the Lord to work through you." "Family" is defined as "our first community and the most basic way in which the Lord gathers us, forms us, and acts in the world," and "church" is defined as "two or three gathered in [Jesus'] name. . . . We give the name *church* to the people whom the Lord gathers, who strive to follow his way of love, and through whose lives his saving presence is made known." Later, page 11 introduces sacramental marriage as a sign of Christ's promise to be faithful to those he has chosen. Note that the bishops do not introduce marriage until they first clarify that Christ's promise to be faithful is the "firm foundation" on which "every" Christian family, "like the whole Church," rests. This clarification is noteworthy because the bishops immediately turn their attention to God's gracious presence in the *love* among members of families that *may not arise from sacramental marriage*—single-parent, blended, and interreligious families, along with childless families. They conclude, "The church of the home can live and grow in every family."

The bishops' rationale for this novel approach to domestic church is spelled out candidly in the proceedings of their 1992 colloquium:

> The theology of marriage is a major source of our theology of family as domestic church. In fact, the term is first used by St. John Chrysostom in his homilies on the "marriage passage" in the Epistle to the Ephesians. In *Lumen Gentium* and other documents the term is consistently linked with Christian marriage. The family (domestic church) is regarded as proceeding from, or being rooted in, marriage. Marriage is the origin of family and, therefore, of the domestic church. This is the position taken in official church teaching.
>
> But there are tensions and limits. On the one hand, this position emphasizes the importance and dignity of marriage. On the other hand, it exposes an apparent weakness in our theologizing. There are "families" in our society that are not rooted in marriage. For example, a woman may have a child, never marry the child's father, and then raise and care for her child (sometimes with the help of other family members) in a loving and stable manner. Then, too, there are many families who are no longer united by marriage, e.g., a divorced parent raising children alone. Single-parent families in our society are customarily regarded as families. But are they domestic churches in the same way as families which are rooted in marriage?
>
> A question was raised ... about the relationship of baptism to the domestic church. Our baptismal vocation is basic and antecedent to any other. Matrimony specifies and gives focus to our baptismal commitment. To what extent does Baptism bring the domestic church into being? If this sacrament is also foundational for the domestic church, is the possibility left open for unmarried persons to create a domestic church?[13]

The difference in the current approach of the U.S. bishops, compared to Roman magisterial statements, stems largely from inductive versus deductive reasoning. It corresponds with the two perspectives on the gap between ideals and reality described earlier: ideally all domestic churches might arise from an intact, sacramental marriage, but, in fact, many families that seem to deserve the name do not.

The U.S. bishops display conscious, consistent commitment to contemporary Catholicism's upholding of baptism as the foundational sacrament of the Church (universal and domestic), and the mark of every Christian's call to holiness—whether that person is ordained or lay, single or married, adult or child. The pope, by contrast, appears to straddle two worldviews—one being that of the U.S. bishops, and the other an older perspective that attends more to the separate spiritualities of lay and ordained Christians than to their sharing in the one Spirit of God, and that sees marriage as a sacrament primarily directed toward procreation and education of children. Thus marriage appears related to baptism as the means of future enlargement of the ranks of baptized Christians, rather than as a specification of baptism directed equally to deepening the faith of spouses themselves. For this reason, the pope seems bound to maintain the pattern of situating domestic church only within sacramental marriage and, moreover, only those with children.[14]

THE PRIMACY OF BAPTISM

While theology and practice of sacramental marriage are surely not peripheral to understanding domestic churches, there are many reasons why baptism must be considered a domestic church's primary sacramental foundation. Such a perspective has several advantages. It affirms baptism as the root of every Christian's vocation to holiness. It can appeal to any Christian denomination, and especially to interchurch families whose members participate in more than one Christian tradition. Reflection on domestic church as founded upon shared baptism can be extended to incorporate families wherein one spouse is already Christian and the other spouse or children are exploring Christianity or formally preparing for baptism, a process that can take several years.[15] This approach can speak to Christian couples whose "irregular" marriages are regarded canonically as "invalid" but whose shared, valid baptism is not called into question by Catholicism. This approach better accommodates bonds of family members (such as siblings) not related by marriage. It creates a door for welcoming ordained and other unmarried adults—who are not sealed off from family life—into reflections on domestic church. It acknowledges that just as the role of "child" is our first entrance into family at a human level, the one permanent and universal role among humans, baptism, which marks us a "child of God," is the first, permanent, and universal experience shared by Christians.[16] For all these reasons, baptism as the sacramental foundation of domestic churches deserves more attention in theological and magisterial literature.[17]

There is a further reason why baptism as the sacramental foundation of domestic church deserves more attention; it has to do with the concept of *imago dei* discussed earlier in connection with the tensions inherent in family life. When marriage is seen as the sacramental foundation of domestic church, the message often conveyed, especially by John Paul II, is that a family is sacramental (i.e., conveys God's image or makes God present) to the extent that it models the reciprocal sort of love often called "communion." Though marriage is often said to image the love between Christ and the Church, the way that love is described often sounds more like the perfect communion within the triune Godhead.[18] But there is an equally important aspect of God's love which is especially apparent when it engages humans. Here the love relationship is decidedly less reciprocal. It entails suffering, dying to the self, and struggling to rise again and again to offer love in the hope that maybe this time it will be accepted and returned. This is the "paschal" sort of love best symbolized in baptism. It is this sort of love that many lay authors find neglected in literature I have categorized as deductive and idealistic.

It seems most accurate from a practical and theological perspective to consider marriage and baptism as an interwoven sacramental foundation of domestic church, with baptism being primary.[19] If the domestic church is interpreted as "two or three gathered together in my name,"[20] one can view baptism as that which symbolically marks persons with Jesus' name and invites them to commit to his mission. Sacramental marriage can be seen as that which often (though not always) gathers persons into families, giving them a unique vocation and a bond that distinguishes one group from another. Like other sacraments family members share, sacramental marriage is a public renewal and specification of one's baptismal commitment. Participation in a domestic church engages members in both the reciprocal, joyous love that is a foretaste of heavenly communion, and the earthly, painful, dying-and-rising, hopeful love celebrated at Easter. A domestic church is a case study in the eschatological image of God's kingdom as "already but not yet."

SEVEN

Is the Nuclear Family the Only
Model of Domestic Church?

---

*We honor all families who, in the face of obstacles, remain
faithful to Christ's way of love. The Church of the home
can live and grow in every family.*[1]

In the sources examined during my research for this book, the nuclear
family image—married father and mother running an autonomous household, with children still living at home—is clearly the dominant model of
domestic church. Single parents and blended or step-family relationships
are seldom mentioned.[2] Where they appear, they may be labeled as "irregular or difficult situations," as in *Familiaris Consortio,* part 4, IV. Married
couples without children of their own,[3] grandparents,[4] adult children,[5]
sibling relations, uncles, aunts, cousins, godparents, and other persons
(not related by blood/marriage/adoption) who are a permanent part of
some households are almost completely absent.[6] Cooperative family communities and multigenerational homes receive only limited attention.[7]
Although most authors make some acknowledgment of these sorts of
family relationships, they do not seem to influence discussion of domestic church very much.[8]

Certainly it is convenient to base discussion of domestic church on the nuclear model. This model validates the experience of family I had when growing up; it also corresponds with Catholic/Christian traditions I have inherited—not only theological principles concerning the indissolubility and procreativity of marriage, but also cultural depictions of the proto-typical Holy Family. It is difficult *not* to focus attention on the formative years of childhood and on strongly influential parent-child and marital relationships. On the other hand, there are limits to this habit of thought. There is risk of absolutizing one pattern of family life as ordained by God; this may result in unwarranted condemnation of patterns characteristic of times and places different from one's own. There is risk of excluding persons who rightly ought to be included in discussion of family and, by extension, the risk of excluding them in political, cultural, and religious institutions addressed to families. And there is risk of failing to recognize important convictions that may already be, or ought to be, operative in a Christian domestic church. Let us examine these risks more closely.

A narrow focus on the nuclear model can blind us to needs and con-tributions of many who ought to be considered in discussion or ministry related to domestic churches. Recall that the U.S. bishops felt the need to clarify from the start of *Follow the Way of Love* that they are members of families even if they do not have spouses and children.[9] They speak can-didly about the fact that some families (perhaps many that John Paul II categorizes as being in "difficult or irregular situations") may not under-stand or believe that they can be a domestic church. This concern is the unifying theme of Prisca Wagua's article on pastoral care of incomplete families in Africa. Wagua explains that members of incomplete families are often denied participation in the sacraments, as when children of unwed mothers are denied baptism.[10]

Though most authors operate with a nuclear pattern of family gener-ally in mind, several warn readers not to absolutize this model. Michael Lawler and Gail Risch contend that too many Christians, especially fun-damentalist Catholics and Protestants, naively presume that only the nuclear family has a natural and biblical mandate.[11] Mary Mulligan re-minds us that sociological definitions of family per se do not lend much insight when one's aim is theological understanding.[12] Lawler and Risch agree: "Being Christian means concretely living a Christian life. Living that life makes a family Christian, *no matter what its structure might be.*"[13]

Lisa Sowle Cahill takes a similar approach; her nuanced remarks are worth citing at length.

> Understanding the family as domestic church requires under-standing "church" properly. The primary values defining the Christian family are the same values that define the "new family in Christ": other-concern and compassionate love that overlooks socially normative boundaries and is willing to sacrifice to meet the needs of others. These values are more important in defining the Christian family than is a particular family structure. This does not mean that all structures are equally valid, since some more than others—especially long-term fidelity to mates and children—will serve human growth and happiness and contribute to a more humane society. But it does mean that structure alone is not the key criterion of Christian identity, and it opens up the possibility that even "nontraditional" families may exhibit the most important Christian family values, and for that reason be considered authentic domestic churches.[14]

When we consider family as a metaphor for the Church,[15] surely we must have something in mind other than the nuclear model. There is much room for reflection on similarities between the parish, diocese, or Church Universal and the extended or multigenerational family.[16] This is especially true given Catholicism's stress on communion among believers of all times and places, and on the need to rely on the wisdom of past generations in discerning God's will.[17] I gained insight into this point when my youngest daughter, Elise, was baptized. I was struck by our family baptismal gown—in which my four siblings and I, most of our fourteen children, as well as the child of a close family friend, have been christened. It is now thirty-nine years old and has traveled up and down the eastern United States several times for baptisms in six states. My parents had driven twelve hours to bring the gown, which had been used about two months earlier at the baptism of Elise's cousin Ryan. My mother had carefully repaired a few spots where the seams were frayed, washed it by hand, and laid it in the sun to dry. "If the gown ever got lost or damaged in the mail or at the dry cleaner, there would be no replacing it," we all agreed. While the baptismal water in which Christians of all times and places are immersed is a potent symbol of the Universal Church, the gown in which each of us has been clothed is a beautiful symbol of our domestic manifestation of that Church.

As the title of this book conveys, I believe the U.S. bishops' choice of "two or three gathered together in my name" best and most simply conveys the theological meaning of domestic church. Varied configurations of domestic church illustrate a principle embraced by Vatican II: "The substance of doctrine is one thing, and the manner in which it is expressed is another."[18]

IS HIERARCHY A NECESSARY FEATURE OF DOMESTIC CHURCHES?

Let us next consider *hierarchy* in relationship to the emerging idea of domestic church. I include the topic in this chapter because hierarchical relationships are often associated with the so-called traditional family. Family dynamics that may involve hierarchy include the role of elder generations in directing younger generations, the relationship of husband and wife, division of labor among male and female household members, and parental authority over children.

In *Blessed Be the Bond* William Everett explains that historically family authority has been dispersed in three patterns: hierarchical, organic (i.e., separate-but-equal or complementary roles), and egalitarian. All three patterns have some precedent in Christian Scripture and tradition, and thus it is not surprising that different visions of authority may be found in documents from a single Christian denomination, even those produced within the same time period.[19]

Everett places *Familiaris Consortio*'s understanding of "little church" in the hierarchical category. He considers the discourse on marriage and family in *Gaudium et Spes* to straddle the organic and egalitarian categories, while St. Paul's writings on house churches show both hierarchical and organic elements. I think Everett is on target with all of his categorizations except that of *Familiaris Consortio*. As I read him, John Paul II tries to incorporate both ancient and recent authorities on marriage and family—some with a hierarchical outlook, others with a bias toward equality of family members. I would place John Paul II's writings in the organic category, with some egalitarian elements. For instance, in *Familiaris Consortio* ## 19–25 references to "equality," "communion," and "friendship" are interwoven in a framework that sees spouses and other family members as "complementary," with "specific gifts" or "roles." The pope pointedly rejects claims of male superiority and offenses against women's dignity. His *Letter to Families* #12 strongly chides fathers who forsake responsibility for unintended pregnancies. On the other hand, *Familiaris Consortio* #23 says that while both men and women have equal rights to work outside the home, societies should take steps to see "that wives and mothers are not in practice compelled to work outside the home," so that they can devote themselves full time to their families. No such protections appear to be in order for men. In a discourse on parents' duty to educate their children in prayer, John Paul II displays his organic bias with a quotation from Paul VI that asks mothers to teach children prayers, to prepare them for sacraments, to encourage them to think of Christ's suffering when they are sick and to invoke the aid of the saints, and to lead them in the family rosary. Fathers have significantly fewer duties. "And you, fathers, do you pray with your children, with the whole domestic community, *at least sometimes?* Your example of honesty in thought and action, joined to *some* common prayer, is a lesson for life, an act of worship of singular value."[20]

Everett's distinctions serve as a warning to be critical in searching for common threads among Christian writings on the family as domestic church. It is easy to selectively produce proof texts that can be used to make (what I consider) inappropriate claims about relationships among members of domestic churches. We do not have to stretch our imaginations too far to foresee that some persons might regard the term "domestic church" as an indication that, for Catholics, levels of hierarchy characteristic of the Church at large ought to be mimicked in families, with fathers assuming the places of highest honor.

A perfect example of such a reaction is displayed in a curious document, *The Priesthood of the Laity in the Domestic Church*, by H. Lyman Stebbins, past president of Catholics United for the Faith.[21] This pamphlet is unusual because, while it consistently grounds the domestic church in the sacrament of baptism, rather than marriage, and makes the progressive claim that "as a little Church, the home is specifically a localization of the Church universal,"[22] it completely misses Vatican II's insistence on the equality of spouses. The document includes one citation of Vatican II (the domestic church passage from *Lumen Gentium* #11), but all other documentation of its argument comes from older sources. Stebbins asserts that, in a Christian family, the father ought to be regarded not merely as pastor of a domestic church, but as the vicar of Christ—and ritually installed as such (a ritual service is provided)—while the mother is considered a helpmeet or associate.

> We really must notice with astonishment, and take to heart, that here two divinely appointed Vicars of Christ on earth [referring to pre–Vatican II citations of Pius XI and John XXIII] are telling fathers of families that *they* are God's vicars in the domestic Church! They, with their wives, have priestly office there, but the office of the father is of higher authority. . . . (9)
>
> . . . we have our little domestic Church built and blessed. What comes next? Well, we have heard that the father occupies in the home the place of God, the place of a vicar of Christ, the place of a bishop, the place of a priest. That's quite a place! It ought to be made ready, be liturgically established, be given a sacramental dimension. In some mode the father should be consecrated and installed in his tiny see, while the general priesthood of the mother and of all the baptized within the household is also recognized, declared, and honored. (18)

Stebbin's pamphlet is an anomaly among recent Catholic writings on marriage and family. The overwhelming consensus of magisterial and lay authors is that hierarchical gender stereotypes are to be considered obsolete: within a contemporary domestic church, husbands and wives ought to consider each other equals. There is not complete agreement as to whether men and women are equally suited to public or household work and care of young children,[23] but generally authors encourage spouses to share household chores and child care, and consider both public and household work to have equal dignity and influence on the Christian family's spiritual development. Thus, even where household tasks are distributed according to apparently organic criteria, spouses are to make distribution decisions together, as friends and equals. We might say the decisive feature of a family functioning as domestic church is not tasks done per se, but the spirit they embody.

EIGHT

Is a Romantic Model of Family Appropriate for Domestic Church?

A theology of domestic church, properly understood, should be a counter-cultural statement. It should radically challenge certain postmodern and Western notions about what a family is for, e.g., a safe haven, a unit of consumerism, an overly-affective domain.[1]

The nuclear model of family is often linked with a "romantic" model that understands the purpose of marriage and family as providing love among members. Love is understood in a way that emphasizes emotional intimacy, affirmation, and companionship. This model has become so prevalent in our culture that some of my students have a hard time grasping the fact that people in many times and places, even today, have not seen finding a "soul mate" as the primary mark of a good marriage.[2] When we study Scripture, especially the Old Testament, the first reaction of many students is that people in ancient times did not think love was important for marriage and family life. (Surely this must have been true in some cases, and is probably still true in some cases today.) What takes time for these students to appreciate is that the Bible speaks frequently of love, but love is often understood with different emphases. Ancient Jewish women hoped that their husbands would be reliable providers for their families and respected members of their community. Texts like Proverbs 31 show that a man would praise his wife for her skill and diligence in managing a household, for caring for the children, who would carry on his family name, and even for her "wisdom" and "kindly counsel." These efforts, and the praise attached to them, should be understood as expressions of marital love. While literature such as the Song of Songs reveals that a romantic, passionate sort of love was not unknown, this aspect of love was typically of secondary concern, as Michael Lawler explains:

> Love between spouses was not exclusively romantic love rooted in feeling and passion; it was the love required in the Torah injunction cited by Jesus, "You shall love your neighbor as yourself (Lev. 19:18; Mk. 12:31; Mt. 19:19). *Though feeling is sometimes part of neighbor-love, it is not always part of it and it is never all there is to it.* Neighbor-love is more radical than feeling, romantic or otherwise. It is . . . a love rooted in the will and expressed in active "loyalty, service, and obedience." The neighbor-love and, therefore, *the spousal love the Bible requires is loyalty/fidelity, service, and obedience or availability to another person.*[3]

Rosemary Haughton traces historical development of family patterns, particularly nineteenth-century development of the bourgeois ideal where-by romantic love is considered the cement that holds families together. Noting economic and psychological needs served by various models of family at the times they developed, Haughton says it is appropriate that the nineteenth-century middle-class romantic ideal has retained such a prominent place in Christianity today, even if family love is not always as sincere as it is made out to be, and even if economic forces still steer decisions to marry and have children. She says it "matters to Christians" that families be places where people learn how to love. Indeed, this purpose ought to be the standard by which Christians evaluate and adapt cultural variations of family life: "[F]or most ordinary Christians, now as previously, the Christian family will be formed according to whatever sociological pattern happens to form family life in general at the time.

IS A ROMANTIC MODEL OF FAMILY APPROPRIATE FOR DOMESTIC CHURCH?

89

Christians need only refuse to accept the general pattern when either they have a special vocation to do something different, or the prevalent pattern makes the growth of love and holiness virtually impossible. This is certainly not the case in our society. Like the first Gentile Christians, we do not need to alter the normal pattern so much as transform it."[4]

For Christians trying to assess the romantic model of family life, accepting the normal cultural pattern, and yet transforming it to align it with Christian priorities, is key. Christians should welcome an emphasis on companionship as a balance to models that have viewed marriage and family as simply economic institutions or legal contracts—with women and children often regarded as property. Still, the romantic model can distort the reality of family life, even serving as a rationalization to jump ship when the going gets tough, under the presumption that family life is not good simply because all one's perceived needs are not being met.

To provoke my students to scrutinize this model, I tell two stories of marriages within my own extended family. The first story is about a nephew I inherited from my husband's side of the family. My nephew has been married twice. In his first marriage, both the bride and the groom came from wealthy families. The wedding was picture perfect, with a bishop officiating. There were at least four showers before the wedding day; once the couple opened their wedding gifts, they had a fully furnished home. It would appear that this young couple didn't want for anything. And yet, about five months after the wedding, my nephew came home to find a note on the kitchen table; it said, "I'm not having fun anymore." His wife wanted, and got, a divorce. Soon after this disaster, my nephew told my husband, "I don't know what happened—we hadn't even been married long enough to have a fight!" Years later, my nephew's mother told me that the young bride apparently had doubts about getting married, but went through with the wedding because it seemed impossible to back out. Given the lavishness of the wedding preparations, this explanation seems plausible. Here, it seems the romantic model provided the impetus to enter a marriage that probably shouldn't have happened, and to leave once it was clear that one spouse "wasn't having fun anymore."

The second story I tell my students is about my aunt Joan and my uncle Tom, who have three adult children and three grandchildren. About twenty years ago, my uncle Tom was doing some home repairs and fell off the roof of his house (surprisingly, since he was a firefighter). He went into a coma. If my memory serves me correctly, it lasted several weeks, perhaps months. When he emerged from the coma, he was a very different person. He had to relearn almost everything. He has never again been able to work professionally and has many permanent disabilities. I suspect that over the years there have been days when my aunt has said to herself, "I'm not having fun anymore." Yet, she took her marriage promises at face value; she and my uncle have been married over forty years. Despite the difficulties she has endured in taking care of her husband and children, my aunt has a reputation as a very optimistic person.

When I tell my aunt and uncle's story, I ask my students to question not only the romantic model of marriage and family, but also the related presumption that these are private affairs. The 2001 "State of Our Unions" report from the Rutgers National Marriage Project says that 80 percent of young adults surveyed agreed that "marriage is nobody's business but the two people involved." Taken together with the 94 percent rate of young people who see marriage as a relationship with a soul mate first and foremost, the portrait of marriage embraced is, in the words of the report's authors, "emotionally deep but socially shallow."[5] A theology of domestic church, in keeping with the best of Christian tradition, reminds us that marriage and family are always public affairs. Far from being nobody else's business, the family's role of teaching people how to love and keep commitments is a matter with many public repercussions, as is the role of providing for the material needs of immediate family members and the surrounding community. Sometimes the public significance of marriage and family are not apparent until we consider the social costs (e.g., foster care, substance abuse and mental-health treatment, a judicial system to handle divorce and child custody disputes, restraining orders, etc.) that are traceable to broken or unhealthy family life. Recent social scientific research published by the Rutgers University National Marriage Project, the University of Chicago Family, Religion, and Culture Project, and the Creighton University Center for Marriage and Family confirm that marriage and family life inevitably have a public impact—especially on children—whether we intend this or not.[6] The question is not whether marriage and family have a public impact, but *what sort* of impact this will be, i.e., helpful or destructive.

From a theological perspective, a sacramental marriage is meant to be a public sign, witnessing God's covenant with humans and Christ's love

IS A ROMANTIC MODEL OF FAMILY APPROPRIATE FOR DOMESTIC CHURCH?

91

for the Church.[7] Covenant love doesn't disappear simply because one party "isn't having fun anymore." I tell my students, "My aunt Joan is not only an example of a loyal wife. She is an example of what it means to be a Christian, and that means being an example of how much God loves us. That's what 'marriage as a sacrament' is all about." The public witness of her domestic church was verified at my brother's wedding. At the reception, there was a series of eloquent toasts. One of the loveliest was when my brother toasted my aunt Joan and uncle Tom, thanking them for their presence and saying that he had them in mind when he pledged to marry his wife "for better or worse." I suspect my aunt's fidelity to my uncle in his time of need was not motivated *explicitly* by a desire to teach her nephew a countercultural lesson of what marriage is about. And yet, providentially, that is how her marriage functioned.

Set in a cultural context where privacy and freedom of choice are celebrated almost as ends in themselves, the romantic model of family love can be interpreted such that it prescribes no particular obligation toward persons not mutually chosen. Christian heritage should provoke domestic churches to regard immediate and extended family members, whether chosen (i.e., spouses and "planned" children) or unchosen (i.e., everybody else) as a blessing, with some gift to offer, rather than a mere burden or untimely inconvenience. The romantic model can be interpreted to permit opting out of obligations toward persons with unforeseen special needs, or who change in ways that we do not choose—especially in ways that affect their ability to provide us affirmation and emotional companionship. For instance, one might argue that my uncle Tom is no longer the same person my aunt Joan married. Care for him has imposed countless physical, emotional, and financial sacrifices on her; moreover, he has not been able to fulfill her emotional and sexual needs as she had hoped, so her marriage promises can be considered void if she chooses. Apparently, my aunt thinks differently.[8]

The romantic model of family has evolved to a point where *deliberately chosen* companionship and emotional affirmation are depicted as the "love" that makes family life worth living. Ironically, this model can fuel new forms of the contractual understanding of marriage and family that proponents of romantic love have historically critiqued. The contracts may not be of the same terms as those of a previous era, but nevertheless the relationships are contractual in character, for they are commitments to relationships on specified terms. Serial marriages and divorces among individuals who "go their separate ways" as their "interests change" are one example.[9] Another example is seen in advertisements that have become increasingly common in Ivy League campus newspapers, seeking "generous" female students (with stipulated heights, ethnicities, and SAT scores) to provide eggs for "loving" infertile couples (in exchange for tens of thousands of dollars). The desire to parent a child of one's own at any cost, which at first glance seems an expression of pride in one's heritage, self-sacrifice, or altruism, can become distorted when infertility therapy becomes a lucrative commodity, but the distortion is shrouded by romantic language of love and generosity.[10] Thus, the danger of conceiving family in romantic terms is that we may completely miss an important message conveyed in the symbol of domestic church—a call to solidarity among *all children* of God and *brothers and sisters* in Christ, not simply those to whom we are related by blood, marriage, or carefully screened adoption.

NINE

Domestic Church and Sacramentality

Rosemary Haughton begins an essay on "Being a Christian Family" with commentary on a passage from *Gaudium et Spes* #48: "Thus the Christian family, which springs from marriage as a reflection of the loving covenant uniting Christ with the Church, and as a participation in that covenant, will manifest to all men Christ's living presence in the world, and the genuine nature of the church." Haughton's reaction to this passage is both amusing and perceptive. Her first comment is that, "It isn't, as it stands, very inspiring. The language is about as rousing as a sleeping pill." Thus, she contends, we may overlook the fact that "what it is actually saying is as full of energy as a nuclear power station." The theologian and mother of ten explains,

> It is saying that when people see a Christian family—you, me, those kids sitting there eating sausages and wondering what to quarrel about next—they will be able to see quite clearly that Christ is alive and at work, here and now. And they will be able to see *how* he lives and works—what the Church is, in fact.
>
> On the face of it this is a pretty ridiculous thing to say. There are days on which anyone who came to a meal in our family (or yours,

probably) would be unlikely to think about anything but how soon it would be over. Other times it might be enjoyable. But—"manifest Christ's living presence"?[1]

If one has any sympathy for Haughton's reaction, then several questions present themselves: Why does it appear ridiculous to claim that the average Christian family "manifests Christ's living presence"? And, if it seems ridiculous to make such a statement, why did the bishops of Vatican II do so? How can this statement, and similar lofty claims about domestic church, be understood?

Indicated in Haughton's allusions to "eating sausages" and "wondering what to quarrel about next" are two reasons why "family life" and "manifesting Christ's presence" might seem, in the minds of many Christians, not to overlap. First, family life seems too mundane and secular to serve a purpose so grand and holy as manifesting Christ's presence. Haughton suggests many people presume that even at its best family life is not the place where we most clearly see Christ alive and at work. That place is the institutional Church, especially the work of "full-time" Christians—those in religious orders, ordained ministers or priests, bishops, and the pope. The rest of us may "help" or "participate" in manifesting Christ and the genuine nature of the Church, but this part-time "work of the Church" is regarded as "something extra to ordinary life, which is just a background to Christian life."[2] Second, family life is often the setting where we are not at our best, but rather where we display our sinful side. Those who live with us see us at our worst. Many people may have trouble associating family life with Christ, at least in part, because terms like "Christ" and "Church" are associated only with things like love, communion, peace, joy, and just rewards.

Thus, if it seems ridiculous to say family life can manifest Christ's presence, it is probably because we assume Christ cannot be present in, or manifested by, the secular and sinful elements of our world. If the idea of domestic church is to have any positive meaning for Christian families, these problematic assumptions must be replaced. To the extent that such assumptions are entrenched at an emotional level, we must call upon the skills of pastoral ministers, liturgists, and religious educators. To the extent that these assumptions are supported by rationalizations—of the meaning of Church, the secular world, and the work of Christ—the discipline of theology exists to offer alternatives. Starting from a different set of assumptions, can we explain how family life reveals Christ alive and at work? Until this is done, Haughton implies, we have neglected the most basic element of a theology of the Christian family.

> [I]f this isn't what Christian families are doing then there isn't much point in calling them Christian families. It would be reasonable, perhaps, to call them families of Christians. That way round, it means that these people in this house are Christians, and that this family is where they live and get part of their education as Christians. Later, if all goes well, the children will take their part in the Christian life, the work of the Church. The work of the Church, in this view, is something in which ordinary Christians can *take part*. . . . They are, in fact, part-time Christians. But part-time Christians can't show the "genuine nature of the Church." In order to "manifest Christ's living presence in the world," you have to be a full-time Christian. You mustn't just *take part* in the work of the Church, you must *be* the Church, so that people can see what the Church is: the body of Christ. . . .
>
> That is why the sentence I quoted is so startling. There it is, in plain language, actually saying that Christians of the most ordinary kind are not just *helping* to "manifest Christ's living presence," or *taking part* in that manifestation, but are actually able to do it themselves. They don't do it by joining a guild or going on a pilgrimage or supporting the Catholic schools—however useful these things may be. They do it simply because they are a Christian family. They show the "genuine nature of the Church." Almost as a matter of course . . .[3]

This chapter is intended to systematically explain why Christian families or domestic churches can manifest Christ's presence, not only when engaged in explicitly religious activities or displaying their best human qualities, but equally when engaged in mundane, secular affairs, and even when they are mired in suffering, immaturity, and sinfulness. Karl Rahner's thought on the meaning of sacrament in general, along with his notions of *liturgy of the world* and *Church as sacrament*, will be my key resources. Rahner did not write much about Christian families, and I have located only a few brief references to domestic church in his work.[4] Still, his thought helps us appreciate that Christian families, as domestic churches, exist to manifest Christ's presence to their own members and to the surrounding world in a manner that is basic and irreplaceable.

In fact, many authors mention sacramentality in connection with domestic church. Usually the connection is treated only briefly, and rarely is Rahner credited for the interpretation of sacrament these authors seem to have in mind.[5] Many other sources speak of family life as "manifesting Christ" or "making Christ present" without using the term "sacrament" per se; for example, *Familiaris Consortio* #54 speaks of the church of the home as a "sign of the presence of Christ." In general, the problematic assumptions exposed through Haughton's comments on "eating sausages and wondering what to quarrel about next" are not examined in depth.

Rahner's theology tackles these problematic assumptions head-on. Contrasting himself with a prevalent theological tradition founded upon the premise that God is encountered primarily in the sacred realm—the domain of the Church, especially its sacraments—Rahner constructs a theology of sacramentality upon the conviction that the so-called secular world is permeated by God's grace. Rahner's sacramental theology is useful in overcoming the obstacles to a theology of domestic church indicated by Haughton, but there are other concerns it can address. I have in mind, first, the *anxiety* of families who believe the Church's sacraments are privileged avenues of encounter with God, but who find it nearly impossible to participate—as families—in worship services customarily available to them. Second, I have in mind the *apathy* of people who find institutional worship meaningless, superstitious, or an attempt to escape from reality, and who believe that if God is to be encountered at all, it is in the ordinary, often troubled existence of family life in the real world.

The plan of this chapter is as follows: first, I will explain Rahner's understanding of sacramentality; next, I will show how it helps correct the problematic assumptions I have identified:

- the assumption that family life is too ordinary and sinful to manifest Christ's presence;
- the assumption that this task mainly pertains to "full-time" or professional Church members and specifically religious activities they lead; and

• the assumption that families deserve the name "Christian" or "domestic church" to the extent that they help or participate in the Church's official, institutional work.

Because Rahner wrote little on Christian family life, I will use marriage and family literature to fill in details of my presentation of domestic churches under the rubric of sacramentality. Among the more important points to be covered in this chapter, I will examine God's presence in ordinary life (aka the liturgy of the world) and propose that domestic churches be seen as the forum where the Church as sacrament does its most basic work. Christian families who deserve the name domestic church have (to some degree) explicitly embraced a sacramental vision, which perceives Christ's presence in all things. Domestic churches aim to embody this vision in everyday life; at the same time, the discipline of ordinary life is instrumental in cultivating a sacramental perspective.

AN OVERVIEW OF RAHNER'S UNDERSTANDING OF SACRAMENTALITY

The Pervasiveness of Grace

Rahner poses his understanding of sacrament as both traditional and new. He is committed to traditional tenets of Catholic sacramental theology, including the belief that the seven official sacraments are privileged signs and instruments of God's grace, that they have been instituted by Christ, and that they cause grace *ex opere operato*.[6] Rahner's understanding of sacrament is heavily indebted to Thomas Aquinas, though Rahner thinks he improves upon Aquinas in two respects: first, he clarifies the relationship of sacraments to the Church; second, he clarifies the traditional axiom that "sacraments cause grace by signifying it" (sacramenta significando efficiunt gratiam).[7] Rahner also credits Aquinas for a principle that, he says, "is all too easy to overlook again and again," and that may be considered the centerpiece of Rahner's own sacramental theology: "God has not attached his power to the sacraments in such a way that he could not also impart the effects of sacramental grace even without the sacraments themselves." Rahner remarks, "Now, taking this as our starting point we can adopt an approach to the entire theology of the sacraments which is the opposite of that usually envisaged."[8]

Rahner was convinced that there exist in Catholicism two very different models used to depict God's grace and, by extension, two very different interpretations of the secular world, the Church, and the sacraments. The first model emphasizes that God gives grace in identifiable historical events, through the authoritative Church, in a completely unmerited way. In addition, the "World" is depicted primarily in a negative way; it is understood foremost as "secular" or "profane," as contrasted to sacred. Rahner explains, "This conceptual model of grace is based on the implicit assumption that grace can be an unmerited gift of God only if it becomes present and only where it becomes present in a secular and sinful world to which it is mostly denied."[9] What place do sacraments have in this model? Rahner puts it succinctly: they are "events at certain points in space and time where grace comes to be in a world otherwise deprived of it. . . . [T]hey produce something otherwise unavailable."[10] The Church, as custodian of the sacraments, becomes a place of refuge where one periodically replenishes one's soul with nourishment needed to tolerate the demands of the secular world, which God, for mysterious reasons, has posed as an entry test for heaven.[11]

The second model of grace, which Rahner prefers, is based on convictions he considers equally traditional, but neglected by Catholicism as he knew it: first, sanctifying grace is present everywhere that individuals have not closed themselves off to God by a truly culpable denial; second, this grace is made manifest and effective (though not always explicitly or consciously) in the concrete events of human history, wherever humans live in a manner that does not imply moral guilt.[12] The pervasiveness of grace is evidenced by the basic human experience of "transcendence." We experience ourselves as knowers, as free and responsible agents, and as persons who yearn for what lies beyond the "horizon" of worldly limitation. These everyday events reveal that yearning for God is a basic element of all human experience—even for those who do not yet recognize God in these experiences. Of course, the "World" is seen much more optimistically in this second model.[13]

For our analysis of domestic church, the significance of this second model of grace is Rahner's explanation of grace as mediated through the concrete events of everyday life.[14] We are beginning to chip away at the problematic assumptions identified previously. But we have not yet explained how Christian families can manifest both Christ's presence and the genuine nature of the Church.

The Necessity of Church as Basic Sacrament

If it is possible to encounter God anywhere, why are the Church and its sacraments needed? For Rahner, they are necessary because through them grace is made

- explicit or thematic
- concrete, historical, incarnational
- a public or communal event
- certain and irrevocable
- specific to particular individuals at decisive moments of their lives

These qualities promote the free and deliberate acceptance of grace that God intends for humans. For Rahner the Incarnation is a climactic moment and the premiere sacramental event. In traditional language of sacramental theology, Jesus' humanity is a visible sign of God's invisible grace. The Church (as the basic sacrament of salvation for the world) and the individual sacraments are needed because they manifest the presence, love, and mercy of our mysterious God, revealed in Jesus the Christ. By introducing people to Jesus throughout the centuries, they have provided humans the opportunity to freely, consciously accept God as the fulfillment of their transcendent striving.

Rahner proposes that the key to understanding how sacraments "cause" grace lies in the scholastic axiom "Sacramenta significando efficiunt gratiam," which even Aquinas did not take seriously enough.[15] As with Christ as the primal sacrament and the Church as the continued public manifestation of God's saving mercy and love, individual sacraments effect or cause grace because they make its presence known. Each sacrament conveys an essential element of God's Word, which has been entrusted to the Church and brings with it the full public commitment of the Church, to specific individuals at decisive moments of their lives. With regard to sacramental reception or fruitfulness, Rahner believes that because our source of grace is incarnational, the true fulfillment or effect of grace is likewise. Grace is not directed to the soul alone, but to the entire human being. Our response to grace is meant to be symbolically expressed or embodied in worldly activity, and such embodiment is the fulfillment of God's sacramental self-communication.[16]

What shall we take away from this for our analysis of domestic church? I suggest the following: If the mission of the Church as sacrament is to make Christ's presence known to specific individuals, concretely, at decisive moments of their lives, and to elicit some sort of incarnate response, then Church and sacrament must somehow reach into everyday life, including family life. It is in keeping with God's plan of revelation that Christian family life function as church of the home and as sacrament.

The Liturgy of the World in Relation to Church as Sacrament

It is important to clarify that for Rahner "any grace-giving event"—here he refers to those occurring in secular rather than specifically religious contexts—"has a quasi-sacramental structure and shares in Christ's character as both divine and human."[17] In contrast to theologies preoccupied with drawing distinctions between sacraments and other Church activities, between religious and secular lives of Christians, and between the Church and the World, Rahner insists there is one sacramental process of salvation with many phases—some institutional, some not—but all equally necessary.[18] Rahner coins the expression "liturgy of the world" to emphasize the continuity of varied sacramental encounters with God.[19] To appreciate Rahner's use of this term, two points must be kept in mind: first, there are not two separate spheres of existence to be distinguished as "sacred" and "secular/profane" according to the presence or absence of God. The difference conveyed by these terms refers to the degree to which God's presence is made explicit and recognized. Conversely, for those who see with the eyes of faith, there is no ordinary experience that cannot serve as an instrument of grace.[20]

It cannot be overemphasized that Rahner considers liturgy of the world and liturgy of the institutional Church interdependent. When grace is encountered in the liturgy of the world, sacramentality pertains especially to its concrete/historical and individual character. Sometimes such events of grace are explicit or thematic, but often this is not the case. For humans to fully embrace their transcendence, quasi-sacramental experiences must be explicitly connected with the historical Jesus. This is one crucial purpose of the Church's liturgy. The institutional Church's liturgy conveys two more important sacramental elements that often remain unclear in the liturgy of the world: the communal character of revelation and salvation and the certainty/irrevocability of God's gracious love and mercy.[21]

Though he does not recommend their conclusions, here Rahner shows regard for those who consider themselves in touch with God even while apathetic about institutional worship. He even admits that it is normal for believers to experience Church liturgies as somewhat contrived manifestations of grace. However, elements of artificiality in the Church's liturgy are best addressed not by abandoning official liturgy, nor by insisting that it be simply accepted as a mysterious truth of the faith, but by pastoral efforts to help people uncover the sacredness of their everyday life, which Church liturgy is supposed to ritualize.[22] As we have seen already and shall examine further, it is precisely this discovery of the sacredness of everyday life that is at stake in our consideration of domestic church. As the 1992 NCCB colloquium put it, "The recognizing and naming of the 'sacred in the ordinary' is the necessary substratum for an awareness of domestic church. Something must first be called holy before it can be identified as a work of the domestic church."[23]

In what might be regarded as a summary of Rahner's understanding of sacramentality, Michael Skelley says that the institutional Church's liturgy is best understood as the "symbol" of the liturgy of the world.[24] The Church as basic sacrament and, by extension, the individual sacraments are the public, historical, concrete, and certain proclamation of God's presence in the world. They bring out of obscurity, to its clearest possible expression, the grace always operative in concrete events of human life, wherever individuals transcend hopelessness and limitation and live as God designs them to be. The Church and its sacraments are not a refuge from the world but, in fact, derive their meaning from the world. The two are related precisely as *sacramentum* and *res sacramenti*, sign and reality signified.[25]

It seems to me that if Karl Rahner had written an essay on domestic churches, he would have described them as the most basic arena where the liturgy of the world finds explicitly Christian, sacramental, and thereby ecclesial, expression. Following Rahner's lead, it no longer appears ridiculous to claim that Christ's presence can be discovered in family life, or that Christian families are a form of church. Instead, we can assert that an explicitly Christian sense of God's presence, love, and mercy are usually cultivated through family life if at all and that, if God is not experienced in the ordinariness and imperfection of our homes, the Good News proclaimed and sacramentally ritualized by the institutional Church will be regarded as foreign and incredible rather than the fulfillment of our most urgent questions and striving.

SACRAMENTAL PERSPECTIVE: THE MOST ESSENTIAL FEATURE OF DOMESTIC CHURCHES

Once a Rahnerian sense of world liturgy and of Church as sacrament is adopted, it is striking how consistently an interpretation of *domestic church as sacrament* is affirmed by literature on Christian family life. One author who deals seriously with the sacramentality of Christian family life related to, but distinguishable from, sacramental marriage is Maureen Gallagher. Gallagher sums up essential components of contemporary understanding of sacramentality: (1) God's self-communication with the world, (2) recognition and acceptance of this in life's ordinary events, which is the task of faith, and (3) celebration of this grace within the community.[26] She contends that despite the pope's use of the term "sacrament" in *Familiaris Consortio* in the narrowly defined sense of the seven sacraments, the conviction that family life as a whole is sacramental is supported by the encyclical wherever family is called domestic church:

> As church is a sacrament, so the family, as domestic church, is a sacrament. And just as the church celebrates sacraments in the community, so does the family ritualize its gifts, its ups and downs, its brokenness, its giftedness. . . . It experiences life every day; at certain times such as birthdays, parties, Sunday dinners or brunches, it takes life in slow motion so its members can come to new realizations, new awareness of what they mean to each other. At such times families take their raw experiences, make them significant and celebrate them. This is the heart of sacramentality. So I propose that by saying the family is "domestic church," the document is implying that the family is sacrament.[27]

Of the three elements of sacramentality identified by Gallagher, the second may be considered the crucial distinguishing feature of domestic churches. Sacramentality is first and foremost an outgrowth of faith, a distinctive way of seeing the world.[28] It is another name for the second worldview depicted by Rahner, which assumes that despite its all too obvious evils and limitations, the so-called secular world is permeated by God's gracious presence. To the extent family members believe that God's Spirit remains constantly present in their families' lives, that no work undertaken in the care of their households falls outside the scope of God's concern, and that whatever good they do in Christ's name (implicitly or explicitly) serves as a medium of grace for others, they have begun to transform their homes into domestic churches.

Mary Perkins speaks eloquently to the idea of sacramental perspective and its link with embodiment. Remarkable for one who wrote before Vatican II, Perkins invites lay readers to consider their homes "little churches."[29] Perkins says God deliberately designed marriage as the "usual vocation" of Christians and humans in general because it is "beautifully suited to the needs of human creatures who are made up by bodies and souls."[30] She says that, ironically, many of us struggle with the vocation of marriage because we have not learned to appreciate the sacramental value of our bodies, nor the fact that we love the God we do not see by loving the family members we do see. Perkins's thoughts are as timely today as they were when she wrote them in 1955:

> The great difficulty about the vocation of marriage for many of us today (especially, perhaps, what are called well-educated men and women) is to learn how to appreciate the sacramental value of the whole physical side of married life, not only of the marriage act, but of all the processes of childbearing and child care and of ordinary household tasks. A great many of us never realized until we were married and had children that human life was so very physical. . . . Our education, our special training, our "careers" had given us to suppose that our bodies were more or less incidental to our human make-up, rather useful instruments, perhaps, or annoying handicaps, but not to be particularly considered in getting ahead either on earth or toward heaven.

We need, then, to devote thought and prayer to the sacramental significance which God himself has given to all the basic functions of married and home life. We need to realize (at least at the depths of our souls, if not explicitly at the end of Monday morning) that cooking and cleaning and tidying and so on are not merely regrettable necessities of family life, but are meant by God to raise our minds and hearts to Him, and to be a part of our reasonable service of Him in the vocation of marriage. . . .

Christian marriage rightly lived is the vocation in which we learn to love God and all our neighbors with the love of Christ, primarily by learning to love one man or woman, and some special children; . . . it is the vocation of trying to use rightly the things that are seen for the sake of the unseen God; and of helping to build up His Kingdom by helping Him to make and form its chosen stones, our children.[31]

Because sacramentality is linked to embodiment, many activities that all families share will take on a symbolic Christian significance where sacramental vision is operative. On the other hand, domestic churches should be willing to make countercultural lifestyle choices if these seem necessary to manifest (what they consider) a true perspective on the world. The physical embodiments of sacramental perspective will vary, and manifestations in particular circumstances will not always be easy to predict, but the impetus to embody sacramental outlook in one's lifestyle will follow almost intuitively.

Thus, to the casual observer, domestic churches may not look much different from other families. Yet, if we accept Rahner's conviction that the grace of God's sacramental communication is effective and fruitful to the degree that it is recognized (and responded to) in the guise of seemingly ordinary signs, then we may say domestic churches are, despite appearances, different from families where God's presence remains undiscovered, unnamed, unconnected with Jesus Christ and his Church, or connected with the institutional church but not with ordinary life. Wherever a sacramental worldview is operative in families, the same activities have a second level of significance uncovered, which can be appreciated with the eyes of faith.[32] Life's high and low points enlighten, confirm, and strengthen these people's relationship with God—or, alternatively, create doubts or breaks in it.

Following Rahner's lead, we can say that in a domestic church, members know (or are coming to know) that one loves God *by* loving one's neighbor, and that to the degree one does not love the family member he sees, he does not yet love the God he doesn't see. In their reflections on spirituality of domestic churches, Mitch Finley and Kathy Finley support this proposal in a chapter on Christian parenting:

> *Perhaps the main characteristic of Christian parenting is the understanding on the part of parents that it is in a faith context that they are called to parent.* Many of the forms of knowledge and the skills that are helpful to any parent are equally helpful to Christian parents. Christian parents have no magic formulas for raising children, no easy ways out of the tight spots all parents find themselves in with their youngsters from time to time. That which especially characterizes the Christian parent is the religious values background that provides a basis for the minor and major decisions that parents must make regularly. . . .
>
> *All that has been said so far can be examined from the perspective of a traditional theological principle which states, "Grace builds on nature."* . . . On the "natural" level—prior to any consideration of religious aspects of parenting—parents need to know their business. They need to read the books of parenting experts, attend parenting classes, join parent support groups. All this amounts to gaining practical ministerial skills. *For all that the Christian parent gains in the way of practical knowledge becomes so many ways of showing God's love to the child in ways the child can feel.* In these ways, love becomes real, not merely a matter of words and fond aspirations. As we relate to our children in the loving ways we learn, we observe in our own actions illustrations of how God loves us.[33]

FAMILY LIFE AS AN ASCETIC DISCIPLINE THAT CULTIVATES SACRAMENTAL PERSPECTIVE

Gallagher's three-point summary of sacramentality suggests that celebration of God's grace (through everyday activities or specifically religious ritual) *follows upon* its recognition. Certainly this is true. However, daily routines, even those not overtly religious, can also *nurture* a sacramental faith perspective. *In other words, we cultivate awareness and love for the God we do not see precisely by learning to love the family we do see.* Our families" ordinary, tangible existence is a necessary phase of the great sacramental process of God's revelation and humanity's response.

This point, which touches on the heart of Rahner's conception of the liturgy of the world, emerges repeatedly among authors in the field of family spirituality. Ernest Boyer explains that our initial intellectual acceptance of revealed truth is just a preliminary step of our sacramental interaction with God. What follows upon it is the long and often difficult task of transforming a truth recognized into one truly felt at the core of one's being.[34] This long stage of conversion, which follows upon initial hearing or assent and reaches its culmination as a supernatural sort of awareness of God's activity in the world, Boyer labels *discipline.*[35] He intends to evoke the idea of discipline Catholics associate with religious orders—those rigorous rituals, time-tested exercises in training the mind and heart to God's presence. The Finleys likewise view the rigorous routines of parenthood as a means of forming a domestic church's spiritual outlook. Their reflections could be adapted to include experiences of adult children caring for infirm parents; of spouses who tend daily to each others' unique, "for better or worse" personal needs and to the continual demands of their shared household; or of siblings compelled to go through the motions of hospitality, generosity, and forgiveness so that they grow up committed to love each other despite their differences:

> No monk rising from his bed of straw in the darkness of night for prayers has more chances for dying to selfishness than parents who rise in the night to care for a hungry or fussy baby or a child who is sick. This is dying to self for the love of one's neighbor. No ascetic practices of fasting and penitence embraced by the saints of old were more valuable in the eyes of God as ways of growing in love than the sacrifices made by parents to be able to spend more time with their children or to be able to provide them with enough food or good schooling. The parent who struggles to keep an open mind about his or her teenager's tastes in music and clothing strives to love in ways that cannot be measured. The parent who trusts a child

a little more this year than last, and lives with the anxiety that comes with letting go just a little bit more, is attempting to grow in his or her trust in God in ways that cannot be matched.[36]

INDIVIDUAL DOMESTIC CHURCHES ARE NOT SELF-SUFFICIENT

Ordinary and extraordinary activities of domestic churches have an irreplaceable role in cultivating sacramental vision among their own members and in providing a forum for members to embody this perspective in daily life. However, individual domestic churches are not self-sufficient in cultivating sacramental perspective. Their origin and continued strength depend on a source outside themselves. Each relies on the resources of (God working through) the larger Church community—including other household communities, past and present—to nurture sacramental perspective at all stages of development: hearing, discipline, and awareness. Following Rahner, we may say God's presence in the liturgy of the world is a truth that must be brought into explicit and convincing expression through the larger Church as sacrament. When the Good News is shared by believers, newcomers are introduced to the possibility of sacramental perspective.

My reading in family spirituality and my own experience, especially eight years with my parish RCIA program in Boston, confirm that proclamation and hearing take place in many contexts. These include worship or formal religious education one may attend out of habit or compulsion, as well as conversations among elder and younger family members or between adults, such as spouses or dating partners. We must not forget that adults can be evangelized by children, as noted by Paul VI in *Evangelii Nuntiandi* #71.[37] Proclamation need not entail drawn-out discussions of religion. There is overwhelming agreement that occasional, but sincere and consistent, words and actions that show awareness of God's presence and concern for everyday life are just as effective.[38]

Michael True notes that conveying a sense of awe at the sacredness of life is not a purely intellectual affair. Those with little doctrinal training or flair for words can serve quite well as mentors of sacramental perspective. True says, "What is said on such occasions—prayers at mealtimes or at bedtime or on important celebrations—is perhaps less important than the fact that parents and children express their gratitude or longing or sorrow *together,* formally or informally. . . . Parents may think they cannot possibly instruct their children on subjects they know so little about themselves. In such efforts, 'it is not half so important to *know* as to *feel,*' for if facts are the seeds that later produce knowledge and wisdom, then the emotions and the impressions are the fertile soil in which the seeds must grow."[39] If people hear a certain message repeatedly, and if this message seems to determine the lifestyle of persons they care about (a lifestyle they already share, in part), they must form some opinion about the message. Those individuals are forced to take the message seriously because they take the messengers and their lives seriously. Even if the message is not accepted immediately, it confronts the hearer, in Rahner's terms, as a standing "offer to freedom" that may be embraced later if life experience renders it believable.

As Boyer notes, many of us Christians first accept the Christian message intellectually, trusting someone else's judgement, with an integrated awareness of God's presence in the world developing through time and experience. For others, emotional bonds and Christian lifestyle routines fall into place before complete intellectual assent is given. In any case, joining the larger church community in worship, catechism classes or Christian schools, fundraising, service and social activities, or religious celebrations of extended family or friends is part of the ongoing discipline that solidifies an individual's sacramental outlook on the world and leads to the formation of new domestic churches.

Popularity of the term "domestic church" is a fitting accompaniment to our growing recognition of how irreplaceable family life is in cultivating sacramental perspective. Christian families do more than simply "support" or "help with" the work of the Church. The work of the Church is not conducted only by professionals or experts. Christian families are not meant to be part-time Christians, but full-timers, no less than the professionals. Following Rahner's lead, we can say that any family experience contributing to explicit recognition of Christ's presence in the world is the work of a domestic church as sacrament.

TEN

Further Consideration of Domestic Church in Light of Sacramental Ecclesiology

Now that we have examined the "problematic assumptions" surfaced by the Haughton piece at the start of chapter 9, we should consider issues raised in previous chapters to see what additional insight Rahner's sacramental ecclesiology can provide. In some cases, we will be taking an element of consensus and enhancing its theological depth. In other cases, we will be highlighting unresolved issues and offering guidelines for moving toward consensus.

THE ECCLESIAL STATUS OF DOMESTIC CHURCHES

I have already made the case that the term "domestic church" should serve, first and foremost, to stimulate believers' religious imaginations to a fuller appreciation of the mystery of Church and of how family life manifests God's presence. At a time when many "families of Christians" have not yet recognized themselves as domestic churches, and theologians have only recently begun probing the concept, it seems premature to dic-tate specific roles that domestic churches may someday have in the insti-tutional Church.

On the other hand, symbolic concepts do hold implications for insti-tutional structure, and so the Church must begin to address this subject. Though Rahner never wrote more than a few sentences on domestic church in any one essay, he has made a daring assertion about domestic churches' ecclesial status. On at least four occasions he speaks of domes-tic church as a "local church." For Rahner and for Catholic ecclesiology since Vatican II, "local church" is a potent expression. The term implies a community that is not simply a part of the Church, but rather the fullness of Church in a particular locale and—so long as it maintains communion with its local bishop or ordinary and with the college of bishops—an authoritative source of religious knowledge. Some of Rahner's strongest claims for domestic church are found in a section on marriage in *The Church and the Sacraments*.

We have already said how remarkable the relation between the indi-vidual parish (local community) and the whole Church is. The local community is not only a member, a province of the whole Church. The whole Church is not only the sum of the parishes. Rather in the local church and its active accomplishment and self-realization, the whole Church in a true sense is manifested as a totality. What hap-pens in the individual parish, especially in the celebration of the eucharist, renders unmistakably and really present, in its ground (the redemptive death of the Lord), the existence of the whole church as the grace-giving presence of God. It testifies unambigu-ously to it and guarantees her nature and reality in the world. In view of this, and seeing that matrimony is an image of the alliance between Christ and the Church, we can say in a true sense of mar-riage that in it the Church is present; to the extent to which mar-riage realizes its own nature, as a valid marriage, sanctified by grace and lived in holiness. It is the smallest community, but for all that, a genuine community of the redeemed and sanctified, whose unity can build on the same foundation as that on which the Church is founded, the smallest of local churches, but a true one, the Church in miniature.[1]

Subsequent scholarly analysis of the domestic church's institutional status has emerged slowly.[2] Attention focuses primarily on three subjects: (1) a need for more open consultation and sharing of authority among hierarchy and laity, (2) the phenomenon of interdenominational domestic churches as communities on the cutting edge of ecumenical progress, and (3) controversial issues pertaining to worship, such as sharing of the Eucharist by interdenominational families and the need for regular celebration of sacraments in Catholic communities lacking their own pastor.

To give some direction to future reflection on domestic churches' ecclesial status, it will be helpful to have some agreed-upon premises in mind. Practical implications of Rahner's theology of Church as sacrament provide the starting points needed. There are two premises that should guide discussion of domestic churches' institutional roles:

- The Church is a living, open system whose institutional forms must be guided by movements of God's Spirit; and
- the laity are not to be regarded as nonexperts or part-timers in the Church.

Richard Lennen explains that, for Rahner, theology of Church as sacrament implies that development, plurality, and reconfiguration of structure are not a threat to the Church's nature, but an essential part of it. Thus, Rahner's theology can be enlisted to address those who may fear that any authority claimed on behalf of domestic churches represents a loss of something essential to the Church's nature and mission. Rahner would argue that variety, not uniformity, best manifests the Church's nature as sacrament of the unfathomable mystery of God and best affirms that the Spirit's movement in the Church is also a mystery.[3] Even the Church's teaching authority is dependent ("not juridically, but in fact") upon the unfolding, unpredictable, charismatic life experience of the whole Church.[4] The Church, its sacramental mission, and its office are unified and permanently established by divine law, but division and specific content of offices should be expected to change because the Church exists in and for a changing world. Willingness to experiment is an essential element of the Church's sacramental nature.[5] Rahner thought the demise of bonds between Church and state would be the most important influence on the Church's future institutional configuration. As in the early Church, small communities built upon personal conviction of members and integrating all aspects of life would be the best way for Christians situated amongst nonbelievers to give each other the support needed to continue their sacramental witness to the world. The prospect of domestic churches becoming key players in the Church at an institutional level seems in keeping with the practical thrust of Rahner's sacramental ecclesiology.

On the other hand, Rahner's sacramental ecclesiology does not imply that domestic churches *must* be vested with hierarchical recognition beyond baptism or with duties over and above Christian witness in ordinary life.[6] Rahner insists that any baptized Christian is charged with the task of being a member of the Body of Christ and making the Church "the visible manifestation of the victory of God's grace in the world"— and is valuable for that task in itself.[7] We should not be satisfied with a negative definition of the lay vocation, saying that lay members are not experts because they are not clergy. The difference between hierarchical and lay roles stems from the degree to which their sacramental communication is rooted in the ordinariness and immediateness of world liturgy, as contrasted to the explicit or symbolic nature of the institutional church.[8] Some of Rahner's strongest statements on the dignity of the lay vocation echo Haughton's interpretation of what Vatican II's claim that Christian families "manifest Christ's presence and the genuine nature of the Church" really entails.

> The mission of the baptised layman to share in the task of the Church does not begin and end with the observance of peaceful Sunday devotions. It does not consist in any primary sense in Corpus Christi processions with notables of the parish or the political party or the good Catholics. It does not mean casting one's vote in favor of the Catholic interest, nor yet in patiently paying the Church's dues. Rather it implies an awareness, so deep and radical that it revolutionizes everything, of the fact that the baptised man is constantly confronted with the task of a Christian precisely in the environment in which he finds himself and in which his life is passed, that is to say in the wholly natural context of his calling, in his family, in the circles in which he lives, in his nation and state, his human and cultural milieu. And this task consists in establishing

the God in truth, in selflessness and love, and thereby making what is truly essential to the Church's nature present in the setting in which he is placed, from the position only he can occupy, in which he cannot be replaced by any other, not even by the clergy, and where, nevertheless, the Church must be.[9]

When Rahner's observations about individual lay Christians are extended to Christian families, we can conclude that domestic churches serve as indispensable ecclesial instruments in God's grand plan of sacramental revelation. Each, in the time and place it uniquely occupies, is charged to manifest Christ and the genuine nature of the Church in a way that cannot be replaced by any other, and where nevertheless the Church must be. Through these instruments, God's presence becomes historical, incarnate, public, and directed to individuals at decisive moments of their lives.

In the future we may see structures in place that would allow domestic churches to have a more formal influence on the Church's official magisterium. In places where priests are in short supply, some might be recognized with the authority to nominate their own ordained leaders or to conduct their own Eucharistic celebrations. Such developments would be in keeping with domestic churches' ecclesial importance and with biblical evidence concerning the earliest house churches. These developments may become increasingly necessary to allow the Church to continue its sacramental mission in the world. But even without these institutional structures, lay members of domestic churches must be seen as equal partners with clergy in the Church's mission.

Rahner's sacramental ecclesiology seems to imply that hierarchy need not be a prominent feature of domestic churches, except in two respects: first, each Christian family should seek to maintain union with its broader local community and its bishop, with the episcopal college, and with traditions of the Church as a whole; it should see this relationship as necessary to maintain the integrity of its sacramental perspective and witness. Second, more mature and convinced believers should take their position of leadership in domestic churches very seriously—which is less a matter of being ritually installed as vicars of Christ in their homes, as H. Lyman Stebbins has proposed, than of consistently speaking and embodying a life of Gospel truth.

ORDINARY FAMILY LIFE AS A CHANNEL OF GOD'S GRACE AND OF HUMANS' EMBODIED RESPONSE

A sacramental worldview provides family life with a rich sense of purpose. It helps meet a deep human need to find lasting significance in mundane tasks, which preoccupy so much of a family's time and attention. James McGinnis and Kathleen McGinnis have pointed out that a common obstacle preventing families from taking themselves seriously as domestic churches is a *lack of imagination,* both as to the meaning of Church and the meaning of their everyday lifestyle choices.[10] In chapter 3 we began to examine the sacredness of ordinary life. Let us further explore family life as a sacramental *source* of grace and as a *response* to it.

Many authors confirm that God's constant presence is revealed to them in family life; they also cite many specific "created graces" and virtues that become real through their families as instruments. Examples include unconditional love, forgiveness, patience, compassion, humility, and knowledge of one's own limitations and of the need to rely on a source of strength greater than oneself. In his chapter "The Sacrament of the Care of Others," Boyer lists spiritual gifts acquired through the discipline of caring: courage, persistence, trust, forgiveness, and the ability to balance holding on to loved ones with letting go. He says the often thankless discipline of caring for loved ones can eventually yield to joy of sharing in God's creation.[11] Elsewhere he writes that participation in recurrent joys and sorrows of family life provides reassurance that God is providentially caring for each of us as individuals, and for the entire human race.[12]

Beginning in Scripture and throughout history, Christian theology, catechesis, and devotional practice have commonly depended upon family-oriented images and analogies to convey truths of revelation. Certainly there are limits in anthropomorphic imagery. Still, it must be admitted that family experiences of childhood, marriage, and parenthood, of being brothers and sisters, of forgiveness, fidelity, joy in creation, celebration, meritorious sacrifice, obedience, unconditional love, death and new life all have the potential to facilitate acceptance of the Good News. For instance, I recall that, in calming my son's fears about the whereabouts of his great-grandmother after she died (and of himself after death), what was most valuable was not simply Jesus' stories about the kingdom of heaven being like a great feast or wedding banquet, but also the fact that he could associate these with our family's dinner parties and his aunt Mary and uncle Tom's recent wedding. As another example, several theologians have called family a sacrament or human image of the triune, relational God.[13] What these authors seem to mean is that experience of family life not only provides images and language helpful to explain this divine mystery, but also disposes us to accept the Trinity and other tenets of Christian faith as credible. Whether it facilitates theological understanding or cultivates virtues such as faith, hope, compassion, and humility, ordinary family life can be interpreted as a sacramental source of grace.

If our source of grace is incarnational, its true fulfillment—that is, our response—should likewise be embodied. A domestic church's embodied sacramental communication occurs both among immediate family members and between each family and its associates in the surrounding world. Small, everyday choices consistently informed by Gospel values communicate Jesus' message and instill commitment to him as nothing else can. Conversely, seemingly insignificant choices that fail to embody Gospel values undermine Jesus' message and impede commitment to him as nothing else can.[14] The process of sacramental communication in which domestic churches partake is incremental and often painstakingly slow. Results are often not apparent for years.[15] Thus Ernest Boyer's application of the term "discipline" to the "sacrament of the routine" in Christian family life is completely appropriate.

TENSION BETWEEN IDEAL AND ACTUAL LIFE OF DOMESTIC CHURCHES

We have seen that a prominent theme in literature on Christian family life is awareness of a nagging, and sometimes marked, distance between ideals and actual life. What insight does Rahner's sacramental ecclesiology contribute to our understanding of this phenomenon? How would he respond to Haughton's suggestion that what is most obvious about Christian family gatherings is not Christ's presence, but quarrels and other shortcomings? For insight on these questions, the best place to turn is Rahner's writings on the sinfulness of the Church.[16] However, not every question about domestic churches' sinfulness will be conclusively answered, for while Rahner insists that the Church is not something separate from the concrete lives of her members, he seems to have in mind the Church over the vast sweep of its earthly history. Though elsewhere Rahner identifies domestic church with local church, it seems that individual domestic churches lack the "critical mass" necessary for his strongest statements about the Church's holiness to be applied to them.

On the other hand, Rahner repeatedly draws upon familial imagery when describing the sinfulness of the Church. His essay "The Church of Sinners" is organized around the themes of the Church as Mother and as harlot-bride of Christ and of believers as her children and members of the "House of God."[17] Elsewhere Rahner says Christians must realistically and soberly admit the failings of the Church just as they do with regard to their families.[18] Based on the sheer frequency of references, it seems Rahner chooses familial images not as arbitrary signs, but as deeper symbols. Following Rahner's own sacramental principle of union between sign and reality signified, and his willingness to consider domestic churches akin to local churches, one is inclined to apply most of his conclusions about "the sinful Church" to the family as domestic church.

Rahner was convinced that the principle of sacramentality implies that the Church cannot be disassociated from the concrete lives of its members, who are simultaneously justified and sinners. Its nature as sacrament has an *ex opere operato* quality—it derives primarily from God's promise of fidelity, not from the worthiness of human ministers. [19] In his essay "Marriage as Sacrament," Rahner carefully examines the union of the Church as *sign* with the *reality* of Jesus Christ signified. He says that both the Church as basic sacrament and marriage as a sacrament signifying Christ's love for the Church exemplify a unity *and* difference between sign (*sacramentum*) and reality signified (*res sacramenti*). The unity between sign and reality lies in the fact that both entities (sacramental marriage and the Church as sacrament) truly *manifest and make effective* Christ's continuing presence in history. The difference lies in the fact that neither is *identical* with the reality signified; both point to a reality beyond, and greater than, themselves.[20]

Rahner's identification of a "unity in difference" in sacramental dynamics partly explains the common failings of marriages, domestic churches, and the larger Church as sacraments. However, this essay cites a difference between individual sacramental marriages (also called "house churches") and the Church taken as a whole. An individual marriage may in fact be an empty sign that does not embody what it should signify; then its sign function is degraded into a lie.[21] In alternate terms, a sacramental marriage may be "valid" or "licit" but not "fruitful." We can assume the same holds true for a domestic church founded upon sacraments of baptism, Eucharist, and marriage. But Rahner believes such a complete break between sign and reality signified is not possible for the Church as a whole. "In the Church as a whole the intrinsic connection between sign and reality signified can no longer radically be destroyed in virtue of the eschatological victory of Christ. Nevertheless, the basic parallelism between marriage and the Church continues to exist."[22] An extension of this sacramental/ecclesial principle of "unity in difference" to domestic church is provided by Frederick Parrella. He reminds us that a sacrament is "bipolar" by nature.

> [A sacrament] embodies grace in concrete form while pointing to a grace that is absolute and eschatological. Thus, one could say that a sacrament not only makes grace present but also fails to make it present—it actualizes grace, yet only in sacramental form. . . . The Church [as sacrament] fails to make Christ fully present not only because the eschaton has not yet arrived and the Church is not yet complete, but also because she is a Church of sinners who share in the same ambiguity of history as every other institution.[23]

Now, with all this in mind, says Parrella, we should not be surprised that "[t]he family is at once both the image of the divine life and of human estrangement." This dialectical view of the family is in keeping with the idea of Church as sacrament. The Christian family, the "domestic sanctuary of the Church," is sacramental in the same "already-but-not-yet" manner.

Rahner's sacramental ecclesiology lends this basic insight to our consideration of tension between ideals and reality in domestic churches: because the Church is not separable from the concrete lives of her members, there is a basic parallelism or identity between sacramental marriages, domestic churches, and the Church as sacrament. All are holy, but none perfectly embodies or symbolizes the ideal reality with which it is unified. Thus, Rahner's thought provides support for the U.S. bishops' claim in *Follow the Way of Love* that domestic churches are no less perfect than parish or diocesan churches. His "unity in difference" principle further enlightens Leckey's discussion of the virtue of stability in Christian family life, by which one presumes that one's family, imperfect as it is, is the place God has designed for each to be inserted into the mystery of Christ.[24]

A family where Christian sacramental vision is operative may experience the same "falling short of ideals" as any other family. But they dare to believe, if nothing else, that God remains with them. In time such a family may find its experiences of limitation make a positive contribution to its faith. Skelley reminds us that although positive events can be explicit experiences of God, negative experiences can be even more so. Our transcendence is most strikingly manifested at those times in everyday life when we are jarred out of complacency and forced to consider truths, freedoms, and values that we normally evade or overlook:

> This takes place, for example, when we face loneliness and isolation, when we act responsibly for our sinfulness, when we are faithful to our commitments at great cost to ourselves, when we freely surrender in self-sacrificing obedience to one another, when we calmly accept sickness and diminishment, when we courageously commit ourselves to justice and peace for all, when we seek reconciliation with our worst enemies, when we sincerely forgive people who break our hearts, and especially when we confront death, our own or that of someone we cherish. . . .
>
> Through such experiences we can discover that God is present in every moment, no matter how "negative" it might be. Their common thread is that they are all experiences of limitation. . . . But precisely because these are such powerful experiences of limitation, they can be equally powerful experiences of transcendence. We could not experience these limits as limits unless we were able also to go beyond them. . . . To perceive that there is something beyond our limits and to affirm the good that we may glimpse only dimly there is to experience God. And to do this again and again is to gradually discover that God is present in every experience, no matter how negative.[25]

Even a cursory reading of recent works on Christian family life reveals that tension between ideals and actuality is a common aspect of a domestic church's spirituality. But how should it be explained? Is it permanent, or something that may be outgrown? Is it due to the family's immersion in the "secular" world and its inability to fulfill the counsels of perfection traditionally associated with religious and ordained vocations? Or is it something that Christians in all states of life share? Does it make any positive contribution to Christian maturity? Rahner's sacramental ecclesiology teaches us that the Church will never fail to manifest Christ's presence in the world, but neither will it ever manifest Christ perfectly. There will always be a unity-and-difference between *sacramentum* and the *res sacramenti*. In the life of the Church in general and even more so in the life of individual domestic churches, there is a permanent tension between ideal and actuality, but that tension can fuel human growth. Indeed, if the tension is greater at the domestic level, the potential for growth may increase proportionately. Following Rahner, we might say the ideal to which humans are called—a free and responsible acceptance of their transcendent or divine fulfillment—can be made symbolically (but really) present in the imperfect medium of family life. Without imperfection, there is nothing to transcend. All this is possible for those who have embraced a sacramental perspective, who see with the eyes of faith. Mary Perkins testifies to just this point, in a description of family dinners reminiscent of the Haughton piece introduced at the start of chapter 9:

> [S]uppose that we began to follow out the sacramental implications of our family meals. . . . Our food and family meals are meant to be the humble human reflections of the sacred meal of the holy Eucharist, which itself is a reflection of the eternal feast of heaven.
>
> In the light of these facts, imagine a meal which the father earned by a piece of "sharp business" in which he did somebody out of the price of a day's food; a meal consisting of food which the mother obtained by pushing in ahead of ten other people for a bargain at the supermarket; which she prepared in a temper and shoved onto an untidy and not-too-clean table; food which looked like something else and contained virtually no real nourishment; a meal to which the children come completely unwashed, knocking each

other over in their hurry; a meal eaten in uncharitable silence, or to the accompaniment of mother's complaints about the neighbors.

Such a meal obviously bears no relation at all to the Table of God. It is not a *sign* capable of teaching the children anything at all about God's banquet. It will certainly give no notion at all of why heaven should be compared to a feast. Such a meal is a completely secular activity, un-Christian, hardly even human.

But think of the possibilities inherent in our family lives if both the bread-winner and the bread-baker were trying to make each meal and everything connected with it more and more fit to be a humble human *sign* and reflection of the banquet of the holy Eucharist. The cooking and the preparation of meals, the day-by-day, year-by-year, often seemingly hopeless task of training the children to cleanliness and decent table manners would take on a real purpose and point, and so would the even more long-drawn out and difficult job of training them to happy and interesting and charitable table conversation. . . .

No matter if such an occasion were to look and sound much like any other family meal where small children are present. . . . None of this would affect the main point, that the parents are trying as best they can, in the light of the sacramental significance of the holy Eucharist, to align everything connected with their daily bread towards the requirements of full and fruitful participation in the banquet which is the sign and pledge of the everlasting wedding-feast of heaven. In any case, God Himself has made the material *signs* of heavenly realities necessarily crude and, in a sense, unworthy of those realities, so that we would take them as signs and signs only and not the realities themselves. St. Thomas points out that Holy Scripture uses crude rather than "noble" things as the basis for its figures and metaphors for this same reason.[26]

Shared Features of Domestic Churches

By way of conclusion, we may consider an unsettled issue taken up previously: articulating *identifying features of domestic churches*. In several years of research and speaking on the subject, I have found that the first question to surface when the term "domestic church" is introduced to new audiences is usually the question of "what counts" as a domestic church. In a tradition such as Catholicism, known for organizing complex phenomena into more easily manageable categories, this is not surprising.

Drawing upon Rahner's sacramental ecclesiology, we may cite several reasons why variety in domestic churches should be expected. God can be found in all human events—sacred and secular, joyful and dark. No one can predict the events through which humans will truly give themselves over to God. Christian families must be "Church" wherever they find themselves. Each family's situational context is a unique place in the world that only it can occupy. A variety of miniature domestic churches best manifests the nature of the Church as sacrament of a mysterious, transcendent God. At the same time, Rahner's sacramental ecclesiology indicates that Christian domestic churches will be alike in elements that are most essential. First, members will accept (with varying degrees of maturity) a sacramental vision that perceives God's presence in all things and interprets the family's life as an instrument of sacred communication with God and the world. Second, they will seek to maintain social, spiritual, and intellectual bonds with the larger Church community instigated by Jesus, to give the best possible assurance of integrity in their sacramental perspective and witness. Third, they will celebrate the liturgical sacraments with this community. They will do so to fulfill a human need to express their implicit daily relationship with God, *as well as* their Christian responsibility to take advantage of symbolic means of communication passed on to them by Jesus and his Church.

ELEVEN

Domestic Church:
The Primary School of Virtue

In chapter 4, we learned that Catholic magisterial writings strongly link family or domestic church and education, especially religious education.[1] Family life is called a "school of deeper humanity"[2] and a "school of social virtues";[3] family is the "first community" called to bring persons "through progressive education and catechesis to full human and Christian maturity."[4] Parents are "appointed by God himself as the first and principal educators of their children and their right is completely inalienable."[5] Put differently, parents' teaching role "is so decisive that scarcely anything can compensate for their failure in it."[6] It is a responsibility so sacred that it is part of the vocation of sacramental marriage.[7] Notably, formation in the home has been recognized not only as crucial to development of natural virtues, but also of evangelical virtues.[8] Vatican II's *Dogmatic Constitution on the Church* tells us, "Married couples and Christian parents . . . should imbue their offspring, lovingly welcomed from God, with Christian truths and evangelical virtues."[9] Speaking of the connection between domestic church and formation of virtue, John Paul II urges, "Catholic parents must learn to form their family as a 'domestic church,' a Church in the home, as it were, where God is honored, his law is respected, prayer is a normal event, virtue is transmitted by word and example, and everyone shares the hopes, the problems, and sufferings of everyone else."[10]

To me, these citations have common-sense appeal; still, their basic premise deserves further examination. If parents are their children's primary religious educators, why is this truth not more universally embodied in ecclesial structures? Relatively few communities have adopted a family-centered, home-based approach to religious formation, at least in the United States.[11] Instead, most of us are familiar with religious education efforts that remove people from their homes, segregate young people from adults (not least, their parents), and then further divide older and younger children. With the development of the Sunday-school movement and Catholic or other Christian schools, scholarship on Christian education throughout the twentieth century has provided proportionately little reflection on Christian families as the most important setting for religious formation. Although there are exceptions, the catechism class, Christian school, or worshiping community have commanded most authors' and ministers' attention.[12]

Some of us are so accustomed to parish or congregation-*centered*, family-*supported* religious education that we have difficulty imagining anything resembling family-*centered*, parish-*supported* religious education. I recently had a graduate student whose final project for her ministry degree involved organizing a discussion series and weekend retreat for parents and their teenage children. She reported that at the first meeting with the planning committee, several volunteers seemed confused and kept insisting that the program wouldn't work because of a lack of appropriate meeting spaces. My student was initially perplexed, but finally realized that the volunteers assumed parents and teenage children had to meet in different rooms. She explained that the whole purpose of the program was to enable parents to be primary religious educators of their children, in keeping with the idea of domestic church. Small groups of parents and their children convened in a single, large meeting space would work just fine—separating the parents and youths would be counterproductive. My student reported that this explanation caught her volunteers completely by surprise—"It was like a light bulb turned on over their heads. It had never occurred to these parents that they could meet in the same room, let alone lead or teach their own children in an explicitly religious context."

There is more at stake than the issue of *who* teaches Christianity and *where* it is taught. We must be very careful that Christian educational literature or practice does not distort our understanding of *how* Christian virtue usually matures. As a by-product of the focus on teaching by experts outside the family, faith formation may be described as an initiate's taking on a new or different life, rather than as a gradual progression in a single way of life.[13] Alternatively, Christian formation may be envisioned not so much as an everyday lifestyle habit, but as a weekly extracurricular activity, like flute lessons or soccer practice, with parents dropping their kids off for an hour or two and picking them up afterward—except during summer vacation, when everyone gets a break from the normal routine! Religious education may even be regarded as something that young people graduate from when they complete confirmation class or their senior year at a Catholic/Christian school. Any of these explanations of religious formation is inadequate to capture the rich potential of Christian families as schools of virtue.

WHAT IS VIRTUE? HOW DO FAMILIES TEACH IT?

Virtue may be considered the most important component of religious formation. A shorthand way of describing virtue is as a "good habit"— one that leads us to be the best people we can be. Philosophers and theologians from ancient to contemporary times have described virtue as a gradual harmonizing of thoughts, emotions, desires, and behavior. Virtue moves us toward habitual pursuit of goals God has designed for human fulfillment. Virtuous habits are formed inductively, through practice, as experience poses new tests of character. Thus, the virtues embody shared human values according to individuals' specific abilities, temperaments, and circumstances.[14]

The measure of maturity in virtue is the degree to which a person seeks to *know* what is good (or, in religious language, to know God's will), consistently *does* it, and *enjoys* doing it. Because virtue is individually tailored, mentors closely related by kinship usually have an advantage over school or parish teachers, who change yearly and must start from scratch to learn a child's background and circumstances. Something similar is true for adults. Experts can teach us much about good lifestyles "in general," based on patterns learned from observing and researching large groups of people—especially in cross-cultural studies that look not only for differences, but also for similarities that point to some shared human nature and universalizable moral values. But the challenge of living virtuously comes in particular, everyday choices—as the saying goes, "The devil is in the details." Family mentors and peers (such as spouses or mature siblings) are uniquely positioned to evaluate subtleties others overlook, to give living examples and tests of "good" behavior in varied contexts, to draw upon past shared experiences to provide consistent explanations or advice about what is good, and to assess whether good behavior is truly becoming integrated as a self-motivated habit, rather than something performed only on special occasions, to win a reward or to maintain a public image.

What does it mean to say that virtue is cultivated by practice? The major Catholic theologian to be reckoned with in exploring virtues is Thomas Aquinas;[15] a study of the *Catechism of the Catholic Church* reveals that his theological categories are still the mainstay of virtue theory.[16] Although Aquinas never wrote a program or curriculum for cultivating virtue, it is possible to infer basic, timeless strategies of character formation based on his explanation of what virtue is. Aquinas presumed that goodness or holiness is intrinsically pleasurable to humans. In other words, God wants what is best for us, and doing God's will as a matter of habit will make us happy in the long run. Yet, we don't always appreciate immediately what is for our own good—that's why it is necessary for our thoughts, desires, and behavior to be ordered or habituated as virtues. Given proper exposure to a good life, through practice, we should be attracted to it.[17] Conversely, if we practice harmful lifestyles too often, we may fall into the habit of treating short-term, limited pleasures as if they were all there is to a good life. Seemingly insignificant experiences can build upon each other to instill both virtues and vices, so it is important to regard everything we do as a sort of "moral exercise."[18] In describing "proper exposure" to a good life, we must be specific. Practicing virtue will allow us to *know* what being virtuous means only if practice is *critical*. Practicing virtue will lead us to desire and love being virtuous only if practice is, for all its difficulty, somehow *enjoyable*.

What does it mean to say virtue is learned inductively? Inductive knowledge works from the bottom up; it begins by experiencing and observing what is happening in various circumstances. Based on these experiences, a person gradually draws conclusions about what is true in general and refines these conclusions with ongoing experience. These conclusions then serve as the foundation for our laws and for the practical advice that we exchange informally. Yet, if it is going to promote virtue, critical practice of good behavior must become more than reflex reaction, blind obedience to authority and law, or rote memorization. Many moral education enterprises adopt elements of reflex formation, obedience, and memorization. These surely have a place in cultivating virtue, particularly in beginning stages. But mastery of rules must not be equated with mature virtue. Those of us who have kin of a certain temperament know well that learning general rules like sharing, cooperation, or taking turns can go through phases of obsession with splitting the last cupcake into exactly equal pieces, keeping a tally of who carried which grocery bags from the car to the kitchen, or setting a timer to referee equal chances to talk on the phone. Because they focus on generalized goods only, rules can over-simplify particularities of life that mature virtue must address.

The inductive sense of virtue to be developed is like fluency in a language, which entails a sense of general patterns and the variety of ways they are concretized, as well as unusual settings that dictate departure from these norms.[19] As in learning a language, learners of virtue must be given firsthand exposure to a living exercise of virtue by mentors. Learners should be encouraged to mimic mentors in these activities. Then, good behavior should be praised so that learners will come to recognize what goodness is and take pride in it.[20] This can take place within the context of ordinary activities that engage learners and mentors together.

In time, probably in response to learners' questions about activity they observe, or protests against acting virtuously, mentors should add explanations tailored to the learner's maturity and past experience. Some explanations will be more logical or formal; others will come in the form of emotionally engaging stories, whether fictional or nonfictional. These will clarify why a certain way of behaving is good, healthy for the body and soul, and perhaps obligatory in particular settings. Explanations should alert learners to the *habit-forming* potential of behavior and the *goals* for which it aims. Mentors might recount their own efforts, or those of loved ones, to form good habits, and how they gradually matured from the same place where the learner currently is. Likewise, the mentor ought to note how the learner has improved with practice. Explanations should stress ways that good behavior makes people (both oneself and others) happy, though perhaps not in the short term.[21] It will be easier for beginners to refine their inductive understanding of what virtuous choices have in common if explanations of good behavior provided by mentors are relatively consistent, including use of consistent terminology.[22]

A strong relationship exists between intellect and affect in the habituation of virtue, because we can fall in love with pursuing a virtuous life long before we fully appreciate what this entails.[23] We are familiar with such faith-based commitments with respect to other loves. For instance, I may develop a commitment to my younger brother's well-being at an early age, though I barely understand the concept of his future needs and have no way to predict what these might actually be. As with love for siblings, love for the good life develops by practice, sometimes under compulsion, and as a by-product of trust and affection for mentors. We already share our lives with these mentors, and we desire to imitate them. Because of emotional attachments, they are in a unique position for persuasion of the forming intellect, so that it interprets experience in one way rather than another. It is to be hoped that right action initially done out of love for mentors[24] will eventually be appreciated as intrinsically good— partly through reason and experience, partly through faith. Role models who have something in common with us stimulate a sense of hope, allowing us to imagine that we can grow to share their lifestyle. Unconditionally committed mentors are most likely to elicit the faith and trust necessary to emulate a lifestyle not yet fully understood and not always enjoyable in the short term. Family, school, and parish mentors (ideally) reinforce each other to gradually socialize children in community narratives, language, role models, rituals, and laws; this molds habits of perception, emotion, and behavior. However, naming family or domestic church the primary "school of virtue" means recognizing that family relationships and everyday activities have an especially lasting influence in cultivating virtuous habits—or, if directed toward harmful goals, vices. All this resonates with Aquinas's convictions about parents' natural responsibility for the education of children (convictions that are reflected in magisterial statements cited previously) and those concerning the order of charity.

Aquinas said *charity*, the greatest and most comprehensive virtue,[25] is "ordered" by familial bonds.[26] Love of family is an expression of love of neighbor, which Aquinas considers "specifically the same act whereby we love God" or "love of the same object under a particular aspect."[27] Charity includes neighbors with whom we have no natural bonds, but family and friends are rightly loved more intensely, he says. We can say charity is perfected through practice, by figuring out how love of neighbor should be embodied among those closest to us. As 1 John 4:20 tells us, if we don't love the kin we see, we can't love the God we don't see. This makes sense in light of Christianity's incarnational and sacramental convictions— God can be encountered via visible, human signs. Whenever we feed our families, welcome annoying siblings or quirky aunts, compromise with toddlers or teenagers (or our parents) about appropriate clothing, comfort loved ones who are physically or mentally ill, or remain committed to family members imprisoned by destructive habits, we are fleshing out our love for God (recall Matthew 25:31 ff.). Moreover, as we learn, by trial and error, to balance these multiple relationships and responsibilities, we refine the crucial virtue of prudence.[28]

Opportunities for personalized evaluation, intellectual and emotional persuasion, and long-term, in-depth role modeling through communal activity are readily available in the context of family life, and hard to duplicate in other settings. Therefore, of all the human communities jointly responsible for teaching virtue, each individual's own family or domestic church is best situated to oversee the task. Given all these considerations, it is fitting to name family as the primary school of virtue.

Can Christian Virtue Be Taught?

A fundamental theological question is whether supernatural virtues, those most associated with Christian life and considered virtuous in the fullest sense,[29] can be taught at all. Aquinas contends that supernatural virtues—unlike natural or "acquired" virtues—cannot be taught, learned by practice, or caused by any human agency, but must be "infused" by God alone, as an accompaniment to sanctifying grace, through water baptism (or, in exceptional cases, through baptism of the Spirit). They are lost as a consequence of mortal sin, and reinfused in the sacrament of penance. Supernatural virtue is something "God works in us without us."[30]

In some respects, Aquinas's convictions seem true to experience. Any veteran of religious education, RCIA ministry, or Christian parenting knows that cultivation of faith, hope, charity, and correlated virtues is not guaranteed, despite our best efforts. They are always a gift from God and manifest themselves in unpredictable ways.

Aquinas also believed that formation of supernatural virtue enlists human agency and free cooperation; he says humans can "dispose" themselves to receive these virtues or to undergo increase in them.[31] The recognition of some role for human effort, guidance, and practice also resonates with present-day experience. We have seen that many authors in the family theology/spirituality genre suggest that supernatural virtues are formed through family life. They describe habits of faith, hope, and love, of humility, patience, joy, and trust in God's providence, of peace and justice— *grounded explicitly in Christian conviction*—as born and cultivated in this context. They value participation in the institutional Church's sacraments, but repeatedly urge readers not to confine attention to spiritual formation within the sanctuary. The spiritual discipline of ordinary family life is not considered an alternative to sacraments; rather, it completes them.[32] Thus, Aquinas's fixation on God "working within us without us" and his distinctions between *disposing* for natural virtue by human *practice* and *causing* supernatural virtue by divine *infusion* (normally via the sacraments) are not replicated in these authors.

How are faith, hope, charity, and correlated virtues "transmitted by word and example" or "imbued" by Christian parents in their children, in the context of domestic churches? Until theologians address this question, they have neglected the most basic point in a discussion of the Christian family as a school of virtue. We must expect contemporary development in sacramental theology and ecclesiology—especially nascent appreciation for domestic church—to impact understanding of how supernatural virtues form, because the tradition running from Aquinas through the *Catechism of the Catholic Church* presumes the Church's official sacraments as the key locus of their infusion.[33] What we need is attention to the liturgy of the world and the domestic church as the surrounding ecclesial context wherein virtues grow and sacraments are celebrated.

Aquinas and like-minded authors apparently presume Christian family life to be a setting where supernatural virtues develop. For instance, similar to the magisterial statements cited previously, Aquinas remarks that being reared from childhood in things pertaining to Christian life allows one to more easily persevere therein.[34] Yet, his theological categories are conceived such that family life does not figure into his explanation of supernatural virtues formed by God "working in us without us." In the natural order, parental education of children is basic to the structure of God's creation; in the supernatural order, appearance and disappearance of virtues need not adhere to natural patterns.[35] Thomas's statements about religious formation in the home sometimes seem too fantastic to believe. Building from the traditional premise that faith necessary for infants to receive the grace of baptism (and, by extension, supernatural virtues) is provided by the Church, Aquinas says that a baptized child is protected from harm by the faith of the Church even if, after baptism, his parents do not believe and "strive to infect the child with the worship of demons."[36] This statement, which probably seems counterintuitive to most of us today, is symptomatic of an understanding of the salvific function of the Church and its sacraments that has been recast by contemporary theology.

To resolve the tension, we must appreciate two points: (1) the sacraments, the Church, and its ministers are fully human, even while God works through them, and (2) God's grace operates beyond institutional Church structures. As we know, Karl Rahner builds his sacramental theology upon the premise that "God has not attached his power to the sacraments in such a way that he could not also impart the effects of sacramental grace without the sacraments themselves." By extension, we can say that supernatural virtues are created not simply by baptism and penance out of context, but also through God's ongoing work in the Church community as basic sacrament and in what Rahner calls the liturgy of the world. These concepts are bridged by the concept of domestic church.

Baptism signifies past, present, and future work of the Holy Spirit in a maturing Christian and makes public and explicit God's gift of the Church to that person. Represented in microcosm by family and sponsors who pledge support to candidates for baptism, the Church serves symbolically and practically as an ongoing instrument of union with Christ, without which the baptizand's active reception of grace and fruitful response to the Spirit in a virtuous life are severely compromised. The supernatural orientation our souls receive develops gradually (except in the most miraculous cases) through movement of God's Spirit in a lifetime of human events, of which only a fraction is overtly religious.

It is not necessary that infusion of supernatural virtue be located exclusively in institutional sacraments in order for God's power to be fittingly manifested. Formation of supernatural virtue can be understood as "God working in us, with us." Aquinas acknowledges the Church's sacraments and their human ministers as instrumental or ministerial efficient causes of grace.[37] We should conceive of this causality as extended through the entire life of domestic churches; after all, the institutional Church and its sacraments are explicit signs of God's work being accomplished quietly in the liturgy of the world, not least through family life. Then, we can reappropriate the premise that the faith infants need to receive baptismal grace is provided by the Church. This occurs especially through domestic church members, who request a child's baptism and pledge to make their home a place of ongoing religious formation. The process is similar for adult converts.[38] Often a relationship with a domestic church, such as a Christian spouse and in-laws, makes their faith possible, and these people commonly serve as sponsors throughout the RCIA process.[39]

Supernatural virtue is a gift from God that enriches and perfects any natural virtues acquired without conscious reference to one's relationship with God. It is always miraculous, dependent on the mysterious movements of God's Spirit and on the gift of faith. This said, it must be admitted that what Christian tradition has called "supernatural" or "evangelical" virtue often matures in a seemingly ordinary way, in an ongoing relationship with a human community of believers. Communities of believers expose learners to a Christian interpretation of truth and goodness and try to persuade them to accept it as the central point of reference for their life's activities. These are appropriate ways of moving learners to respond to God's Spirit fruitfully and with increasing integrity. Like any human community, a Church community—at the household level or larger levels—employs all available resources to elicit and solidify in its members a self-motivated commitment to its understanding of the good life. These include reasoned explanation, persuasion of the affections, role models, disciplinary routines, and rituals of praise or shame. Among these human resources we will certainly include the sacraments, consistent with Aquinas's belief that the institutional sacraments are generally necessary for infusion of supernatural virtue.[40] The Christian virtue engendered by the Church as "teacher and mother" is formed by God's enlistment of the same practices and mentoring relationships that cultivate natural virtue in any human community.[41]

FAMILY AS A SCHOOL OF VIRTUE AND SACRAMENTAL PERSPECTIVE

Throughout this investigation I have proposed that what makes a family a domestic church is a habit of interpreting its ordinary life—for better or worse—as the means through which family members are to seek, know, and love the God made known in Jesus Christ. This is the most distinctive and unifying characteristic of Christian domestic churches. If we want to give the habit a theological name, we can adopt contemporary language of sacramentality or use the more traditional concept of charity. If we choose the latter, we should balance the conviction that charity is a gift from God with the recognition that in many cases it is "disposed" for (or even mediated, as Rahner might say) through everyday relationships and activities. Their miraculous purpose as God's instruments is perceived with faith and celebrated in sacrament.

For our purposes "sacramental perspective" and the "supernatural habit of charity" can be seen as terms from different arenas of Christian tradition that try to describe the same phenomenon. Both have been described as a distinctive "vision" and as requiring outward expression in activity.[42] Sacramental perspective denotes a habit of finding God in all things, of dealing with worldly matters in light of their ultimate relationship with God. Like the architectonic virtue of charity as traditionally defined, it refers all things to God and thus presupposes faith. Both concepts are well captured in the biblical image of loving God by loving your neighbor.

Let me attempt to further connect themes of virtue, sacramentality, and domestic church. My example may seem to demonstrate that participation in the institutional sacraments is not necessary for cultivating charity. I prefer to regard the incident as a delayed reaction to a sacrament, in this case, the Holy Thursday Eucharistic liturgy.

During Holy Week of 1998, I was less than a week away from defending my doctoral dissertation. Tension had been high in our house for months, and though the end was in sight, I had a number of last-minute details to polish up before the big day. Wouldn't you know it, sometime Tuesday night or Wednesday morning my son Seth, then five years old, began throwing up. He wasn't old enough to make it to the toilet or a bucket very often. It wasn't his fault, but as it continued all day Thursday, I began to lose patience. I had so much to do! I didn't have time for this inconvenience. I didn't have time for *him*. Certainly I took care of him, but I resented doing it. Needless to say, I missed mass on Holy Thursday evening. But that night, while cleaning him up for what seemed like the hundredth time, I found myself washing his feet. And all of a sudden, it hit me—that was the Gospel message for the day. "If you do not wash each others' feet, as I have washed your feet, you will have no share in my heritage" (John 13). Basically, you still don't know what it means to be my disciple. After writing an entire dissertation on domestic church, you still don't get the point about loving God by loving your neighbor! I began to cry, which is out of character for me. My attitude changed. My washing actions remained observably the same, but I saw them in an entirely different light.

As well as any I can come up with, this incident illustrates the respective roles of the Church at large, the domestic church, sacramental liturgy, and ordinary activity as cooperative causes—with divine intervention—in the gradual formation of explicitly Christian sacramental vision, or supernatural virtue. This example points to continuity between natural and charity-informed virtue, as well as to the distinctive character of each. Their exercise may differ not so much materially as in the degree to which agents explicitly refer them to their relationship with God, as interpreted through Christian Scriptures and community tradition. In this case, it seems to me that the sacramental liturgy and the liturgy of the world were interdependent causes of charity, or rather an increase in charity. We don't have here a case of "God working in us without us." True, if I hadn't heard that Gospel and participated in the Holy Thursday liturgy in years past, I wouldn't have had the necessary reference point to understand what it meant to wash the vomit off my son's feet. But if I hadn't washed the vomit off my son's feet, I wouldn't have had the necessary reference point to appreciate all those Holy Thursday Eucharists I had participated in before.

Renewed attention to charity as friendship with God,[43] considered in conjunction with a more contemporary understanding of sacraments such as baptism and reconciliation, should allow us to acknowledge its incremental formation and decline—comparable to friendship in the natural order—as a general rule. Sudden, miraculous growth (or sudden destruction through mortal sin) could be acknowledged as an occasional event, but we must be careful that our theology of virtue does not portray it as the norm of moral and spiritual development. Moreover, human friendships—preeminent among them family relations—and all the ordinary activities they entail must be acknowledged for their crucial role as mediating instruments of friendship with God.

DOMESTIC CHURCHES ARE NOT SELF-SUFFICIENT AS TEACHERS OF VIRTUE

Even if families are seen as the primary "school of virtue," broader community reinforcement certainly remains crucial in teaching virtue. Communities beyond family can convey to a learner that the vision and lifestyle proposed by loved ones is not just something they made up, but something others are convinced of as well. Communities beyond family can devise customs, incentives, and laws that make exercise of virtue easier. But a large community's role in cultivating virtue is discrete in scope. The school, neighborhood community center, or parish, even with professional staff, cannot normally be expected to replace the individualized mentoring in virtue that family customarily provides.

Professional religious educators should see their primary job as providing families with encouragement, resources, and logistical support for larger community cooperation, as needed to fulfill their educational role knowledgeably and in fidelity to their tradition, rather than haphazardly. Formal instruction by professionals should concentrate on what they have the resources to do best—presenting the highlights, depth, and breadth of Christian tradition. Professionals should be especially responsible for compiling and disseminating accurate information on church doctrine, history, Scripture, worship, saints, and so forth. Information should be presented to children, but equally (if not more) to parents and other adults.

Literacy, if not fluency, in Christian tradition is important in cultivating charity and correlated virtues, for several reasons. Christian tradition provides a distinctive hermeneutic of experience that invites believers to see God at work in the world and in their lives. A person's ability to refer ordinary human affairs to their final end, their relationship with God, is the essence of charity. Christian tradition offers continuity of language as well as persuasive role models of faith, hope, and charity, both of which aid inductive discernment of what supernatural virtue entails.

Since virtue requires engaging the emotions, professional educators and ministers should, of course, be warm and loving people and should find engaging ways to link learners' everyday lives with the lives of Christians past. Some may succeed in creating ongoing relationships with students or parishioners, a "church family" or a "home away from home." Those who interact with learners only on a short term or occasional basis should aim to be role models, but should not expect to duplicate the service of families in what they do best—individually-tailored training in virtuous living.

TWELVE

Domestic Church: A Missing Link in the Consistent Life Ethic

In literature on Christian family spirituality, one prominent theme may be described as a perceived call and ensuing struggle for *consistency* in attitude and practice of faith, manifested in extraordinary and ordinary events of family life. Chapters of books often follow a pattern of reflection on a range of household events, which are seen as occasions to grow in love and service for God. In many cases the link between love of God and love of neighbor is described in very material terms, and with focus on the common good, rather than the family in isolation. These authors and their families have accepted the Church's invitation, as Wendy Wright puts it, "to be obedient to a vision of persons and the world" that, following modern Catholic social teachings, considers the person "not only sacred but social."[1]

Obedience to this vision invariably results in a countercultural lifestyle; it impacts upon choice and use of possessions, physical living space, leisure time, food and dress, work (both inside and outside the home), education, conflict resolution, rewards and punishments, gift giving and celebrations, hospitality, and, of course, prayer and worship. Some of the better-known Christian models of this lifestyle are seen in the Parenting for Peace and Justice Network spearheaded by James McGinnis and Kathleen McGinnis of St. Louis, Missouri,[2] and in families associated with the Catholic Worker movement.[3] A secular model is seen in the "voluntary simplicity" movement—and many thoughtful Christians have embraced this trend.[4] Though these spokespersons may not draw the connection themselves, they have clearly adopted the premise of virtue ethicists that every human action is a moral exercise. Even very ordinary lifestyle choices cultivate virtuous or vicious habits; they mold both the actors and their communities.

These authors conceive of their families' lifestyle choices as part of an evangelizing or prophetic mission.[5] They hope their lifestyle will not only assist those in need, but also inspire acquaintances to share their vision. Concern to cultivate their religious vision in their own children holds a special measure of urgency. They are convinced that God has entrusted them with this vocation and that household lifestyle will make a decisive difference in their children's ability to respond to fellow human beings in keeping with their God-given dignity.[6]

In a chapter titled "Circles of Care," Wendy Wright explains that many of us manifest generous nurture and care for our families, even when sacrifice is entailed. Building from this natural foundation, we can and should be challenged to extend our care to the wider circle of God's human family. She suggests that parents are best positioned, with some strategic forethought, to teach their children to widen the circle of their concern:

> Parents are the first teachers of their children. We may send our kids off to school for the 3R's and to music and dance academies for aesthetic instruction, but they learn most about who they are and how the world is put together from us. They learn this almost by osmosis. They learn it by assimilating our attitudes toward ourselves and the domestic and global families of which we are a part. Sometimes the immediate life of the family seems only remotely concerned with the big issues of the world, and the big issues are left for "big people" (especially those in positions of leadership) to be concerned about. Certainly in our complex world, children cannot be expected to grasp the totality of our political, economic, and social realities. How many adults can? But these big issues do have small

manifestations that touch us daily in family life. Parents can explore these as teaching moments or avail themselves of the many small ways natural in family life to let the attitude of domestic caring spill out into a larger sphere.

There are three simple things, at least, that parents can teach their children: the beauty and variety of the human family; the suffering of our family; and that we as families can act in many ways to alleviate suffering and restore the dignity of all God's people. Such lessons would do much to create a generation of Christians whose compassion is aroused by the miracle of God's creation, our world, and its inhabitants.[7]

Wright is not alone in observing that many people experience family life as "only remotely concerned with the big issues of the world," which are left to the world's leaders. James McGinnis and Kathleen McGinnis have found that the world's "big issues"—individualism, materialism, violence, sexism, racism, militarism—are often overwhelming. "'What's the use; what can one family do?' is too often the plaintive reply of persons who choose to do nothing because they can't do everything."[8] The McGinnises say such families need three things: they need to have their imaginations stretched, they need inspiration, and they need the support of like-minded families and larger communities.[9]

In recent years, quite a few authors have drawn attention to Catholic social teaching in conjunction with the emerging concept of domestic church.[10] In particular, they ask us to consider the family's role as an active agent, not simply a passive beneficiary, of the Church's pursuit of social justice. The McGinnises say that "reorienting family thinking about themselves" is requisite for empowering families to become agents of transformation of the world's social ills, and that "helping families to see themselves as domestic church has wonderful possibilities along this line."[11] However, they warn that a person's interpretation of "Church" is critical in this context. "Church must not be seen primarily as a safe harbor where we protect ourselves from the winds of the world, as many of us experienced growing up in Catholic ghettos. As the gospel parables indicate, the church of God is to be a leaven in society, deeply involved in transforming the world, God's instrument in the completion of God's kingdom or reign."[12] Though younger generations of Catholics may not have been raised with a ghetto mentality, their sense of Christianity's social mission is often dulled when they assimilate the cultural gospel, which preaches that religion is a private matter. If a sense of Church as leaven and instrument for God's kingdom can be conveyed such that ordinary believers embrace it, then the next step of encouraging families to view themselves as domestic churches should "help families move more fully into the world rather than retreat from it."[13]

Such an appreciation of Christian family life ushers us into uncharted territory. Students in my theology of marriage course and my social justice course often seem perplexed when I introduce a social mission as an element of Christian marriage, or a family's everyday lifestyle choices as social justice issues. Almost inevitably, the association is new to them. Some are resistant to the idea, apparently because they have been schooled in the habit (vice?) of considering both marriage and religion private matters, or because they do not readily connect Christian faith with counter-cultural lifestyle choices.[14] For instance, I once asked a young married couple who deliberately sought to live a justice-oriented lifestyle to discuss their experience with my marriage class. This particular weekend section of the course drew mostly adult students, many of whom were older than the two guest speakers. The young couple described choices like carpooling, exchanging tools with neighbors, trying to invest their retirement savings in socially conscious mutual funds, purchasing a home in a racially integrated neighborhood, and recycling everything they could, even though this monopolized much of their garage space. When my students gave written evaluations of the lecture, they surprised me with some of their negative comments—for instance, describing the speakers as "naive" or "preachy," or the entire discussion as an "intrusion" that didn't belong in the course. On the other hand, some students have latched onto this approach with gusto. In my social justice course, one assignment option is to adopt a lifestyle change that expresses solidarity and a pursuit of justice, and then keep a journal documenting the experience in connection with course materials. Many students report that their lifestyle change—e.g., recycling, packing lunch each workday so that money saved on restaurants can be given to a charitable cause, or taking the bus to work (to help the environment, to save money for a worthy cause, and to spend time with people who may not earn enough money to own a car)—is difficult initially, but becomes easier with practice.

Often students add to their original lifestyle change as the semester progresses—for example, they might start by recycling glass and cans, but later add plastic, paper, or even a backyard compost pile. My experience has been that (at least some) students who are introduced to this approach in a college course now look for opportunities for their families to concretely express solidarity with the needy, or to connect community-minded lifestyle choices they are *already* making with the Christian faith they profess in quiet daily prayer or at Sunday worship.

Yet, many people still need to be reached with this message. Julie Hanlon Rubio is reserved in assessing the impact of *Familiaris Consortio* and subsequent magisterial statements on the average family's sense of personal investment in the Church's public life. She contends that while magisterial statements have made advances in promoting domestic churches as agents of the Church's social mission, potent principles have not been developed fully either at the magisterial or the grass-roots level:

> Catholic social teaching is primarily addressed to larger society, not to the family. However, tradition holds that the family is a domestic church with a personal and social vocation.... This social mandate of the family is perhaps the greatest strength of Catholic social teaching on the family. ... Still, because Catholic social teaching does not concentrate its attention on families and because Catholic family teaching does not concentrate on the family's social mission, this aspect of Catholic teaching is not as fully developed as it might be.... Because [John Paul II's] theology of the body gives so much weight to the marital relationship, it tends to obscure the social calling of the family. The radical idea that persons can find true fulfillment only in community is obscured in the quest to promote the view that man and woman find fulfillment only in relationship with each other....
>
> What counts as Catholic teaching on the family is associated with encyclicals focusing on the personal rather than on the social. Thus most Catholics would doubtless affirm that their major moral duties are to love their families, to obey the Church's teaching on sexuality, and to stay together for life. They would justify their stance by arguing that this is the main thrust of Catholic teaching on the family. [15]

In this context—where some Christian families feel called to nurture a vision of humans as sacred and social through deliberate lifestyle choices, while others regard the world's social ills as only tangentially related to their home life; where those with the training to do so search for words and images that might arouse in Christian families a sense of confidence and responsibility as agents of the Church's social mission— it is valuable to consider the consistent life ethic, or "seamless garment" approach, associated with the late Joseph Cardinal Bernardin.[16] Themes of sacramentality and virtue undergird and are enlivened by Bernardin's practical and politically-oriented ethic.[17] Most important for our purposes are recurrent themes of the *sacredness of ordinary life,* of the *Church's mission to cultivate a distinctive vision* that sees visible things in relation to the invisible God, and of *love of neighbor as the embodiment of love for God.*

An Overview of Bernardin's Consistent Life Ethic

The consistent life ethic promoted by Bernardin in various venues from 1983 until his death in 1996 has been offered to the Catholic Church as a foundational point of reference for moral reflection, pastoral practice, and strategic engagement in civil society.[18] Simultaneously, it has been offered to civil society, especially in the United States, as a moral stance or vision (with public policy implications) that can be found compelling by rational persons of good will from across the political and religious spectrum. The consistent ethic of life centers around a deep appreciation of human beings as the *image of God* and aims to specify moral mandates that derive from a community's commitment to respect human dignity. The result is a linking of concern for a whole spectrum of threats to human life and well-being: poverty, inadequate health care and education, abortion, domestic violence, defense spending, capital punishment, euthanasia, consumerism, and more.

Bernardin sees it as incumbent upon the Church's leadership not only to instigate principled, critical dialogue on life issues, to advocate public policy that protects human life, and to sponsor projects/organizations that serve human needs, but also, perhaps most importantly, *to cultivate a constituency committed to a moral vision that sees human life as sacred,*[19] a community of persons who see violence against even one human life as a momentous event. In the long term, says Bernardin repeatedly, *attitude* is the place to root an ethic of life, though he insists any attitude or moral vision will hold implications for public policy.[20]

Among family spirituality texts surveyed throughout this book, only one cites Bernardin directly.[21] But these sources demonstrate that for many Christian families the impulse for a consistent life ethic resonates with their most fundamental faith convictions and with their sense of themselves as domestic churches. These families are equally concerned to cultivate a constituency that respects human life as sacred—better yet, they are already doing so among their own families and friends. Explicit familiarity with the consistent life ethic approach found in academic, magisterial, and lobbying environments may help Christian families appreciate the significance of their often unrecognized and unrewarded grass-roots efforts. Reciprocally, family spirituality literature provides for a missing element of Bernardin's thought—an explicit recognition of the moral agency of Christian families, not focused so disproportionately on their *passive* role as an audience for bishops and government policy makers, but as *active* teachers and decision-makers in their own right, upon whom cultivation of a consistent pro-life vision and constituency largely depends. In this literature, and among Catholic Worker families and other intentional communities, we find viable models of how the consistent life ethic can be embodied on a daily basis, to include persons of all ages. It is valuable theoretically and strategically to bring these two groups of writings into conversation. Because families are a basic cell of civil society and Christian families are a basic cell of the Church, the consistent life ethic cannot have its intended impact unless the formative agency of families is engaged.

Many Bernardin commentators have wrestled with the practical meaning of consistency in Catholic ethics. Some suggest Bernardin's project is flawed because Catholic ethics is profoundly inconsistent in the methodologies it uses for social and personal ethics.[22] Others say that in a fallen world, consistent respect for life may not be possible; we may be forced to make tragic choices.[23] I can appreciate these concerns, but because I tend to approach Bernardin's work with my "virtue" hat on, I am comfortable with the image of consistency. To me, it is another word for integrity,[24] or, in the language of Aquinas, the "unity of the virtues."[25] When we talk about forming attitudes, vision, and public policy choices that consistently respect human life, we are talking about cultivating virtuous habits; thus, everything we explored in the previous chapter about families as the first school of social virtues is pertinent here. According to virtue theory, many strategies are needed to cultivate mature virtue. These include consistent *practice* to habituate the passions and will along with the intellect, observation and imitation of virtuous *mentors,* and individually tailored, well-timed, prudent *fraternal correction.* Aquinas believed that *law* is a teacher of virtue because it articulates what a community considers good and compels people to practice good habits. But even if we accept this premise, we must remember that the role of law, important as it is, remains discrete. It is not sufficient in itself to solve all our cultural ills concerning life issues.[26] Sometimes this is hard to remember in our legalistic and bureaucratic culture.

If these tools are indeed necessary, then we who are sympathetic to Bernardin's approach must carefully examine the agency of families as schools of virtue. When we think of the public life of the Church—as an instigator of critical dialogue and a prophetic witness for human dignity—we must think not simply of stories in the *New York Times* about the late Cardinal O'Connor and his disputes with Catholic politicians, or whether Catholic hospitals can host certain medical procedures, or whether *Ex Corde Ecclesiae* implementation will require a pro-life litmus test for Catholic university faculty. We must direct the same attention to the more mundane, everyday public impact of the Church at the micro-level, the household level designated by the expression "domestic church." Lifestyle choices at the household level will not often make the front page of the *New York Times,* but for most of us they have at least as much (if not more) lasting influence on character.

In describing the novelty of the consistent life ethic approach, Bernardin sometimes said that "[t]hinking systemically about life issues is not something all are in the *habit* of doing" (emphasis added).[27] Wearing my "virtue" hat and my "family" hat, my immediate question is, why not? Where should people learn these habits? How can people be brought up from childhood to think about life issues holistically or systemically, so that it seems second nature to do so? It has been said that it's much easier to form a good habit than to break a bad one. Why should the habit of respect for life be any different? Those of us who are sympathetic to the "seamless garment" approach should dwell on this piece of advice, and we should ask ourselves: What is the large-scale Church's role in fostering the constituency and virtue necessary to sustain the life ethic, and what is the domestic church's particular scope of expertise?

Believe it or not, in his best-known speeches on the consistent life ethic, Bernardin never explicitly raises the issue of targeting or organizing *families,* the basic cell of civil society and of Church, as witnesses of the life ethic and as nurturers of constituents with consistent pro-life vision. As I see it, families *must* be targeted to complement, with their resources and expertise, what bishops, politicians, the media, and other leaders lack in persuasiveness and specificity of witness.

Bernardin knew from experience that the seamless garment approach could be embraced by persons of varied religious persuasions or of no religious affiliation. He believed this was true because the sanctity or dignity of human life is a fundamental moral experience.[28] And yet, by itself, this fundamental experience has not been sufficient to guarantee consistent protection of human life in practice. It is akin to the natural inclination to virtue Aquinas describes. It is a potential or power intrinsic to humans, but it is a power that can be used more than one way. It must be *trained* in order to develop virtuous habits.

Bernardin indicates (implicity, not explicitly) two reasons why this fundamental experience of human sacredness does not develop into a consistent habit of thought and lifestyle. First, the fundamental experience of human dignity *may be undermined or distorted by narrow self-interest of individuals and groups.* He says a culture that teaches us to value youth and immediate gratification leads some to question the very existence of "vision and values which transcend time and individual choice."[29] In the not distant past it was "assumed that pain and sacrifice were part of the human experience and contributed to the meaning of life," however, many dismiss that assumption today.[30] In a context where people experience (or are led to believe) that material resources are in short supply, it is difficult to get individuals or special interest groups to muster support for life-promoting causes that do not appear to impact on them personally.

In contrast, the sustaining attitude of the life-ethic requires a sense of *solidarity,* a persistent commitment to the common good. It requires a sense of solidarity not only between privileged and underprivileged groups—specifically the ability of the privileged to see persons whose dignity is threatened "not just as statistics, but as our brothers and sisters"[31]—but also solidarity among members of privileged groups. By this I mean friendships among families consciously committed to a lifestyle in keeping with a consistent life ethic. As the McGinnises note, one obstacle to integrating social ministry and family life is *isolation.* "High mobility combines with an individualistic ethic to make real community difficult. Without the support and challenge that community can provide, few people, especially beleaguered parents, are about to go forth to transform the world."[32] Jack Nelson-Pallmeyer enthusiastically describes his ten-year experience with a neighborhood-based intentional community near Minneapolis: "An essential insight is that we need each other. Alone we feel disconnected, overwhelmed, fragmented, and sometimes powerless. We choose to be part of an intentional community because we offer one another encouragement and because our collective vision and united action make us stronger and more effective."[33] Certainly there is untapped potential for Church parishes to facilitate friendships among social-minded families. Other Church-related institutions, such as Christian schools and hospitals, could attempt to facilitate such intentional support systems among their employees' families. Dedication of institutional resources to support the public life of domestic churches would be a priceless contribution to the public life of the large-scale Church.

Solidarity includes willingness to *sacrifice* limited goods, to reject a narrow vision of self-interest. Bernardin says, correctly, "The truth is that consistent respect for human life will cost us something."[34] Again, "Although some of those who oppose the concept seem not to have understood it, I sometimes suspect that many who oppose it recognize its challenge. Quite frankly, I sometimes wonder whether those who embrace it quickly and wholeheartedly truly understand its implicit challenge."[35] The countercultural lifestyles of the McGinnises, Catholic Worker families, voluntary simplicity advocates, and like-minded families are testimony to the challenge, but also to the fact that sacrifice for the common good can be the path to happiness. This testimony is much needed; otherwise, the life ethic will not sell.

A second reason the basic moral experience of human sacredness remains incomplete is because even for those who are sympathetic to the seamless garment approach, *it is difficult to translate a general belief or principle of human sacredness into specific, concrete choices.*[36] The difficulty is compounded in a context of increasing global interdependence and sophisticated technology. Translation from general moral principle to specific action requires the virtue of prudence. In the case of the consistent life ethic, translation also requires some imagination. The McGinnises explain, "Many people do not know what to do even when they are willing to do something. 'Action on behalf of justice' and 'peacemaking' are simply equated, for many people, with either marching in demonstrations or contributing to hunger relief efforts; most people are afraid of or disagree with the former and are already doing the latter. 'So what can we do?' they ask."[37] As with any virtue, learning consistent respect for human dignity calls for virtuous mentors to imitate.

As a manifestation of integrity or "unity of the virtues," the consistent life ethic involves persuading people intellectually and emotionally to accept a vision of human fulfillment that is not shortsighted or narrowly self-interested. It requires training the passions so that people desire and enjoy what is truly good, even if there is sacrifice involved, so that alternative models of "the good life" are no longer attractive. It entails training inductive reasoning skills needed to recognize situations that place moral demands on us and to prudently tailor general moral principles to the circumstances at hand. It involves imitating role models and being persuaded to pursue their distinctive lifestyle. It involves devising community laws and explicit, consistent language and traditions that train maturing persons to think and act appropriately.

For Christians the life ethic should be informed by the virtue of charity. Bernardin and like-minded persons "see God hiding in the poor";[38] they see life-promoting acts of love toward neighbor as service to "brothers and sisters" in Christ. Thus, the consistent life ethic reflects a rich sacramental sense of the graced quality of everyday life, of the divine presence hidden within finite media that prophets and apostles have uncovered and which sacramental encounters highlight.[39] The Church, as a community that continues the prophetic tradition in a manner engaged with the world, has a mission to uncover the transcendent dimensions of every human act and train people to see them.[40]

FAMILY AS A MISSING LINK IN THE CONSISTENT LIFE ETHIC

If the consistent life ethic is indeed a form of virtue (either natural or distinctively Christian) or sacramental vision (whether anonymous or explicitly Christian), then families, as the basic cell of both civic society and church, should be considered indispensable to cultivating it, for reasons identified previously. A family's life-affirming choices, both countercultural and more ordinary, carried on communally, consistently, and self-consciously, should be recognized as forms of witness and discipline that, more than any other human factor, mold the moral vision, practical reasoning, and widened circle of care of those engaged.

However, comparing Bernardin to authors in the family spirituality and theology genres, one finds that ordinary citizens and believers—persons with no official ministry or leadership position in government or the church—do not figure prominently in his speeches on the consistent life ethic. When they do appear, they are often described in *passive* roles—as beneficiaries of social justice, as the audience for bishops, or as electoral constituencies who once every few years vote to elect or remove the real decision makers from office.

Families are rarely mentioned in Bernardin's consistent life ethic speeches, except as victims of violence and injustice, or as persons with "real problems to face in this delicate area of respecting unborn life."[41] Many other groups—bishops especially, along with priests, religious educators, Catholic universities, Catholic hospitals and other service providers, and Catholic elected officials—are described as potential leaders of dialogue, teachers, and role models of the consistent life ethic. Though it has a limited scope and effect, civil law is said to have important potential for establishing pro-life consensus.[42] Even the popular media is said to "have a special responsibility in framing a correct vision of life in our society."[43]

To my knowledge, none of Bernardin's speeches on the life ethic describes families as having any such responsibilities. This occurs despite the fact that the life ethic's sustaining vision is often described in terms of responding to the suffering of our "human family," or seeing the poor not just as statistics, but as "brothers and sisters." His challenge to boundless love and forgiveness, regardless of worthiness, implicitly presupposes we have learned something of these phenomena through our experience of family. Bernardin does not take the next logical step and explicitly acknowledge families as having significant responsibilities to help frame a correct moral vision among the churches and in civil society.

Turning specifically to the Christian family or domestic church, we can say Bernardin misses the opportunity to articulate domestic churches' role within the public mission of the Church as a whole. I have not located any references to domestic church in his speeches on the consistent life ethic. The oversight is curious, considering Bernardin's interest in the concept during his tenure as chairman of the U.S. bishops' Committee on Marriage and Family.[44] This omission occurs despite Bernardin's acknowledgement of the principle of subsidiarity[45] and the limited expertise and authority of bishops with regard to specific applications of the life ethic.[46]

In fairness, we must take into account the fact that Bernardin's speeches were often written in reponse to questions posed by event organizers or by his critics.[47] He more than once remarked that citizens "will make all the difference" to the success of the consistent life ethic.[48] Still, Bernardin's lack of attention to family or domestic church as agents responsible for cultivating a constituency with a consistent pro-life attitude may be considered symptomatic of the fact that lifestyle choices at the level of household or family tend not to be raised in Catholic social ethics.

I venture to guess that when most of us think of our actions as citizens, we think of voting, paying taxes, and jury duty. Occasionally we may think of ourselves as concerned citizens while attending a meeting of the local school committee, or lobbying our elected officials when issues that affect us are at stake. Our culture does not teach us to think of our home lives as part of the arena of our citizenship; this part of our lives is sectioned off as private. In classic Catholic political theology "political" life is a broader term and does encompass our family roles. But this definition is lost on the average person in American culture today.

So, when Bernardin tells his audiences that citizens will make all the difference, it is likely that he has not provoked them to think about what the life ethic means for their day-to-day lifestyle. When he addressed audiences such as the American Bar Association, or the National Press Club, or the Association of Catholic Medical Schools, or the Fordham University community, they likely *heard* him talking to them in their public roles as lawyers, journalists, doctors, or university professors. But these are roles many leave at the office (at least, they try to). The same may have been true when Bernardin addressed his fellow bishops, or a conference of social action directors, or the National Right-to-Life Convention. When Bernardin talked about cultivating constituencies, some of them may have thought of their public roles as lobbyists, event planners, or public speakers.

A consistent life ethic must be just that—consistent. It's not a nine-to-five sort of thing, still less an item for business only in election years. Those of us who are sympathetic to the consistent life ethic must take up the challenge of demonstrating what it means enfleshed as a "24/7" life-style. Bernardin has done a wonderful job of articulating linkage of various life issues at the macro level. The next step is to instigate examination of the microlevel, the household level.

For instance, what will we (not) buy the kids for their birthdays? Whom will we invite (or neglect to invite) to our home? How low on the food chain were our meals today? Is our babysitter being paid a living wage? Should I refrain from gossip, as a habit of violence? Are the punishments I use with my kids mostly violent and retributive, or crafted to promote reconciliation and responsibility? When we plan our family budget, are donations to charity a dedicated line-item or something allocated from whatever money is left over? Is a family vacation to Disney World an example of good stewardship? Are we willing to invest the time to visit our elderly neighbor regularly so that she does not feel alone and that her life isn't worth living? Do we threaten to throw a teenage daughter out of the house if she ever comes home and announces she is pregnant? Do we remember persons in distress—both from the evening news and close to home—in our family bedtime prayers? Does our family recycle trash even if it means driving a few miles to the local depot? Would we discontinue using a birth control method we discovered to have abortifacient properties, or would we continue because it was convenient and effective? Do my spouse and I make our career plans based on how much flexibility they will allow for us to volunteer in a neighborhood adult literacy program? If we are in the market for a home, are "racially diverse neighborhood" or "close enough to work to allow us to live with one car" among the features we look for—or are we more concerned to find "walk-in closets," "wired for cable," and "convenient to shopping mall and golf course"?

John Carr, who has worked in social ministry at the diocesan and national levels, speaks to this challenge in an essay on the underappreciated natural alliance between social justice and family ministries. He praises Catholicism's recent magisterial statements on both social justice and family life as strong, clear, and complementary, but says coordinated response to these statements has been less than exemplary because integral links between widespread social ills and family life do not receive sufficient attention:

> I'm impressed with not only how far we've come in these areas, but also how far we have yet to go. Family life ministers and social justice ministers need to acknowledge the differences in style, agendas, and structures of our two ministries. We have not worked together or supported one another as much as we should. In my view, we have traveled parallel paths without enough contact or collaboration. Too often we stereotype each other. Social justice people can appear to be focused on a huge, almost overwhelming agenda. Our urgency can get in the way, as well as our occasional grimness and singlemindedness. Too often we seem more focused on global issues than local relationships. Family life ministers, on the other hand, face similar stereotypes. We may seem preoccupied with the everyday challenges of marriage preparation and family ministry, seeing justice concerns for families as issues which could alienate constituents. Family life folks sometimes seem to talk a different language, avoiding conflict at all costs and focusing on dynamics and warmth rather than on organization and change.
>
> However, I think we have more in common than we think. . . . [O]ur issues intersect. The issues at the center of a social justice agenda are among the greatest threats to family life. . . . We also need to acknowledge that there is no effective response to these problems that does not build upon the strengths of American families. Social solutions which ignore the central role of families simply won't work.[49]

Linking social justice and family ministries will entail relearning our habitual ways of thinking about our public and private lives, and about the public witness of the Church.[50] We who are leaders or teachers in any capacity must look for opportunities to help our audiences make these links, because often our secular and ecclesial traditions have habituated us to *not* make these links. Julie Hanlon Rubio observes that, in modern Catholic social teaching, families are said to have responsibility for the poor and oppressed, but are seldom challenged to make any specific sacrifices comparable to those to which nations have been called. Rubio concludes that "[t]he absence of reflection on appropriate levels of sacrifice weakens those parts of the social teaching that speak to families. Because what is expected of families in the social realm is so vague, this part of Catholic social teaching is rendered virtually meaningless in the lives of Catholic families."[51] An example is allocation of financial resources, a subject Bernardin raised often in speeches on the consistent life ethic, but inevitably in discussions of national health care or welfare or military spending, not in connection with family spending. Rubio asks, "How do commitments to solidarity and the common good affect family's choices about how to spend their money? To ask the question in the context of social ethics seems almost absurd. Some might argue that ethicists should not concern themselves with decisions about clothes, cars, homes, vacations, food, and entertainment, because these are issues of personal or pastoral concern. Ethicists are at home analyzing the budgets of nations or corporations, not the budgets of families. Perhaps discomfort about the issue is revealing." [52] Rubio says academics are wrong to ignore this ethical arena, even though each family spends relatively little compared to a corporation or nation. She astutely observes, "Spending money is one of the most significant ethical domains in most people's lives."[53]

In "What Families Can Teach," Marilyn Martone proposes that the ethical import of family *nurturance* is vastly underappreciated in Catholic social ethics and examines the consistent life ethic as a case in point. Martone's first premise is that the consistent life ethic depends upon sustained nurturing of virtues. On this point we have found in Bernardin significant agreement, albeit little explicit attention. Her second premise is that family life is where most of us learn these virtues. On this point Bernardin is silent. Martone wisely observes that when we think of "life issues," we too often think of isolated moments such as the "moment of conception" or the "moment of death." She argues that this approach treats ethical decisions out of context.

What often gets lost in this way of thinking is that life is not a single moment in time, but a long continuum of moments. We are conceived and born, nourished and nurtured over an extensive period. This nurturing is not often thought of as part of the ethical realm. We take it for granted or we cover it with such broad strokes (husbands, love your wives; children, obey your parents) that there is little practical content showing us how to do it well. Yet it is this very nurturing that forms the crux of a consistent ethic of life. We learn to respect life by having been nurtured into this respect. . . .

The consistent ethic of life should not revolve around issues but around a consistent nurturing of others. This would include not just the "big issues" such as war, abortion, and euthanasia, but the very mundane activities of daily care. We need to ask ourselves if we are life givers in our day-to-day activities.[54]

Martone's essay helps us understand the family's sphere of expertise in addressing challenges posed by the life ethic—replacing self-interest with a sense of solidarity, fostering a willingness to sacrifice limited and misguided pleasures in view of the long-term common good, and translating general principles into specific lifestyle choices.

As professionals (scientists, academics, health-care and social-service providers, lawmakers and lobbyists, workers in the criminal justice system or the media, etc.) many of us contribute to civil discourse on life issues and perhaps have an opportunity to implement life-sustaining public policy. These activities influence the religious and moral attitudes of our communities, our professional acquaintances, and our families.[55] However, the reverse is equally true. Relations with our loved ones play a less glamorized, but equally important, role in forming commitment to care for others, willingness to sacrifice when necessary for the good of all, and skill in responding to multiple human needs simultaneously.[56] Indeed, our family lives may often contribute significant motivation and practical skills needed for serving the wider community in our professional roles. The virtues Martone examines as prerequisites for the life ethic—faithfulness, courage, and prudence—can be considered among domestic churches' most important contributions to the Church's comprehensive pro-life witness.

Martone's description of *faithfulness* addresses the need to cultivate solidarity and a willingness to sacrifice immediate gratification in view of the long-term, common good. She says faithfulness may be the most important life-sustaining virtue because it "assures us we will be there for each other, not just when we feel like it but all the time." She continues,

> It is not sufficient to condemn certain acts as being against life. . . .
> It is imperative that we nourish life, and to do this we must recog-
> nize the importance of faithfulness, since nourishment involves a
> commitment of time. . . . We need to ask ourselves how we as a
> society are faithful not just to fetuses but to pregnant women, new
> mothers, the handicapped, the sick, the dying—to each other.[57]

Martone describes courage as "constantly giving of oneself without the certitude of knowing the end result, but resolving you will always be there for the other regardless of the pain and suffering involved." She contin-ues, "In order to be faithful, we must be courageous. . . . Sustaining life is courageous activity. There are no givens, just commitment. We need to examine how we go about developing courage in our personal lives."[58] In their treatment of courage, the McGinnises explain that willingness to risk reaching out to those in need requires self-confidence, and seemingly insignificant gestures of affirmation and care offered in the home have far-reaching impact on courage.

> The affirmation that can be experienced within the family is abso-
> lutely essential for the realization of the church's social mission.
> Neither children nor adults can be concerned about others unless
> they feel good about themselves first. They cannot deal well with
> difference—whether racial, economic, or religious difference—
> unless they feel comfortable about their own identity. They cannot
> take risks on behalf of others and participate in social change unless
> they have a good self-concept and some self-confidence. They will
> be unable to be different from the crowd and stand up for what they
> believe unless they feel good about themselves.[59]

If courage and faithfulness redress narrow self-interest, prudence provides the reasoning skills needed to translate the life ethic's general principles into practical living. Martone remarks that the importance of prudence is underrepresented in theological discussion of life issues.[60] She believes the practical reasoning parents exercise on a daily basis can become the basis for thinking about life issues with prudence. Martone recalls Aquinas's view that in practical matters we can attain only "practical truth," which is superior to opinion but not absolute truth. Prudence is a skill, not a science. She continues,

> Sustaining life requires fulfilling and balancing the needs of many. . . . Sustaining life involves not so much eliminating doubt as learning to function in the midst of doubt. We are not always sure what is the best way to sustain life, yet because we need to act, we must make a choice in the here and now. . . . Monday morning quarterbacks might come up with better decisions but they were not on the playing field at the moment of action. Life-sustainers are always on the playing field.[61]

Any family of good will can contribute to the cultivation of prudence, courage, faithfulness, and other virtues (such as temperance, generosity, justice) requisite for a sustainable pro-life ethic. Christian domestic churches can cultivate these virtues as informed by Christian charity. As Bernardin's experience testifies, explicitly Christian faith is not a prerequisite for embrace of the consistent life ethic among persons of goodwill; by extension, neither is the virtue Christians call charity. Vision and values that transcend time and individual choice, and which interpret human events in relationship to God, are not a monopoly of Christians. However, among Christians, the virtue we call charity solidifies and broadens that moral vision by explicitly identifying love of God with love of neighbor. If, as Bernardin claims, Catholic hospitals and similar institutions can provide their personnel with training and formation to see God hiding in the poor and treat them with dignity,[62] surely mature members of domestic churches can do as well or better for their loved ones.

In his study of recent magisterial statements on the family, conducted in conversation with socioscientific literature, Donald Miller shows a point of agreement—the premise that families are the primary agent of both religious and civic socialization.[63] This principle is very traditional, but it must be examined anew in each historical and cultural context. I am convinced that the contemporary American context dictates not only the need for a consistent life ethic, but also the need for families to cultivate self-consciously the constituency needed to sustain it. In ecclesial circles, true recognition and use of the resource of domestic churches, with an appreciation of their overlapping religious and secular roles, may do more than anything else to cultivate a constituency with the attitude necessary to sustain the consistent life ethic.

Frankly, without mobilizing teachers and role models at the level of family and neighborhood, I see no way to persuade a sufficient constituency to sustain comprehensive life-supporting policies. As Bernardin knew, customary attitudes that in previous generations kept shortsighted self-interest in check are increasingly called into question. Neither bishops nor elected officials have the sway over consciences that they once had. Thus, while advocacy of bishops, lobbyists, and pro-life elected officials is valuable in promoting and analyzing the life ethic and rooting it in an impressive communal tradition, their impact on attitudes and lifestyle is limited in intensity and everyday usefulness. For the consistent life ethic to be persuasive, and for its general principles of human dignity and solidarity to be translated into everyday choices, role models who embody these ideals must be readily visible at the grass-roots level. With these role models in place, chances for the consistent life ethic to win over new adherents among Christians and persons of other faiths would be much increased. Speaking for many of the spiritual authors we have examined, Leonard Doohan writes, "In fact, the teachings of the Church on social justice remain largely ineffectual without the responsible commitment of the family."[64]

When he responded to critics who feared his consistency agenda would erode support for important single issues, Bernardin said that the Church *as a whole* can and must give comprehensive witness to the sanctity of human life, and that each member must do what is possible, with their given resources and within the scope of their vocation, to contribute to this witness.[65] These premises can give us insight into domestic churches' current and potential impact on the Church's public mission. To those who ask, "What can one family do?" the answer is this: no one is called to do everything, but each person, each household, can do something. In fact, each household can do many things. Comprehensive protection of life in all its conditions and manifestations is possible to the extent that the Church, in all its conditions and manifestations, is unified around this complex, but single, issue. Both the McGinnises and Bernardin say that in order to protect human dignity we need to have our moral imaginations expanded or stretched;[66] we need to cultivate a habitual, conscious, explicit connection between life issues. As I see it, it is equally necessary to expand our ecclesial imaginations. Comprehensive witness to life is indeed overwhelming or impossible for a random group of unrelated persons and projects. Yet comprehensive witness could be possible—and potentially very persuasive—if a Church comprising countless, diverse domestic manifestations is consciously and explicitly unified in witness across the spectrum of life issues.

Bernardin observed that "because this vision encompasses the full range of human life issues from conception to natural death, it is difficult to create a stable constituency for it."[67] This being the case, advocates of the consistent life ethic must enlist the agency of families, the civic and ecclesial institution that most consistently and concretely nurtures virtue in humans from conception to death.

CONCLUSION

This book has taken as its premise that there is a doctrinal vacuum surrounding the term "domestic church" in Roman Catholicism, and that this vacuum needs to be redressed. I believe I have demonstrated the range and significance of issues and questions provoked by this classic, yet timely, concept. I do not suppose I have completely redressed the doctrinal vacuum surrounding domestic church but hope that I have made a useful contribution to that end.

Because magisterial, pastoral, and spiritual authors deserve credit for reintroducing the idea of domestic church to Roman Catholics, I looked to these sources first for issues worthy of theological examination. They have not disappointed us in this regard. My exploration of domestic church in connection with sacramentality, virtue, and the consistent life ethic is very much a reply to questions raised by these authors. On the other hand, I believe literature on domestic church has often been lacking in terms of comprehensiveness and theological precision, and I have tried to redress these weaknesses. If nothing else, I hope that introducing the likes of Rahner, Aquinas, and Bernardin into reflection on domestic church will raise standards of future exploration.

Combining insights from these varied fields guards against simplistic, overly abstract, or distorted interpretations of domestic church. For instance, the consistent life ethic corrects for sectarian and elitist tendencies that surface among some proponents of virtue and "family values." It also provides some of the concrete moral norms that some commentators have found lacking in virtue ethics,[1] and which authors such as James McGinnis and Kathleen McGinnis, Michael True, and Julie Hanlon Rubio have found lacking in literature on the Christian family's social mission.

As Marilyn Martone rightly observes, virtue ethics provides a corrective to moral analysis that neglects the ethical significance of nurturance. Virtue theory's recognition that human development is usually slow and incremental (also a common theme in the family spirituality genre) balances the style of theologians whose preference for describing the family in terms of its ideal form may intimidate neophytes or alienate realistic veterans of church and family life.

There is a common human temptation that has shown itself in discourse on Christian family life. This is the temptation to evaluate moral prowess or fidelity to Christian tradition simply on the basis of isolated (and often extraordinary) choices. Martone, Rubio, and others warn us that Christian families have been poorly catechized if they consider their mission as domestic churches fulfilled simply by not getting divorced or cheating on their spouses, not using contraceptives, and not aborting or euthanizing vulnerable family members. If consistency or integrity is not the foundation of one's moral life, it is easy to have delusions of grandeur about oneself or one's mentors, and it is tempting to relax on the laurels of a few notable achievements.

An appreciation of the sacred significance of ordinary life, contributed by sacramental theology, can undergird domestic churches' pursuit of virtue and justice and help ensure that this interest does not fall out of fashion, like many educational theories and political agendas. Among the sources examined, sacramental ecclesiology offers the most potential for developing a renewed sense of each Christian family not simply as a group of Christians who happen to live together, but as a small ecclesial community responsible for manifesting Christ's presence in a particular locale. The sources brought together for this study confirm John Paul II's assertion that "future evangelization depends largely on the domestic church."

In this book I intended to bring together fields of theological inquiry that have not always interacted as fruitfully as they might. Recurrent themes among family spirituality literature, sacramental ecclesiology, virtue theory, and the life ethic are multiple and profound. Points of convergence indicate distinctive, unifying characteristics of domestic churches and serve as a solid foundation for future theological and practical work on the subject. What are these points of convergence?

- First, the full range of authors consulted testifies to Catholicism's *appreciation of the potentially sacred significance of ordinary human activity, seen with the eyes of faith,* and insists that this potential not be taken lightly. This premise is captured well in recurrent attention to the biblical theme of loving God by loving neighbor.

- All of these authors recognize human limitation, immaturity, and sinfulness along with human dignity. They recall for us the *need to rely not on ourselves as individuals, but on God's strength, which is often made present or incarnate in family communities God has provided,* whose wisdom and support move us toward the fullness of life for which we were created.

- All sources indicate that *faith convictions are incomplete if they remain unthematic, abstract, or simply spiritualized.* They are to be made explicit, particular, and concrete. They are meant to be embodied in ordinary life and called to mind publicly, explicitly, and with celebration in sacrament.

- Finally, these varied resources can be enlisted to give *strong affirmation to the lay vocation and its indispensable role in the Church's mission.* If taken to heart, they provide a much-needed *correction to the false and harmful dichotomy between religious and secular life.*

We cannot help but conclude that domestic churches represent the Church's best hope for reading the signs of the times and responding to them in light of the Gospel.

NOTES

1. *Dogmatic Constitution on the Church/Lumen Gentium* #11, in *The Documents of Vatican II*, ed. Walter M. Abbot (New York: America Press, 1966). For those younger readers who did not live through it, the Second Vatican Council (aka Vatican II) was a convocation of the world's Catholic bishops that took place in Rome in a series of sessions from 1962 to 1965.

2. National Conference of Catholic Bishops, *Follow the Way of Love* (Washington, DC: United States Catholic Conference, 1994), 8. Hereafter the National Conference of Catholic Bishops will be referred to as either the U.S. bishops or the NCCB.

3. John Paul II, *The Role of the Christian Family in the Modern World/Familiaris Consortio* (Boston: St. Paul Books and Media, 1981), #49. For those readers who are not familiar with them, either Latin or English titles may be used for Roman Catholic Church documents. Generally they are better known by whichever title is shortest, and this is often the Latin title. This book will use both English and Latin titles in the first citation of each source. Latin titles will generally be used in subsequent citations.

4. Michael Fahey, "The Christian Family as Domestic Church at Vatican II," in *The Family,* ed. Lisa Sowle Cahill and Dietmar Mieth, Concilium Series, vol. 4 (London: SCM Press; Maryknoll, NY: Orbis Books, 1995), 85–92, at 92.

5. A notable initiative is the Family, Religion, and Culture Project, directed by Don Browning at the University of Chicago Divinity School, and published in a series of eleven volumes through Westminster/John Knox Press. A second phase of the Chicago project is being published by William B. Eerdmans Press as the Religion, Marriage, and Family Series. Other examples include the Center for Marriage and Family at Creighton University, directed by Michael Lawler, the National Marriage Project at Rutgers University, directed by Barbara Dafoe Whitehead and David Popenoe, the Center for Work and Family, sponsored by the Carroll School of Management at Boston College, and two ongoing research projects on sex, marriage, and family and on children, sponsored by the Center for Interdisciplinary Study of Religion at Emory University.

ONE. WHY DO WE NEED THEOLOGY OF DOMESTIC CHURCH?

1. NCCB, *Follow the Way of Love* (1994), 8.

2. For a related discussion, see David Thomas, "Family Comes of Age in the Catholic Church," *Journal of Family Ministry* 12, no. 2 (Summer 1998): 38–51. In the article "Family" in the *New Dictionary of Catholic Social Thought,* ed. Judith Dwyer (Collegeville, MN: Liturgical Press, 1994), 371–381, Margaret Farley mentions domestic church only briefly, but considers the expression "a quantum leap in the church's positive affirmation of the family" (374).

3. *The New St. Joseph Baltimore Catechism,* no. 2 (New York: Catholic Book Publishing Co., 1962–1969), 101–103. For those younger generations who are not familiar with it, the *Baltimore Catechism* was first published by the Third Plenary Council of Baltimore in 1885. The three-volume series, intended for children in fourth through tenth grade, was the most popular catechism for children in the United States until the Second Vatican Council (1962–1965). This standard textbook, combined with teaching methods based on rote memorization, fostered a common religious vocabulary and identity for generations of American Catholics. It is not uncommon to find adult Catholics raised with the *Baltimore Catechism* who can still quote the memorized questions and answers.

4. Throughout this book, I allow for insights to emerge concerning the Church as a whole, not simply particular Christian families. In the chapter "The Church as Family," in *The Lay Centered Church* (Minneapolis, MN: Winston Press, 1984), Leonard Doohan observes that "family" has emerged as a dominant model or image used in magisterial documents to depict the Church. Citing several conciliar examples, he concludes, "[N]ot only does Vatican II see the Church as a family, but it also sees the family as a domestic Church. There is, in fact, a dynamic relationship between family life and Church life. . . . Family living is linked to the essence of Christian living so that the lack of family living is a lack in Christian living. Family must be domestic Church. Church must be family" (68, 73). For examples of the "Church as family" metaphor, see *Familiaris Consortio* #73 and NCCB, *Follow the Way of Love,* 28.

Kathleen O'Connell Chesto, creator of the FIRE program (*Family-Centered Intergenerational Religious Education* [Kansas City, MO: Sheed & Ward, 1988]) warns: "Everything the church tries to teach parents about God and sharing their faith gets so 'churchified.' To be holy, a family thinks they have to do churchy things. The whole idea of making a family 'the domestic church,' which is a popular catchphrase among church leaders, is church language. It says to me that the origin of holiness is the church, and the family who wants to be holy must imitate that. But that's backwards. I don't think we need families to be domestic churches; I think we need churches to be families. As church, we keep inviting families to come to us to learn how to be church; maybe we need to go to them and learn how to be family. Maybe then we will better understand and communicate the meaning faith can have in their lives" ("Faith Is Best Served Family Style: Interview with Kathleen O'Connell Chesto," *U.S. Catholic* 60, no. 6 [June 1995]: 6–12). Chesto's concern about the institutional church needing to learn to act more like a healthy family has merit, as does her concern that family spirituality be more than mimicking churchy rituals at home. Still, we humans need words and rituals to articulate the holiness of ordinary life, and among my students (as well as persons they have interviewed for class assignments) I have found that the term "domestic church" seems to serve that need well. See my article "Domestic Churches: Sociological Challenge and Theological Imperative," in *Theology and the Social Sciences*, ed. Michael Barnes, The Annual Publication of the College Theology Society, vol. 46 (Maryknoll, NY: Orbis Books, 2001): 259–276.

5. NCCB, *Follow the Way of Love*, uses this Scripture passage to define Church and, by extension, domestic church. "Jesus promised to be where two or three are gathered in his name (cf. Matthew 18:20). We give the name *church* to the people whom the Lord gathers, who strive to follow his way of love, and through whose lives his saving presence is made known. A family is our first community and the most basic way in which the Lord gathers us, forms us, and acts in our world. The early Church expressed this truth by calling the Christian family a *domestic church* or *church of the home*" (8). Cf. National Conference of Catholic Bishops, *A Family Perspective in Church and Society* (Washington, DC: United States Catholic Conference, 1988), 22.

6. NCCB, *Follow the Way of Love*, 8.

7. Ibid.

8. *Familiaris Consortio* #49.

9. Paul VI, *On Evangelization in the Modern World/Evangelii Nuntiandi* (Boston: St. Paul Books & Media, 1975), #71.

10. See Lisa Sowle Cahill, *Family: A Christian Social Perspective* (Minneapolis, MN: Fortress Press, 2000), chap. 2; Vincent Branick, *The House Church in the Writings of Paul* (Wilmington, DE: Michael Glazier, 1989); Robert Banks, *Paul's Idea of Community: The Early House Churches in Their Historical Setting* (Grand Rapids, MI: William B. Eerdmans, 1980); J. H. Elliott, "Philemon and House-Churches," *Bible Today* 22 (1984): 145–150; Herman Hendrickx, "The 'House Church' in Paul's Letters," *Theology Annual* 12 (1990–1991); Normand Provencher, "Vers une théologie de la famille: L'église domestique," *Église et Théologie* 12 (1981): 9–34, at 15 ff.; Hans-Josef Klauck, "Die Hausgemeinde als Lebensform im

Urchristentum," *Münchener Theologische Zeitschrift* 32, no. 1 (1981): 1–15; Carolyn Osiek and David Balch, *Families in the New Testament World: Households and House Churches* (Louisville, KY: Westminster/John Knox Press, 1997).

11. According to Mary Ann Foley, the fact that Christians eventually departed from the Jewish tradition of family-centered prayer as their primary worship style "suggests that the family was not understood in the first place as a 'sign of intimate union with God.'" Nevertheless, married couples who evangelized and families who offered their homes for community worship served as "an instrument for the achievement of such a union (with God)." However, this function of Christian couples and families deteriorated as a growing, legalized Church sought larger public spaces for gathering and worship. Foley explains, "One result was a growing sense that the sacred and secular were different spheres, and since family life was most often seen as clearly within the 'secular' sphere, it became more difficult to recognize the sacred dimension of that life." ("Toward an Ecclesiology of the Domestic Church," *Église et Théologie* 27 (1996): 351–373, at 352–353.)

12. See Cahill, *Family,* chap. 2; Michael Lawler, "Towards a Theology of Christian Family," *INTAMS Review* 8, no. 1 (Spring 2002): 55–71.

13. Religion and spirituality have become so extremely privatized that, in my teaching and in other settings, I have heard some people criticize the premise that parents should teach their faith to their children, expect them to participate in regular worship as a family, or rely upon religious traditions to set disciplinary limits for children. This is regarded as "imposing" one's own opinions on others. Instead, it is suggested that parents let their children choose their own religion when they grow up, without steering them in favor of any particular religion.

14. For patristic sources, see Cahill, *Family,* 48–60; Provencher, "Vers une théologie de la famille," 19 ff.; Michael Lawler, *Family: American and Christian* (Chicago: Loyola Press, 1998), 97; Joann Heaney-Hunter, "The Domestic Church: Guiding Beliefs and Daily Practices," in *Christian Marriage and Family: Contemporary Theological and Pastoral Perspectives,* ed. Michael Lawler and William Roberts (Collegeville, MN: Liturgical Press, 1996), 59–78, at 62 ff.; Vigen Guroian, "Family and Christian Virtue: Reflections on the Ecclesial Vision of John Chrysostom," in *Ethics After Christendom: Toward an Ecclesial Ethic* (Grand Rapids, MI: William B. Eerdmans, 1994), 133–154; idem, "The Ecclesial Family: John Chyrsostom on Parenthood and Children," in *The Child in Christian Thought* ed. Marcia Bunge (Grand Rapids, MI: William B. Eerdmans, 2001), 61–77; Paul Evdokimov, *The Sacrament of Love: The Nuptial Mystery in the Light of the Orthodox Tradition* (Crestwood, NY: St. Vladimir's Seminary Press, 1985), 121–123.

15. John Chrysostom, "Homily 20 on Ephesians," cited in Guroian, "Family and Christian Virtue," 134.

16. John Chrysostom, "Homily 26 on Acts 12:1–2," cited in Guroian, "Family and Christian Virtue," 139. Provencher ("Vers une théologie de la famille," 20) notes this biblical passage applied to Christian families by Clement of Alexandria in *Stromates* 3, 10 (ed. J. P. Migne, *Patrologica Graeca* 8, 1170).

17. Augustine, "Sermo 94," (*Patrologiae Cursus Completus: Series Latina*, ed. J. P. Migne [Paris: Migne, 1844–1864], 38:580), cited in Bernard Häring, "The Christian Family as a Community for Salvation," in *Man before God: Toward a Theology of Man* (New York: P. J. Kenedy & Sons, 1966), 154.

18. Proceedings of Vatican II, recorded in *Acta Synodalia Sacrosancti Concilii Oecumenici Vaticani II*, reveal precisely this dynamic. See analysis of these texts by Michael Fahey in "The Christian Family as Domestic Church at Vatican II."

19. See Guroian and Evdokimov texts cited previously; also Evdokimov, "Ecclesia Domestica," *L'Anneau d'Or*, no. 107 (1962): 353–362; idem, "The Theology of Marriage," in *Marriage and Christian Tradition*, with George Crespy and Christian Duquoc (Techny, IL: Divine Word Publications, 1968), 85–87; Guroian, "An Ethic of Marriage and Family," in *From Christ to the World: Introductory Readings in Christian Ethics*, ed. Wayne Boulton et al. (Grand Rapids, MI: William B. Eerdmans, 1994), 322–330, originally published in Guroian, *Incarnate Love: Essays in Orthodox Ethics* (Notre Dame, IN: University of Notre Dame Press, 1987); John Meyendorff, *Marriage: An Orthodox Perspective* (Crestwood, NY: St. Vladimir's Seminary Press, 1984); and Stavros Fotiou, "Water into Wine, and Eros into Agape: Marriage in the Orthodox Church," in *Celebrating Christian Marriage*, ed. Adrian Thatcher (Edinburgh and New York: T & T Clark, 2001), 89–104, at 102 ff.

20. A valuable introduction is found in the video *Holy Matrimony* (Brooklyn, NY: Greek Orthodox Telecommunications, 1993). The video explains that the crowns also recall the martyrs in heaven, who witnessed to the faith at great cost to themselves. It is understood that marriage involves a mutual martyrdom, as spouses set aside selfish and individualistic ways.

21. So says Guroian in "Family and Christian Virtue," 143.

22. Alexander Schmemann, *Of Water and the Spirit* (Crestwood, NY: St. Vladimir's Seminary Press, 1974), 145.

23. Horace Bushnell, *Christian Nurture* (1861; reprint, Cleveland, OH: Pilgrim Press, 1994).

24. Bushnell, *Christian Nurture*, 10.

25. Bushnell, *Christian Nurture*, 63; see commentary by Margaret Bendroth in "Horace Bushnell's Christian Nurture," in *The Child in Christian Thought*, ed. Marcia Bunge (Grand Rapids, MI: William B. Eerdmans, 2001) 350–364, at 356.

26. Cahill, *Family*, chap. 3. For Protestant references to "little church" and similar metaphors see also Foley, "Toward an Ecclesiology of the Domestic

Church," 356–360; Thomas Martin, "The Family as Domestic Church: Why There is a Family Perspective on Social Issues," in *Using a Family Perspective in Catholic Social Justice and Family Ministries,* ed. Patricia Voyandoff and Thomas Martin, Roman Catholic Studies, no. 6 (Lewiston, NY: Edwin Mellen Press, 1994), 19–38; Max Stackhouse, *Covenant and Commitments: Faith, Family, and Economic Life* (Louisville, KY: Westminster/John Knox Press, 1997); John Witte, *From Sacrament to Contract: Marriage, Religion, and Law in the Western Tradition* (Louisville, KY: Westminster/John Knox Press, 1997); and William Johnson Everett, *Blessed Be the Bond: Christian Perspectives on Marriage and Family* (Philadelphia: Fortress Press, 1985).

27. John Calvin, *Commentary on 1 Corinthians,* cited in Cahill, *Family,* 71.

28. Thomas Taylor, *Works,* cited in Cahill, *Family,* 71.

29. Martin, "The Family as Domestic Church," 32.

30. Ibid., 33–34.

31. Martin recounts, "John Etherington, for example, 'was fined and imprisoned by the High Commission on a charge of expounding the Scripture to others besides his own family' in 1626. As early as 1583 the Puritans had prohibited 'all preaching, reading, catechism, and other suchlike exercises in private places and families whereunto others do resort, being not of the same family'" ("The Family as Domestic Church," 31).

32. Cahill, *Family,* chap. 5.

33. J. Deotis Roberts, *Roots of a Black Future: Family and Church* (Philadelphia: Westminster Press, 1980), 80, 86.

34. Fiordelli's oral and written interventions, as well as patristic sources he drew upon, are documented in Fahey's "Christian Family as Domestic Church at Vatican II." For a history of the Christian Family Movement, see Jeffrey Burns, *Disturbing the Peace* (Notre Dame, IN: University of Notre Dame Press, 1999).

35. However, parallel references are found in two other Vatican II documents, the *Decree on the Apostolate of Lay People/Apostolicam Actuositatem* (#11) and the *Pastoral Constitution on the Church in the Modern World/Gaudium et Spes* (#48).

36. John Paul II, *Catechesis in Our Time/Catechesi Tradendae* (Boston: St. Paul Books & Media, 1979), #68.

37. See bibliography.

38. See Jan Grootaers and Joseph Selling, eds., *The 1980 Synod of Bishops "On the Role of the Family"* (Leuven, Belgium: Bibliotheca Ephemeridum Theologicarum Lovaniensium LXIV, 1983).

39. *Familiaris Consortio* ## 21, 38, 48, 49, 51–54, 59, 61, 65, 86; *The Vocation and Mission of the Lay Faithful in the Church and in the World/Christifideles Laici* (Boston: St. Paul Books & Media, 1988), #62; *Letter to Families* (Boston: St. Paul Books & Media, 1994), ## 3, 5, 13, 15, 16, 19; *The Gospel of Life/Evangelium Vitae*

(Boston: St. Paul Books & Media, 1995), #92. John Paul II's weekly general audiences on sexuality, marriage, and celibacy are collected in four volumes, published by the Daughters of St. Paul. They are *Original Unity of Man and Woman* (Boston: St. Paul Books and Media, 1981), *Blessed Are the Pure in Heart* (1983), *Reflections on* Humanae Vitae (1984), and *The Theology of Marriage and Celibacy* (1986). References to family in other contexts from John Paul II's election in October 1978 through December 1982, apart from these general audiences and *Familiaris Consortio*, are compiled by Seamus O'Byrne in *The Family: Domestic Church* (Athlone, Ireland: St. Paul Publications, 1984).

40. *Catechism of the Catholic Church* (Libreria Editrice Vaticana, 1994), ## 1656–1658, 1666.

41. See works by Clerici, Lwaminda, Owan, and Wagua in the bibliography.

42. See bibliography. Perhaps academic interest in domestic church was furthered by a 1993 request for study of the topic by the National Conference of Catholic Bishops to the Catholic Theological Society of America. A CTSA task force convened in response to this request presented panel discussions at the organization's 1994 and 1995 annual meetings. The task force completed its study in the fall of 1997 and forwarded its report to the U.S. bishops. A concluding report and panel discussion were offered to fellow members at the 1998 CTSA annual meeting.

43. Carlo Caffara, "The Ecclesial Identity and Mission of the Family," in *The Family Today and Tomorrow* (Braintree, MA: Pope John XXIII Center, 1985), 1–22.

44. Angelo Scola, "The Formation of Priests in the Pastoral Care of the Family," *Communio* 24 (Spring 1997): 57–83, at 76.

45. Donald Miller legitimately observes, "Often the Church's elaboration of its notion of family focuses attention on two constituent parts: the nature and function of marriage as the root of the family, and the proper use of sex within marriage. One might even get the impression that *family* and *marriage* are coterminous. Such a reduction, when it happens, is detrimental to the family which exists as an institution ideally rooted in, but at times separate from, marriage. My suggestion is that the Church needs to develop more fully the theology of the family as such without separating it from its appropriate relationship to marriage and marital sexuality." Donald Miller, O.F.M. *Concepts of Family Life in Modern Catholic Theology from Vatican II through* Christifideles Laici (San Francisco: Catholic Scholars Press, 1996), 227.

46. William E. May, "Family as Domestic Church: Contemporary Implications," in *Marriage, the Rock on Which the Family Is Built* (San Francisco: Ignatius Press, 1995).

47. National Conference of Catholic Bishops, Committee on Marriage and Family, "A Theological and Pastoral Colloquium: The Christian Family: A

Domestic Church," (summary report of colloquium held at Notre Dame, IN, June 15–16, 1992), 8.

48. Ibid., 9.

49. Fahey, "The Christian Family as Domestic Church at Vatican II," 91.

50. Mitch Finley and Kathy Finley, *Christian Families in the Real World: Reflections on a Spirituality for the Domestic Church* (Chicago: Thomas More Press, 1984), 11. An example of such oversight is seen in a recent book edited by Avery Dulles and Patrick Granfield, *The Theology of Church: A Bibliography* (New York: Paulist Press, 1999). In a 198–page bibliography, organized under fifty-three different subject headings, there is no heading for domestic church.

51. Ennio Mastroianni, "Christian Family as Domestic Church: A Brief Theological Inquiry," 24 (preparatory paper for NCCB Committee on Marriage and Family's colloquium on domestic church held at Notre Dame, IN, June 15–16, 1992).

52. See NCCB, *A Family Perspective on Church and Society* (Washington, DC: United States Catholic Conference, 1988), especially chap. 3. These evaluations would ask questions such as: Do parish programs segregate family members (e.g., by age or gender) rather than uniting them? Do they minister to the needs of individuals in isolation, or as members of a family system? Do they enable families to share responsibility, or leave them in passive roles? Do they evidence negative stereotypes concerning particular family situations (e.g., single-parent, interfaith, or dual-career families)? Do they interrupt the family dinner, or otherwise monopolize precious family time?

53. In *Magisterium: Teaching Authority in the Catholic Church* (New York: Paulist Press, 1983) Francis Sullivan comments, "[S]urely university professors of theology are not the only ones who can rightly be called teachers in the Church. What about catechists, what about those who teach Christian doctrine in schools, what about parents who are the teachers of the faith in the 'domestic church'?" (45). Joann Heaney-Hunter writes, "[L]ocal church communities . . . must be prepared to support the inevitable changes in their own structures that could result as families take more responsibility for their own vocation in faith" ("The Domestic Church Proclaims the Gospel of Life," *Living Light* [Fall 1995]: 27–38, at 31). Wendy Wright elaborates:

> That the Christian family is understood to be an authentic, and indeed, the primary unit of church does not necessarily mean that the family mirrors in miniature the institutional church in its structure or simply that family members embrace official church teaching. Nor does it mainly mean that "religion starts at home" (although this is undoubtedly often the case). Rather, to be the domestic church means that the family . . . is an authentic community of believers. What members of the family know to be their own experience of the

sacred in the particularities of marriage, sexual intimacy, procreation, parenting; the building, sustaining, and decay of intimate relationships; the struggles of providing, sheltering, and feeding—this experience is authentic and must be part of the knowledge of the gathered church. . . . In other words, church teaching and Christian witness must come directly, at least in part, from the lived experience of family. . . . The family, for its part, must learn to trust the fact that it is a living and authoritative cell of the Church. (*Sacred Dwelling: A Spirituality of Family Life* [New York: Crossroad, 1989], 24–25)

For more on this theme, see Bernard Boelen, "Church Renewal and the Christian Family," *Studies in Formative Spirituality* 2, no. 3 (November 1981): 359–369, and Foley, "Toward an Ecclesiology of the Domestic Church."

54. See Joann Heaney-Hunter and Louis Primavera's marriage preparation program, *Unitas* (New York: Crossroad, 1998).

55. See works by Kilcourse, Örsy, Falardeau, and Lincoln in the bibliography; also Rosemary Haughton, "The Experience of Family," in *The Knife Edge of Experience* (London: Darton, Longman & Todd, 1972), 115–120; the entire Fall 2000 issue (vol. 6, no. 2) of *INTAMS Review,* published by the International Association of Marital Spirituality in Brussels, Belgium, and the web site of the Association of Interchurch Families, *www.aifw.org.*

56. Among suggestions in the summary statement of the 1992 NCCB Theological and Pastoral Colloquium are "sponsor a 'national stay at home and pray together' day" and "ask liturgists to examine again the suitability of celebrating Eucharist in the home" (17).

57. See Leif Kehrwald, "Using a Family Sensitivity in Parish Ministry," in *Using a Family Perspective in Catholic Social Justice and Family Ministries,* ed. Patricia Voyandoff and Thomas Martin, Roman Catholic Studies, no. 6 (Lewiston, NY: Edwin Mellen Press, 1994), 167–179; Mercedes Iannone and Joseph Iannone, "Family Learning Teams and Renewed Understanding of the Parish," in *Family Ministry,* ed. Gloria Durka and Joanmarie Smiths (Minneapolis, MN: Winston Press, 1980), 228–248; Chesto, *Family-Centered Intergenerational Religious Education.*

58. Wendy Wright says, "My impression . . . is that families do not often think of themselves as church. At best, families either simply claim agreement with official church doctrine or import 'churchy' rituals or prayers into their homes hoping this will impart religious meaning to their shared life. Most Christian families seem not to feel their very family-ness as sacred. They fail to name their most profound moments of shared memory—birth, death, sexual intimacy, estrangement, forgiveness, gathering, the daily struggles to be with and for each other—with words associated with religion or spiritual life" (*Sacred Dwelling,* 24). Commenting on magisterial attention to family, evidenced by the U.S. bishops'

designation of the 1980s as a "decade of the family," Christine Firer Hinze writes, "As the new decade of the 1990's dawned, this Catholic theological vision of the family continued to germinate. Meanwhile, many Catholic families went about their lives unaware either of the family decade that had just transpired or of the lofty and provocative mission that their leadership had begun to propose for them" ("Catholic: Family Unity and Diversity Within the Body of Christ," in *Faith Traditions and the Family*, ed. Phyllis Airhart and Margaret Lamberts Bedroth [Westminster/John Knox Press, 1996], 53–72, 64).

59. NCCB, "A Theological and Pastoral Colloquium," 11–12.

60. NCCB, *Follow the Way of Love*, 6–7.

61. Wright, *Sacred Dwelling*, 11–12.

62. Cristina Traina, "Oh Susanna: The New Absolutism and Natural Law," *Journal of the American Academy of Religion* 65, no. 2 (Summer 1997): 371–401, at 372; Cahill, "Natural Law: A Feminist Reassessment," in *Is There a Human Nature?* ed. Leroy S. Rouner (Notre Dame, IN: University of Notre Dame Press, 1997), 78–91. We can include among these efforts the Charter of Family Rights compiled by the 1980 Synod of Bishops, reprinted in *Familiaris Consortio* #46. Cahill adds that this point is at the heart of Thomistic natural law theory, dependent on both universal laws and practical wisdom. She says that Thomistic natural law was not dreamed up in a vacuum, but was based on experience as Aquinas observed and interpreted it; his interpretations in turn were molded by judgments of human experience provided in his Catholic heritage and philosophical resources. Cahill concludes, "What is novel about contemporary appeals to experience—feminist and otherwise—is not their existence as such, nor the fact that they aim to accomplish social and political goals, but their self-conscious quality and their attentiveness to diversity of experience and to the social location of the one who experiences and interprets" (15).

63. Rosemary Haughton, *The Theology of Marriage* (Cork, Ireland: Mercier Press, 1971), 89.

64. Finley, *Christian Families in the Real World*, 15.

TWO. WHAT SORT OF TERM IS "DOMESTIC CHURCH"?

1. NCCB, "A Theological and Pastoral Colloquium," 12.

2. Wendy Wright, "Living the Already But Not Yet: The Spiritual Life of the American Catholic Family," Warren Lecture Series in Catholic Studies, no. 25, University of Tulsa, March 21, 1993. Cf. Everett, *Blessed Be the Bond*, 25, 59–60.

3. Wright, "Living the Already But Not Yet," 15.

4. Ibid., 10.

5. Ibid., 16.

6. Ibid., 14.

7. NCCB, "A Theological and Pastoral Colloquium," 13, 8, 9.

8. Fahey, "The Christian Family as Domestic Church at Vatican II," 86–87.

9. This link in Fiordelli's thought is further suggested by his interest in the notion of "local church" elsewhere in the Council's debate on the schema on the Church. Fahey's article reports, "Bishop Fiordelli once again addressed the council fathers during the Fiftieth General Congregation (October 17, 1963). . . . Fiordelli gave an eloquent defense of Roman Catholicism's need to stress local or particular churches, using a formula that was adopted almost verbatim in the definitive text of the *Dogmatic Constitution on the Church:* 'Ecclesia vero universalis articulatur in ecclesias particulares'" (In fact, the Universal Church is expressed in particular churches) (Fahey, ibid., 88).

10. *Familiaris Consortio* #49.

11. However, *Gaudium et Spes* #48 states, "The Christian Family, which springs from marriage as a reflection of the loving covenant uniting Christ with the Church, and as a participation in that covenant, will manifest to all men Christ's living presence in the world, and the genuine nature of the Church."

Foley argues correctly that in *Familiaris Consortio* John Paul II is not consistent in his discussion of domestic church as an ecclesial entity. Mingled with strong statements about domestic church (e.g., "a specific revelation and realization of ecclesial communion") are various passages that distinguish "family" from "Church," with the latter term referring to the Church's hierarchical leadership. At times, "family" is described as passive vis-à-vis "Church," as persons who receive or accept the Church's services and instruction. Foley points to *Familiaris Consortio* #4 as an example: "It is, in fact, to the families of our times that the church must bring the unchangeable and ever new Gospel of Jesus Christ, just as it is the families involved in the present conditions of the world that are called to accept and to live the plan of God that pertains to them." In Foley's analysis, "[t]he church brings the Gospel; the family accepts and obeys" ("Toward an Ecclesiology of the Domestic Church," 364–365).

12. NCCB, *Follow the Way of Love,* 10.

13. Mastroianni, "Christian Family as Domestic Church," 29–30.

14. For a striking discussion of this point, see Prisca Wagua, "Pastoral Care for Incomplete Families: A Forgotten Ministry in Africa," *African Ecclesiastical Review* 38, no. 2 (April 1996): 114–124.

15. The NCCB colloquium on domestic church also regards the symbolic meaning of domestic church as prior to the juridical: "The term, domestic church, discloses meanings both about family and church. It does not exhaust the total meaning of either reality. It is a word, a symbol, which we use to unfold and

peer into the Mystery of God abiding within our lives.... Domestic church makes a positive statement about family. It is neither poetic flourish nor metaphor. It acknowledges the religious dimension of family experience.... It describes an essential aspect of Christian family life, namely, its ecclesial dimension.... The symbol of domestic church helps us concretize two basic teachings of Vatican II, namely, that the church is a community of people, and that the church is in the world. It is important, however, to be precise. The Christian family is not *the church*. It is the church *embodied in the home or household"* ("A Theological and Pastoral Colloquium," 9, 12).

THREE. A SMALL CHURCH COMMUNITY

1. Paul VI, *Evangeli Nuntiandii* #71.
2. Gregory J. Konerman, "The Family as Domestic Church," in *Church Divinity*, ed. J. Morgan (Bristol, IN: Wyndham Hall Press, 1990/1991), 60; Finley, *Christian Families in the Real World*, 13; NCCB, *A Family Perspective on Church and Society*, 21. Within publications of the NCCB there has been some fluctuation on this point. In *A Family Perspective* (1988) we are told, "The family is not merely like the Church, but is truly Church" (21). To substantiate this point, the text refers to Karl Rahner, whom we shall examine later. However, proceedings of the 1992 NCCB colloquium reflect a modified, more cautious approach: "The symbol of domestic church helps us concretize two basic teachings of Vatican II, namely, that the church is a community of people, and that the church is in the world. It is important, however, to be precise. The Christian family is not *the church*. It is the church *embodied in the home or household*. The Council's intent was to present the Christian family as the smallest unit of the whole church. This is a basic concept ecclesiologically" (12).
3. NCCB, *Follow the Way of Love* (1994), seems to deliberately avoid the suggestion of *A Family Perspective* (1988) that any *single* Christian family "is truly Church." The more recent text states, "As Christian families, you not only belong to the Church, but your daily life is a true expression of the Church. Your domestic church is not complete by itself, of course. It should be united with and supported by parishes and other communities within the larger Church" (8).
4. The source of the original Latin text is Fahey, "The Christian Family as Domestic Church at Vatican II," 89.
5. Here Mastroianni follows the Abbot translation of *Lumen Gentium*. The Flannery translation (Grand Rapids, MI: William B. Eerdmans, 1975) uses stronger language at #1, saying that the Church is "in the nature of" a sacrament. Mastroianni departs from Abbot at #11, which states that "the family is, so to speak,

the domestic church." Flannery's version reads, "[i]n what might be regarded as the domestic church." Fahey prefers "The family is, as it were, the domestic church" (89).

6. Avery Dulles notes that while *Lumen Gentium* #11 inserts the qualifier *veluti* in describing family as domestic church, John Paul II frequently uses the term *ecclesia domestica* without adding *veluti* (*Catechesi Tradendae* #68; *Familiaris Consortio* #49, 52; *Evangelium Vitae* #92). Source: *The Splendor of Faith: The Theological Vision of Pope John Paul II* (New York: Herder & Herder, 1999), 112.

7. Mastroianni, "Christian Family as Domestic Church," 28.

8. Boelen, "Church Renewal and the Family," 366.

9. NCCB, "A Theological and Pastoral Colloquium," 8–9. Even though she uses the expression "domestic church," Foley thinks that the term is potentially misleading. "It is all too easy to perceive the adjective as a diminutive, which refers to something less than the 'real' church. Moreover, the related term 'domesticated' reinforces the idea that this form of Church is not to be taken seriously" ("Toward an Ecclesiology of the Domestic Church," 373). Similar concerns are raised by Adrian Thatcher, who opts to avoid the term: "[Domestic church] is of course close to 'domesticity' which may send several wrong signals about cosiness, separate spheres, the place of wives, and so on. That is why the term is generally avoided in this volume" (*Marriage after Modernity* [Washington Square, NY: New York University Press, 1999], 169).

10. Boelen, "Church Renewal and the Family," 367, 369.

11. Foley, "Toward an Ecclesiology of Domestic Church," 369–370. In his treatment of the Christian family as "little church," Stavros Fotiou, writing out of the Orthodox tradition, similarly invokes the concept of local church: "The family also tries to live according to the love God has for people, which is Christ's love for the church. It thus tries to know love in its universality, as a completed whole, just as each local church experiences the full truth of the church. Here, the part has full knowledge of the whole because it experiences the whole truth. The family knows God's faithfulness towards humanity and receives a taste of his endless philanthropy. Love is not bounded by this world's limits of time and place, but becomes a window that opens on eternity and the final kingdom" ("Water into Wine," 103).

12. Provencher, "Vers une théologie de la famille," 33. Writing in 1981, Provencher does not grapple with the increasingly prevalent phenomenon of parishes / religious communities without a priest in residence. The identity and cohesiveness of these "local churches" does not appear to be solely dependent on regular "official" celebrations of Word and Eucharist—although such celebrations remain uniquely significant signs of communion with God and with the larger Church. While the situation of priestless parishes is neither theologically nor

pastorally ideal, it does provide a conceptual model for thinking about domestic churches as "local church."

Foley suggests another conceptual model when she discusses J.-M. R. Tillard's application of "communion ecclesiology" to our current ecumenical situation. Here, the various Christian churches are not united by the "full and perfect visible communion of the Eucharistic celebration," but nevertheless are united in a sort of communion. "Specifically, [Tillard] points to the fact that Christians pray in essentially the same way; even when not technically sacramental, this prayer is an essential source of ecclesial communion" ("Toward an Ecclesiology of Domestic Church," 369–370).

13. Provencher, "Vers une Theologie de la Famille," 33.

14. *Familiaris Consortio* ## 52, 65.

15. I.e., between two baptized Christians of different denominations. Ministers who work with these couples now prefer the expression "interdenominational" marriage; many use "interchurch" to designate couples and families who are actively involved in the churches of both spouses.

16. Lincoln, "Ecclesiology, Marriage, and Historical Consciousness," *New Theology Review* 8, no. 1 (February 1995): 58–68, at 63. Notable in this context are comments by Ernest Falardeau in "The Church, The Eucharist, and the Family," *One in Christ* 33, no. 1 (1997): 20–30, at 26:

> [I]nterchurch couples should be seen not as the exception, but as the rule. What I mean is that most Churches until now have said that Christians should marry in their own Church. It is quite natural for Churches to say this because their self-understanding is that they are the Church and the other Churches are not.
>
> The problem with that perception is that it is not true. The Church of Christ may "subsist" in our Church, but it "exists" in all of the Christian Churches. The Church is not many Churches. It is one Church—but a divided one.
>
> Interchurch couples are not the exception, they are the rule. They symbolize and exemplify the Church as it is: one but divided. However, interchurch couples do more than indicate what the Church of Christ is in reality, they also point the way to unity, which is love. . . .
>
> Those of us who are involved in pastoral ministry to interchurch couples are well aware that these couples and their families are on the cutting edge of the ecumenical question. It has taken the Churches some time to realise that, but I believe the realisation is beginning to "sink in."
>
> The distinct contribution which interchurch families bring to the ecumenical movement is the love they have for one another. It is pre-

cisely love that will bridge the gap between the Churches. It is not theology or negotiation in dialogue or moving juridical boundaries. It is love. Interchurch families show the Churches how to love one another, how to bridge the gaps created by history and theology and years of estrangement. They are truly catalysts for Christian unity.

17. Haughton, *The Knife Edge of Experience*, 115–120.

18. Notably, 92 percent of permanent deacons are married and have been, on average, for thirty-six years. (Eugene Hemrick, "Deacons' Wives: An Overlooked Force in Ministry," *Pilot*, August 30, 1996, 11). Hemrick adds, "Given the diaconate's growth rate, we could see its numbers growing to equal those of the diocesan priesthood in the not-distant future." It will be interesting to observe whether and how the average Catholic's appreciation of the concept of domestic church may deepen if, in future generations, experiences of clerics (and, by extension, of Church) may just as likely be of a seasoned husband and father as a celibate man.

19. NCCB, "A Theological and Pastoral Colloquium," 14.

FOUR. A SENSE OF MISSION

1. John Paul II, *Familiaris Consortio* #2.

2. Ernest Boyer, *A Way in the World: Family Life as a Spiritual Discipline* (San Francisco: Harper & Row, 1988), 68–69.

3. Some will bristle at the suggestion that ordinary family activities stand in need of religious legitimation from some "expert" source outside the family itself (see Kathleen O'Connell Chesto's comments in chap. 1). It is true that the religious significance of family life does not need to be granted from the top down. Many Christians have discovered this significance without much support from their religious leaders. On the other hand, many others have not been able to perceive religious value in their ordinary family lives because little in their official religious formation has alerted them to the possibility of doing so.

4. On this concern, see Achiel Peelman, "La famille comme réalité ecclésiale," *Église et Théologie* 12 (1981): 95–114, at 102ff.

5. *Familiaris Consortio* #86.

6. *Familiaris Consortio* #17ff. See also *Letter to Families* #13 on family and "civilization of love."

7. *Familiaris Consortio* #17.

8. *Familiaris Consortio* #11: "God is love and in Himself He lives a mystery of personal loving communion. Creating the human race in His own image and continually keeping it in being, God inscribed in the humanity of man and

woman the vocation, and thus the capacity and the responsibility, of love and communion. Love is therefore the fundamental and innate vocation of every human being."

9. For in-depth attention to this theme, showing points of convergence with socioscientific data, see Miller, *Concepts of Family Life in Modern Catholic Theology*.

10. See *Familiaris Consortio* ## 42, 44.

11. *Letter to Families* #16: "If it is true that by giving life parents share in God's creative work, it is also true that by raising their children they become sharers in his paternal and at the same time maternal way of teaching.... Through Christ all education, within the family and outside of it, becomes part of God's own saving pedagogy."

12. A corrective is provided by Frank O'Loughlin, who notes that "in a society which is culturally Christian, the family is seen as being at the same time the basic cell of society and of the Church.... In a society which is not Christian, however, such as our own contemporary society, the relationship between family and church and between family and society are different.... This means that, in our contemporary situation, to be a Christian member of Australian society involves one in two processes of initiation: that of Australian society and that of the church. They are not separated processes; they intersect; if this were not so, the church would end up a sect rather than a church" ("Theology of the Family," *Compass* 29 [Spring 1995]: 33–40, at 37).

13. NCCB, *Follow the Way of Love*, 21, and Leckey, *The Ordinary Way*, 53, say the *Rule of St. Benedict* provides a model for family consultation.

14. *Familiaris Consortio* ## 57–61.

15. Leckey, *The Ordinary Way*, 71, 73.

16. Ibid., 70.

17. Wright, *The Sacred Dwelling*, 31–32.

18. James McGinnis and Kathleen McGinnis, *Parenting for Peace and Justice: Ten Years Later* (Maryknoll, NY: Orbis, 1990).

19. NCCB, *Follow the Way of Love*, 9–10. This 1994 document envisions a significantly broader scope for domestic churches' mission, compared to *Lumen Gentium*'s reintroduction of the term in 1964. *Lumen Gentium* #11 cites "heralding the faith to their children" and "fostering vocations proper to each child, with special care if it be to religion."

20. NCCB, *Follow the Way of Love*, 10.

21. Haughton, *The Knife Edge of Experience*, 111–112, 114; see also Haughton, *Problems of Christian Marriage* (New York: Paulist Press, 1968), 21, 29.

22. Haughton, *The Knife Edge of Experience*, 103–104.

FIVE. THE SIGNIFICANCE OF ORDINARY, IMPERFECT FAMILY LIFE

1. NCCB, "A Theological and Pastoral Colloquium," 13–14.

2. A colorful example comes from St. Jerome: "She that is unmarried is careful for the things of the Lord that she may be holy both in body and in spirit; but she that is married is careful of the things of the world, how she may please her husband. . . . Do you think there is no difference between one who spends her time in prayer and fasting and one who must, at her husband's approach, make up her countenance, walk with mincing gait and feign a show of endearment? Then come the prattling of infants, the noisy household, children waiting for her word and waiting for her kiss, the reckoning up of expenses, the preparation to meet the outlay. . . . The wife flies like a swallow all over the house. She has seen to everything. Is the sofa smooth? Is dinner ready? Tell me, pray, where amid all this is there room for the thought of God?" ("Against Helvidus: The Perpetual Virginity of Blessed Mary," in *Nicene and Post-Nicene Fathers of the Christian Church*, vol. 6, *St. Jerome: Letters and Selected Works* [Grand Rapids, MI: William B. Eerdmans, 1954], 344–345, cited in Wright, *Sacred Dwelling*, 10–11).

3. Boyer, *A Way in the World*, 28–34.

4. *Gaudium et Spes* #43. See also the theme of the "secular" character of the lay vocation, found in documents such as Vatican II's *Decree on the Laity* and John Paul II's *Christifideles Laici*, for instance, in #15.

5. Finley, *Christian Families in the Real World*, 15.

6. Everett, *Blessed Be the Bond*, 18–20. In a similar mindset, John Paul II centers his lengthy treatment of the role of the Christian family in *Familiaris Consortio* around the theme "Family, Become What You Are!" (#17ff.) For a discussion of ideal images of family as an evaluative device, see Miller, *Concepts of Family Life in Modern Catholic Theology*, especially 175–200 and 224–228.

7. *Familiaris Consortio*, part 4, IV. See also John Paul II's 1994 *Letter to Families* #5.

8. In this category I would place Caffarra, "The Ecclesial Identity and Mission of the Family," in *Family Today and Tomorrow* (Braintree, MA: Pope John XXIII Center, 1985), 1–22); May, "The Christian Family: A Domestic Church"; Scola, "The Formation of Priests in the Pastoral Care of the Family"; Alessio and Muñoz, *Marriage and Family: The Domestic Church* (New York: Society of St. Paul, 1982); Stratford Caldecott, "The Family at the Heart of a Culture of Life," *Communio* 23, no. 1 (Spring 1996): 89–100; Germain Grisez, "The Christian Family as Fulfillment of Sacramental Marriage," *Studies in Christian Ethics* 9, no. 1 (1996): 23–33; and Adrian Van Kaam, "Family Formation and the Threefold Path," *Studies in Formative Spirituality* 2, no. 3 (November 1981): 461–485. While these texts show

a strong preference for idealized language, nearly all authors, myself included, use idealized language to some extent.

9. Richard Hogan and John Levoir, *Covenant of Love* (San Francisco: Ignatius Press, 1985), 44–45 (emphasis added).

10. The ideal image of love Hogan and Levoir seem to have in mind is love within the triune Godhead. The love that exists between God and humans is decidedly less reciprocal, but this point is ignored. In chapter 6 we will revisit these points and discuss whether marriage (modeled on reciprocal communion of love within the trinity) or baptism (modeled on the unreciprocated sacrificial love of Jesus) is the primary sacramental foundation of the domestic church.

11. For alternate perspectives on this theme, see Marcia Bunge, ed., *The Child in Christian Thought* (Grand Rapids, MI: William B. Eerdmans, 2001).

12. NCCB, "A Theological and Pastoral Colloquium," 11.

13. *Familiaris Consortio* #5: "Following Christ, the Church seeks truth, which is not always the same as majority opinion." See also #34 on "gradualness of the law," and *Veritatis Splendor* #33 (Boston: Pauline Books and Media, 1993), which warns against use of statistical or scientific research to legitimate relativistic morality.

14. Boyer, *A Way in the World*, 53–56; Wright, *Sacred Dwelling*, 23, 120 (which includes interesting connections with the experience of pregnancy), 151; Wright, "Living the Already But Not Yet", 14–15; Linda Woodhead, "Christianity for and against the Family: A Response to Nicholas Peter Harvey," *Studies in Christian Ethics* 9, no. 1 (1996): 40–46, at 45.

15. Konerman, "The Family as Domestic Church," 63; Wright, *Sacred Dwelling*, chap. 8; William Roberts, "Theology of Christian Marriage," in *Alternative Futures for Worship: Christian Marriage*, ed. Bernard Cooke (Collegeville, MN: Liturgical Press), 47–63, at 49.

16. *Letter to Families* #13. Similarly, he states in *Familiaris Consortio* #6 that the family is immersed in a historical situation that "appears as an interplay of light and darkness." He adds: "[H]istory is not simply a fixed progression toward what is better, but rather an event of freedom, and even a struggle between freedoms that are in mutual conflict, that is, according to the well-known expression of St. Augustine, a conflict between two loves: the love of God to the point of disregarding self, and the love of self to the point of disregarding God."

Family spirituality writers with a strong concern for social justice (Mitch Finley and Kathy Finley, Jim McGinnis and Kathleen McGinnis, Michael True) give much attention to the Christian family or domestic church as a necessarily counter-cultural community. The Finleys summarize the Christian family spirit as being "in the world but not of the world" (*Christian Families in the Real World*, chap. 9).

NOTES TO PAGES 57–62

17. Perkins, *Mind the Baby* (New York: Sheed & Ward, 1949), 41–51.

18. See also *Familiaris Consortio* #65, which speaks of a "daily journey toward progressive actuation of values and duties." Miller comments on the U.S. bishops' understanding of family as a "developing system" and John Paul II's remarks on the "law of gradualness" (*Concepts of Family Life in Modern Catholic Theology* 160, 183)

19. *Familiaris Consortio* #34.

20. In "Familiaris Consortio: A Review of its Theology," in *The Changing Family*, ed. Saxton et al. (Chicago: Loyola University Press, 1984), 23–46, Michael Place says that John Paul II's adoption of contemporary theological language of growth, juxtaposed with more traditional language of moral absolutes, creates unresolved tensions in his own writings and, more importantly, sends mixed signals to pastoral ministers "in the trenches" dealing with birth control issues, persons improperly disposed for marriage, mixed marriages or second marriages, etc.

21. Willie Teague, "What *Is* a Christian Family?" *Weavings* 5 (January–February 1988): 26–31, at 28.

22. Ibid.

23. Ibid., 31. John Paul II does mention some trials of the Holy Family—their poverty and their exile to Egypt under threat of persecution (*Familiaris Consortio* #86, *Letter to Families* #21).

24. Based on the premise that the Benedictine monastery considered itself a household and a family, Leckey's *The Ordinary Way* examines Benedictine observances of intimacy, equality, authority, prayer, solitude, play, study, stability, and hospitality for their relevance to lay family life. Similar efforts are found in NCBB's *Family Perspective on Church and Society*, 22; "A Vowed Life," chap. 10 in Wendy Wright's *Sacred Dwelling;* Janet Edward Anti's "Motherhood as a Monastic Discipline," *Studies in Formative Spirituality* 7, no. 1 (February 1986): 7–19, David Thomas's "Downhome Spirituality for Ordinary Families," *Studies in Formative Spirituality* 2, no. 3 (November 1981): 447–459; and Ed Willock's "Postscript on Poverty and Marriage," in *Be Not Solicitous*, ed. Maisie Ward (New York: Sheed & Ward, 1953), 246–254.

25. Leckey, *The Ordinary Way*, 4. But, see 1 Timothy 3 and Titus 1:1–8, which list qualifications of the Church's ordained ministers; such persons should be good managers of their households and their children—"children who are believers and who are not known to be wild or insubordinate" (Titus 1:6).

26. Merton, *The Monastic Journey*, ed. Patrick Hart (Kansas City, MO: Sheed, Andrew, McNeel, 1977), 68; cited in Leckey, *The Ordinary Way*, 120. Remarks on this theme are offered by Thomas, "Downhome Spirituality," 457: "Marriage and family place people together, but their presence to and for each other is not enforced. It must be freely chosen—day after day. This makes the creation of

genuine community in the family a *task*, an essential feature of family spirituality. It demands its own asceticism in that in choosing the spouse or other family members, 'outsiders' are left out. I am not calling for a disregard for persons outside the family—that would be a horrible twisting of any Christian spirituality— but I am emphasizing that the concrete embodiment of one's Christian love will move from that which is near to that which is more distant. While there is not space to develop it here, the point is to be critical of a tendency which 'spiritualizes' the goal of the Christian life as a general love of neighbor, but never really demands the intense love of a single person. It is also to emphasize that the love within the family is 'for better or worse.' It is a love steeped in fidelity."

27. Leckey, *The Ordinary Way*, 123.

28. NCCB, *Follow the Way of Love*, 6; see also Finley, *Christian Families in the Real World*, 79. An engaging collection of stories of Catholic families struggling with various crosses—and increasing in awareness of God's love through the struggle—is *Be Not Solicitous*, ed. Maisie Ward, cited above.

29. For a review of the importance of concepts such as "truth" and "image of God" in John Paul II's writings on the family, see Hogan and Levoir's *Covenant of Love*, especially 39–81.

30. *Familiaris Consortio* #85 (emphasis added).

31. An essay on the spiritual life of a Christian family rendered homeless by war is "Flight into Egypt," by D. H., in Ward, *Be Not Solicitous*, 95–110.

32. The U.S. bishops, by contrast, appropriate the sorts of insights and gentle style that appear less instinctive for John Paul II. In *Follow the Way of Love*, several examples are found:

> No domestic church does all this perfectly. But neither does any parish or diocesan church. All members of the Church struggle daily to become more faithful disciples of Christ.
>
> We need to enable families to recognize that they are a domestic church. There may be families who do not understand or believe they are a domestic church. Maybe they feel overwhelmed by this calling or unable to carry out its responsibilities. Perhaps they consider their family too "broken" to be used for the Lord's purposes. But remember, a family is holy not because it is perfect but because God's grace is at work in it, helping it to set out anew every day on the way of love. . . .
>
> Wherever a family exists and love still moves through its members, grace is present. Nothing—not even divorce or death—can place limits on God's gracious love.
>
> And so, we recognize the courage and determination of families with one parent raising the children. Somehow you fulfill your call to create a good home, care for your children, hold down a job, and under-

take responsibilities in the neighborhood and church. You reflect the power of faith, the strength of love, and the certainty that God does not abandon us when circumstances leave you alone in parenting.

Those who try to blend two sets of children into one family face a special challenge to accept differences and to love unconditionally. They offer us a practical example of peacemaking.

Families arising from an interreligious marriage give witness to the universality of God's love which overcomes all division. When family members respect one anothers' different religious beliefs and practices, they testify to our deeper unity as a human family called to live in peace with one another. (10–11)

33. Hogan and Levoir's *Covenant of Love,* 31–38, summarizes the importance of this concept in John Paul II's theology. This term allows him to provide a synthesis of Christian theological tradition and insights of phenomenology—one that preserves concepts such as "universal human nature" and "universal moral norms," but also allows for human experience to be considered a source of revelation and authority. References that demonstrate the centrality of *imago dei* in John Paul II's anthropology and ethics are *Veritatis Splendor* ## 2, 10, 14, 19, 32, 39, 41, 86, 99, 102, 111, 117; *Evangelium Vitae* ## 34, 35, 36. For more background on *imago dei* in recent magisterial writings on family, see indexed references in Miller, *Concepts of Family Life in Modern Catholic Theology.*

34. See John Paul II, "Redemption as New Creation," in *Redemptor Hominis* #8, (Boston: St. Paul Books & Media, 1979); see also *Evangelium Vitae,* 34–36.

35. See comments on John Paul II's Wednesday lecture series entitled "Theology of the Body," in Hogan and Levoir, *Covenant of Love,* 44: "When we act as God acts and manifest those acts in and through our bodies, the body is not only a sacrament of our own persons, but is also a physical image of God, an outward sign of how God acts. We are not just images of God in our interior structure, in the powers of thinking and choosing, but also physically in the body."

36. See *Veritatis Splendor* #19, 39, 99, 111.

37. *Familiaris Consortio* ## 6, 33, 86; *Letter to Families* ## 14, 18, 23.

38. Several of these issues are raised by Teague, "What *Is* a Christian Family," and Luigi Clerici, "The Church as Family: African Church Communities as Families of Jesus and God—A Biblical and Ecclesiological Reflection," *African Christian Studies* 11, no. 2 (June 1995): 27–45.

39. In a chapter devoted to divorce and single parenthood, Wendy Wright comments, "We forget that we have a faith in a God who not only creates us but a God who enters into *all* our humanness. We cling to a God who encountered the most terrible of all human suffering and who absorbed the fullness of evil that humankind can muster. Our God embraced all this so utterly that divine

forgiveness and ultimately, the power of love which *is* God, triumphed. Life over death. Joy over sorrow.

"Yet it was *through* the process of losing all that this came to be. I would never suggest that God *wills* our suffering, our divorces and the deaths of those we love. Nor would I ever counsel those in families where abuse or sorrow exists to 'accept it with patience' or 'to be Christlike.' The mystery of our faith consists in the discovery that God is greater and larger and more sustaining than anything else, that God is with us when we are least able to recognize that divine presence. . . . The joyful discovery of the Christian is that even in emptiness, in the void, a constant and more joyful presence truly lives" (*Sacred Dwelling*, 78–79; cf. 130–132 on "suffering together" as a transformative gift).

40. An exception is *Familiaris Consortio*'s pastoral guidelines for persons "imperfectly disposed" for marriage (#68), which speaks of baptized nonbelievers cooperating with God's will even if this is not done consciously and explicitly. "They have thus already begun what is in a true and proper sense a journey towards salvation, a journey which the celebration of the sacrament [of marriage] and the immediate preparation for it can complement and bring to completion, given the uprightness of their intention." Of course, there is another agenda at stake here—the pope is putting forth a rationale for upholding the belief that any valid marriage of two baptized persons (whether or not they consider themselves Christians) is automatically a sacrament, and therefore indissoluble.

41. NCCB, "Theological and Pastoral Colloquium," highlights the urgency of this issue. "The term, domestic church is an example of idealized language. When offered as a vision of family life, it can challenge our limited imaginations. But it can also discourage those who fall short of where they would like to be. The strategic question for pastoral ministers is not how to move people from here to perfection, but how to help them take just the next step along the way" (13).

42. Wagua, "Pastoral Care for Incomplete Families," 123.

43. Kris Owan, "African Marriage and Family Patterns: Towards Inculturative Evangelization," *African Christian Studies* 11, no. 3 (September 1995): 3–22, at 18.

44. Leckey, *The Ordinary Way*, 70; Wright, *Sacred Dwelling*, 132. On family acceptance and forgiveness as an image of God's, see David Thomas, "Down-home Spirituality for Ordinary Families," *Studies in Formative Spirituality* 2, no. 3 (November 1981): 447–459, at 450–451.

45. Wright, "Living the Already But Not Yet," 7. Cf. her chapter on "welcoming and letting go" in *Sacred Dwelling*.

46. O'Loughlin, "Theology of the Family," 35–36; Roberts, "Theology of Christian Marriage," 49; Patricia McDonough, "Dying and Rising with Christ," *Catholic Telegraph* 168, no. 44 (November 5, 1999).

47. Wright, "Living the Already But Not Yet," 7.

48. *Familiaris Consortio* #6.

49. See Wright, *Sacred Dwelling,* chap. 9, "Transfiguration." This chapter brings the subject of family violence into conversation with Eastern Orthodox interpretations of deification (i.e., humans becoming like God), which include images of light and darkness.

50. Wright, *Sacred Dwelling,* 19–22 (emphasis added).

SIX. DOMESTIC CHURCHES FORMED BY BAPTISM AND MARRIAGE

1. NCCB, *Follow the Way of Love,* 8.

2. Karen Sue Smith and Sarah Randag, "Please Pass Down the Faith," *U.S. Catholic* 63, no. 11 (November 1998): 17–21.

3. Wagua, "Pastoral Care for Incomplete Families," 118.

4. See http://www.aifw.org.

5. Sarah Mayles, "My Experience as an Interchurch Child," at http://www.aifw.org/journal/2000jul05.htm.

6. Finley, *Christian Families in the Real World,* 20, 48, 86.

7. Similar statements appear in *Familiaris Consortio* ## 54, 56.

8. We read in *Letter to Families* #16, "Through Christ all education, within the family and outside it, becomes part of God's own saving pedagogy, which is addressed to individuals and families and culminates in the paschal mystery of the Lord's own death and resurrection. The 'heart' of our redemption is the starting point of every process of Christian education, which is likewise always an education to full humanity." I prefer this formulation to others described above.

9. However, section #38 goes on to connect baptism, teaching, and the domestic church: "Thus in the case of baptized people, the family, called together by word and sacrament as the Church of the home, is both teacher and mother, the same as the worldwide Church."

10. *Familiaris Consortio* ## 9, 55, 65, 69; *Catechesi Tradendae* ## 22, 23, 43.

11. Both options appear to have, at first glance, much common-sense value, but theoretical difficulties arise from each. "Process" explanations of sacraments have trouble dealing with the traditional doctrine that sacraments give grace *ex opere operato* (see *Familiaris Consortio* ## 67, 68). *Ex opere operato,* Latin for "from the work done," is a concept used to specify how a sacrament achieves its effect "not because of the faith of the recipient and/or the worthiness of the minister, but because of the power of Christ who acts within and through it" (definition from Richard McBrien, *Catholicism* [San Francisco, Harper Collins, 1994], 1239). With reference to marriage in particular, a process explanation of sacramental effectiveness opens the door to liberal attitudes toward divorce and the

granting of annulments. If sources other than the experience of sacramental marriage are acknowledged as the root of evangelical discernment pertaining to family life, this means that families not rooted in sacramental marriage can be acknowledged among the ranks of domestic churches. While the U.S. bishops and many lay writers seem comfortable with this idea, I have not found any clear statement from John Paul II in *Familiaris Consortio* or *Letter to Families* saying that he accepts it.

12. In *Familiaris Consortio* #21 (cf. #19) John Paul II explains these relationships as follows: "Conjugal communion constitutes the foundation on which is built the broader communion of the family, of parents and children, of brothers and sisters with each other, of relatives and other members of the household. This communion is rooted in the natural bonds of flesh and blood, and grows to its specifically human perfection with the establishment and maturing of the still deeper and richer bonds of the spirit: the love that animates the interpersonal relationships of the different members of the family constitutes the interior strength that shapes and animates the family communion and the community." Germain Grisez makes a similar argument in "The Christian Family as Fulfillment of Sacramental Marriage," 33: "Since children participate in their parents' marriage insofar as they come to be and are nurtured in it, Christian children participate in the sacrament of marriage insofar as their parents bring them up as members of Christ." These statements are problematic; both suggest that other familial bonds are somehow not direct or immediate, but rather channeled through the marital bond.

13. NCCB, "A Theological and Pastoral Colloquium," 10–11.

14. For example, John Paul II states that "[w]hen children are born, the married couple becomes a family in the full and specific sense" (*Familiaris Consortio* #69). He repeatedly uses the expression "a community of life and love," interchangeably to refer to marriage or family, whereas *Gaudium et Spes* #48 and #50, the source of the citation, use it only to define marriage. While it is not wrong to say that family is a community of life and love, the pope's use of the citation suggests that, in his mind, marriage, parenthood, and family/domestic church must necessarily exist together. William May's chapter on domestic church in *Marriage: The Rock on Which the Family Is Built* and Germain Grisez in "The Christian Family as Fulfillment of Sacramental Marriage" provide similar arguments. An exaggerated formulation is found in Caffara, "The Ecclesial Identity and Mission of the Family":

> It is obvious that we set out from the pre-suppositions: 1) that only marriage containing the elements of *unity* and *indissolubility* can form the basis of the family; and 2) that the *family* community is an expansion

of the *husband-wife* community. In fact, we can uncover the identity of
the family by beginning precisely with the following question: In what
does this very expansion of the *husband-wife* community into a *family*
community consist? What does this expansion consist of in its *specific*
identity and nature? How, precisely, does the husband-wife community
get *transformed* into a family community?

The answer is so obvious and simple that it might make us wonder
if beginning with this question in order to uncover the identity of the
family is perhaps *too* simple to put us on the right track: for the answer
is the *child*. It is the *child* who transforms the husband-wife community
into a family community, and it is therefore the act of *procreation* which
expands the husband-wife community so that it becomes a family community. (6)

15. In fact, we might revise the statement from *Follow the Way of Love* cited
in the epigraph at the start of this chapter: "Baptism brings all Christians into
union with God. Your family life is sacred because family relationships confirm
and deepen this union and allow the Lord to work through you" (8). We could
say, "Family life introduces Christians to union with God. Baptism is sacred
because it confirms and deepens this union and helps you recognize the Lord
working through you."

16. Reflections on family and domestic church should give more attention
to childhood, along with marriage and parenthood. Mary Mulligan raises this
issue in "Family, Become What You Are," *New Theology Review* 5, no. 2 (May 1992):
6–19, at 12. A valuable essay on the subject of perpetual childhood is Karl Rahner's "Ideas for a Theology of Childhood," *Theological Investigations*, vol. 8 (New
York: Seabury Press, 1977), 33–50. In this essay Rahner argues, "[C]hildhood is
not a state which only applies to the first phase of our lives in the biological sense.
Rather it is a basic condition which is always appropriate to a life that is lived
aright." See also Rahner's "Christmas, the Festival of Eternal Youth," *Theological
Investigations*, vol. 7 (New York: Herder & Herder, 1971), 121–126, and Bunge, *The
Child in Christian Thought.*

17. Grisez acknowledges some limits in interpreting marriage as a sign of the
Church: "[I]t seems to me, though the couple's one-flesh union aptly signifies the
union of Christ with his Church considered as a whole, the Christian family completes the sacrament by more aptly signifying the union of Christ with his Church
considered as a gathering of many members—God's 'large family,' in which Jesus,
the Father's natural Son, is 'the firstborn'" ("The Christian Family," 33).

18. See Frederick Parrella, "Towards a Spirituality of the Family," *Communio* 9, no. 2 (Summer 1982): 127–141, at 132–137. There is some truth in this

perspective. As Parrella notes, "Christ reveals a God of infinite love, one who relates infinitely and whose very nature as Person is constituted by such infinite relation. Therefore we are God's image only in so far as we stand in relation to others."

19. With the caveat, introduced earlier, that the effect of these sacraments not be understood simplistically and legalistically, apart from active faith and ongoing fruitful participation in Christian living. Singly or in combination they are not sufficient, in isolation, to create a Christian domestic church.

20. In his argument for children as the fulfillment of a sacramental marriage, Grisez adapts this definition to suit his purposes: "The three or more family members are gathered in Jesus" name, and he lives in their midst. Thus, the family is a community called together by God, an *ekklesia*, a church" ("The Christian Family as Fulfillment of Sacramental Marriage," 33).

SEVEN. IS THE NUCLEAR FAMILY THE ONLY MODEL OF DOMESTIC CHURCH?

1. NCCB, *Follow the Way of Love*, 12.

2. One exception is chap. 7 of Mitch Finley and Kathy Finley's *Christian Families in the Real World*, "Spirituality and the Single Parent." The Finleys say, "The single parent family is a true family and a legitimate form of domestic church. For all the ways in which it is unique, it remains a genuine family, a small cell of Christian life" (86). See also Wright's chap. 5 in *Sacred Dwelling*; J. E. P. Butler's chapter "Abandonment" in Ward, *Be Not Solicitous*, 87–94; Vera Krokonko, "The Spiritual Journey of a Single Parent," *Studies in Formative Spirituality* 7, no. 1 (February 1986): 45–62; Gerri Kerr, "Making It Alone: The Single-Parent Family," in *Family Ministry*, ed. Gloria Durka and Joanmarie Smith (Minneapolis, MN: Winston Press, 1980), 142–167; "Ministry with Single Parents" and "Ministry with Step Families," chaps. 9 and 10 in *The Family Handbook*, ed. Herbert Anderson et al. (Louisville, KY: Westminster/John Knox Press, 1998).

3. A short piece on such families is "Stripped for Action," by Paul Zens, in Ward, *Be Not Solicitous*, 142–147; see also Haughton, *Problems of Christian Marriage*, 24–25. More scholarly pieces are Joseph Selling, "The Childless Marriage: A Moral Observation," *Bijdragen* 42 (1981): 158–173 and Helen Stanton, "Obligation or Option: Marriage, Voluntary Childlessness and the Church," in *Celebrating Christian Marriage*, ed. Adrian Thatcher (New York: T & T Clark, 2001), 223–239.

4. Miller provides one of the best treatments of the subject of elder parents: "While a couple may no longer be rearing their own children, they very likely may be in significant contact with their grandchildren or the children of relatives and friends. Thus, the couple's role as socializer and educator of dependent children

does not necessarily end when their last child leaves home. Likewise, their parental role with their adult children continues, and as the theories concerning family life-cycles note, may go through numerous stages as both the parents and their offspring mature. The Church's vision of family challenges the post-childrearing couple to maintain a creative and dynamic sense of ministry appropriate to their new life stages." Furthermore, "Since the economic necessities of twentieth-century family life require that both parents in many families work outside the home, the financial, temporal, psychological, and physical realities of family life may make involvement in extra-familial activities difficult if not impossible during the child-rearing years. Thus the engagement in social services and apostolic ministries may not be a practical possibility for a couple until their children are grown, or even until they reach the age of retirement. The relationship of the family as a social unit and as a domestic church to the larger society and the Church may very well find its most productive external expression in a couple's later years" (*Concepts of Family Life in Modern Catholic Theology*, 212–215).

5. *Familiaris Consortio* #77 (the section on difficult circumstances) states that "children's marriage . . . takes them away from their family." This is not consistent with #27, which deals with the contributions of elder generations of families, who "continue to take an active and responsible part in family life, though having to respect the autonomy of the new family." Good treatments of the transition to adulthood are found in Haughton, "The Loss of the Child," chap. 6 in *Beginning Life in Christ: Gospel Bearings on Christian Education* (Westminster, MD: Newman Press, 1966); O'Loughlin, "Theology of the Family," 35 ff.; and James McGinnis and Kathleen McGinnis, *Parenting for Peace and Justice.*

6. On these groups, see Joanmarie Smith, C.S.J., "Grandmothers, Aunts, 'Aunts,' and Godmothers," in *Family Ministry*, ed. Durka and Smith, 168–181.

7. John Paul II briefly mentions "associations of families for families" in *Familiaris Consortio* #72. James McGinnis and Kathleen McGinnis provide information on the Christian Family Movement, Family Clusters, and the Parenting for Peace and Justice Network ("Family as Domestic Church," 132–134).

Extensive treatment of cooperative family communities is found in Boyer's *A Way in the World*, chaps. 11 and 12. While he does not consider shared living arrangements imperative for Christian families (in fact, he demonstrates that it is very difficult to make them work well), he argues that Christian families will find themselves overwhelmed with their mission or discouraged by isolation if they do not enlist support of like-minded persons. Jack Nelson-Pallmeyer enthusiastically recounts his experience with an intentional community of Minnesota families in *Families Valued* (New York: Friendship Press, 1996). An account of raising a family within a Catholic Worker community is provided by Molly Walsh, "Our Two Families," in Ward, *Be Not Solicitous*, 70–86.

8. One exception is Miller, *Concepts of Family Life in Modern Catholic Theology*, especially chap. 4.

9. NCCB, *Follow the Way of Love*, 6–7. Haughton (*Problems of Christian Marriage*, 42) and, in more depth, Leckey remind us that religious communities are also families. Leckey says, "One might question the appropriateness of relating this model to families where the sexes are usually mixed. My response is that the conversation between theology and the social sciences increasingly points to the fact of *personhood* as the fundamental human reality. The implication of this for reflections on family life is that families are communities of persons, as are monasteries" (*The Ordinary Way*, 7).

10. Wagua, "Pastoral Care," 118. Kris Owan says other groups are marginalized because Christians have not allowed indigenous African traditions to be rethought in light of the Gospel: the marriages of couples who fail to have children are called into question, and widows are expected to stay away from celebration of the mass for six months following the burial of their husbands ("African Marriage and Family Patterns," 18–20).

11. Michael Lawler and Gail Risch, "Covenant Generativity: Toward a Theology of Christian Family," *Horizons* 26, no. 1 (Spring 1999): 7–30, at 12ff.

12. Mulligan, "Family: Become What You Are," 7. Mulligan is commenting on the definition of family as "an intimate community of persons bound together by blood, marriage, or adoption, for the whole of life," adopted by the NCCB in *A Family Perspective on Church and Society*, 19.

13. Lawler and Risch, "Covenant Generativity," 17.

14. Cahill, *Family*, 134.

15. See *Familiaris Consortio* #73 on the diocesan family.

16. The NCCB colloquium says, "The spousal unit is a domestic church, to be sure, but the domestic church, if it is truly to be 'foundational' for the whole Church—must be much more. The extended family or multigenerational family seems to be a more adequate expression of domestic church" ("A Theological and Pastoral Colloquium," 12; cf. 9). On this subject see also NCCB, *A Family Perspective on Church and Society*; Doohan, "The Church as Family," in *The Lay-Centered Church*; idem, "Family," in *Laity's Mission in the Local Church* (San Francisco: Harper & Row, 1986); Patrick Brennan, *Reimagining the Parish* (New York: Crossroad, 1990), 115–120; and Gerald Foley, *Family-Centered Church: A New Parish Model* (Kansas City, MO: Sheed & Ward, 1995).

17. *Familiaris Consortio* includes one eloquent section devoted to the elderly. The pope argues that pastoral activity must help make good use of the elderly "in the civil and ecclesial community, in particular within the family." The elderly can contribute "a witness to the past and a source of wisdom for the young and for the future." Furthermore, "the life of the aging helps to clarify a scale of human

values; it shows the continuity of generations and marvelously demonstrates the interdependence of God's people" (#27). The pope might have also discussed the faith of elderly persons, who struggle with weaknesses of body and mind and increased awareness of their own mortality, and who still manage to face life with joy and hope, as testimony of the Good News.

18. This statement was made by Pope John XXIII in his opening address to the Council. See Xavier Rynne, *Vatican Council II* (Maryknoll, NY: Orbis Books, 1999), 47.

19. Everett, *Blessed Be the Bond*, 29–30.

20. *Familiaris Consortio* #60 (emphasis added).

21. H. Lyman Stebbins, *The Priesthood of the Laity in the Domestic Church* (Fairhaven, MA: National Enthronement Center, 1978). I obtained this pamphlet on loan from the Franciscan University of Steubenville.

22. Stebbins, *The Priesthood of the Laity*, 17.

23. Miller clarifies that in recent Catholic magisterial statements the institution of *family*, especially its social role, appears more open to variety and development than does the institution of *marriage*, where traditional "natural" roles place boundaries on discussion (*Concepts of Family Life in Modern Catholic Theology*, 91–92).

EIGHT. IS A ROMANTIC MODEL OF FAMILY APPROPRIATE FOR DOMESTIC CHURCH?

1. NCCB, "A Theological and Pastoral Colloquium," 12.

2. The 2001 "State of Our Unions" report published by the National Marriage Project at Rutgers University finds that in a sample of 1003 persons aged twenty to twenty-nine, 94 percent of never married persons agreed that "when you marry you want your spouse to be your soul-mate, first and foremost." The report is available at the web site http://marriage.rutgers.edu.

3. Lawler, "Towards a Theology of Christian Family," 59 (emphasis added).

4. Haughton, *The Knife Edge of Experience*, 102–103, 111–112.

5. See http://marriage.rutgers.edu.

6. See the web site for the National Marriage Project, cited above; the Family, Religion, and Culture Project can be found at http://divinity.uchicago.edu; the Center for Marriage and Family site is http://www.creighton.edu/Marriageand-Family. The web site for the Emory University Center for Interdisciplinary Study of Religion's forthcoming projects on sex, marriage, and family and on children is http://www.law.emory.edu/cisr.

7. This insight will be further explored in chap. 9.

8. In their anthology of readings pertaining to courtship and marriage, *Wing to Wing, Oar to Oar* (Notre Dame, IN: University of Notre Dame Press, 2000), Amy Kass and Leon Kass include a selection of traditional religious wedding vows and contemporary vows. None of the contemporary vows includes a promise to maintain the marital commitment "for better or worse, in sickness and in health, as long as we both shall live." None of them includes a promise to accept children into the relationship, let alone a promise to be of service to the Church or community. Instead, the vows implicitly suggest that the couple promise to remain married as long as they both are "happy" and "fulfilled"—however the individuals choose to define these terms. One vow reads, "I love you because you are the one person with whom I can be totally myself. You have accepted me as I am. I will try, in every way possible, to make you as happy as you have made me." Another reads, "I want for you that which brings you the greatest personal fulfillment. I promise to encourage and support you as you strive to attain the finest of which you are capable." A third says, "I will try never to do anything which will embarrass you, for I want you always to be proud of me and our relationship. I will care for my body so that my good health will be an asset to our relationship. I will strive for intellectual growth so that I may be an interesting and mentally stimulating companion" (525).

9. I must bracket for now the heartbreaking cases of persons who divorce, sometimes more than once, because they discover that their spouse is abusive. For now, I have in mind what behavioral scientists label as "low-level conflict," such as "emotional distancing, boredom, or a change in one spouse's priorities"— in other words, "not having fun anymore." According to research summarized in Stephen Post's *More Lasting Unions* (Grand Rapids, MI: William B. Eerdmans, 2000), "[Paul] Amato and [Alan] Booth emphasize that about 70 percent of divorces terminate low-conflict marriages that have some shortcomings but are still reasonably tolerable for spouses and far better for children than divorce. Unprecedented and excessively high individual expectations make many good marriages not 'good enough.' While low conflict marriages now routinely become divorces, this was not always the case. . . . Although estimates vary somewhat, divorces resulting from high-level, persistent conflict make up, at most, one fourth of all cases. It seems possible, then, that many marriages could be saved if parents were better prepared for the realities of marriage, regularly supported in marriage (for example, in conflict resolution), and better educated about the consequences of divorce for their children" (15, 17).

10. In their feminist critiques of the infertility therapy industry, Maura Ryan and Lisa Sowle Cahill wisely raise concern about commodification and exploitation of children along with women, both pleasantly packaged in language of

"personal fulfillment." While many older children, non-Caucasian children, and handicapped children wait for "loving" families to adopt them, couples might mortgage their homes, max out their credit cards, and endure painful and intrusive therapies with low success rates in the quest to create a certain type of child to love. See Maura Ryan, "The Argument for Unlimited Procreative Liberty: A Feminist Critique," in *Perspectives on Marriage,* ed. Kieran Scott and Michael Warren, (Oxford: Oxford University Press, 2001), 187–201; Lisa Sowle Cahill, *Sex, Gender, and Christian Ethics* (Cambridge University Press, 1996), 217–254; and Amy Laura Hall, *Conceiving Parenthood,* forthcoming from William B. Eerdmans Press.

NINE. DOMESTIC CHURCH AND SACRAMENTALITY

1. Haughton, *Problems of Christian Marriage,* 39–40.

2. Ibid., 40–41.

3. Ibid.

4. On the other hand, Rahner recognized the importance of Vatican II's recovery of domestic church before most theologians of his day: "[T]he love that unites married spouses contributes to the unity of the Church herself because it is one of the ways in which the unifying love of the Church is made actual. It is just as much formative of the Church as sustained by the Church. The term, "Church house," signifying the sort of local Church which is constituted by a family unit, is more than a mere pious image. . . . This passage [*Lumen Gentium* #11] deserves greater attention, and not merely in the context with which we are concerned" ("Marriage as a Sacrament," in *Theological Investigations* [hereafter *TI*], vol. 10 [New York: Seabury Press, 1977], 199–221, at 212, cf. 221). Similar references are found in Rahner, *The Church and the Sacraments* (New York: Herder & Herder, 1963), 111–112; "The Sacramental Basis for the Role of the Layman in the Church," in *TI,* vol. 8 (New York: Seabury Press, 1977), 51–74, at 70; and *Foundations of Christian Faith* (New York: Seabury Press, 1978), 420–421.

5. Two sources that cite Rahner extensively in discussing sacramentality of domestic church are Thomas Knieps-Port le Roi, "Marriage and the Church: Theological Reflections on an Underrated Relationship," in *Celebrating Christian Marriage,* ed. Adrian Thatcher (Edinburgh: T & T Clark, 2001), 105–118; and Maureen Gallagher, "Family as Sacrament," in *The Changing Family,* ed. Stanley Saxton et al. (Chicago: Loyola Press, 1984), 5–13. Consult the bibliography for the following authors, who give a fair amount of attention to sacramentality of family: Ahr, Boyer, Everett, Häring, Konerman, Miller, Parrella, Perkins, and William Roberts.

6. See especially Rahner, *The Church and the Sacraments*, 24–75.

7. Rahner, "Introductory Observations on Thomas Aquinas' Theology of the Sacraments in General," in *TI*, vol. 14 (New York: Seabury Press, 1976), 149–160.

8. Thomas Aquinas, *Summa Theologica* III 64.7, cited in Rahner, "Introductory Observations," 158.

9. Rahner, "On the Theology of Worship," in *TI*, vol. 19 (New York: Crossroad, 1983), 141–149, at 142.

10. Ibid.

11. Rahner vividly caricatures the experience of Christians whose conception of grace falls into the first model in "Considerations on the Active Role of the Person in the Sacramental Event," in *TI*, 14:161–184, at 162–163.

12. Rahner, "Considerations," 166. Grace is always present in one of three ways: as a *pure offer to freedom* wherever it is not yet decisively possessed, as this *offer to freedom accepted* by the justified person, or as this *offer rejected* by the sinner. John Galvin clarifies that in scholastic categories, Rahner emphasizes uncreated, rather than created, grace: "For an accurate grasp of Rahner's theology of grace, it is essential to keep in mind that he attributes priority to uncreated grace. Many Catholic theologians see divine indwelling as a consequence of the presence of created (sanctifying) grace. . . . Such theologians refer to 'actual graces' to account for the operation of grace in instances in which sanctifying grace is not (yet) present. Rahner, on the contrary, is prepared to speak of God's self-communication even in situations in which the divine offer has not yet been accepted. This enables him to consider created grace in all its forms as effect of God's self-communication, at least as offer. He thus explains both 'actual graces' and 'sanctifying grace' as diverse effects of the one divine self-gift. The result is a more personal and more unified conception of our relationship to God, one in which 'grace' refers primarily to God's presence within us, at least as offer" ("The Invitation of Grace," in *A World of Grace: An Introduction to the Themes and Foundations of Karl Rahner's Theology*, ed. Leo O'Donovan [Washington, DC: Georgetown University Press, 1995], 66–67).

13. Rahner acknowledges that the unmerited quality of grace may seem more apparent in the first model, but insists it is no less a part of his theory ("On the Theology of Worship," 143). Michael Skelley provides helpful commentary: "Rahner's own model of the operation of grace in the world starts out from the assumption that it is not necessary for the world to be normally deprived of grace in order for grace to be a gift. We do not need to think that the experience of grace must be something foreign and unfamiliar, something given only to a few on relatively rare occasions, for it to be remarkable. Grace is not less of a gift because it is universally available. The fact that the self-gift of God is lavished on us so extravagantly does not make grace any less marvelous, extraordinary, unex-

pected, or undeserved. The self-communication of God will still be a gift, no matter how profligate God might be with it. If anything, the gratuity of grace is enhanced by the generosity of God" (*The Liturgy of the World: Karl Rahner's Theology of Worship* [Collegeville, MN: Liturgical Press, 1991], 58).

14. Rahner elaborates, "[W]e must stress one thing: this grace is not a particular phenomenon occurring parallel to the rest of human life but simply the ultimate depth of everything the spiritual creature does when he realizes himself—when he laughs and cries, accepts responsibility, loves, lives and dies, stands up for truth, breaks out of preoccupation with self to help the neighbor, hopes against hope, cheerfully refuses to be embittered by the stupidity of daily life, keeps silent not so that evil festers in his heart but so that it dies there—when in a word, man lives as he would like to live, in opposition to his selfishness and to the despair that always assails him. This is where grace occurs, because all this leads man into the infinity and victory that is God. Something else must be said about this grace which is the depth and mystery of everyday life. It attained its clearest manifestation in Jesus of Nazareth, and precisely in the kind of life in which he became like us in all things, in a life full of ordinariness—birth, hardship, courage, hope, failure, and death" ("How to Receive a Sacrament and Mean It," in *Readings in Contemporary Sacramental Theology*, ed. Michael Taylor, S.J., [New York: Alba House, 1981], 71–80, at 73).

15. Rahner, *The Church and the Sacraments*, 36, and "Introductory Observations," 113ff.

16. Rahner, "Personal and Sacramental Piety," in *TI*, vol. 2 (Baltimore: Helicon Press, 1963), 109–133, at 119–120: "The supernatural grace of salvation is grace of Christ. It is not merely merited by him, but bears also something of the distinctive trait of him who as God-*Man* has introduced it in a definite manner into the world. . . . This grace . . . has an incarnational tendency. . . . It is meant to be . . . the sanctifying formative principle of the whole body-soul life of man, *coming right down into his concrete, tangible daily life,* where it therefore receives its 'expression' and takes on its corporality" (emphasis added). Though it does not employ the concept of sacramentality per se, these themes are operative in an important essay, "Reflections on the Unity of the Love of Neighbor and the Love of God," in *TI*, vol. 6 (Baltimore: Helicon Press, 1969), 231–249. Rahner asserts, "[E]xplicit love of neighbor is the primary act of love of God. . . . It is radically true, i.e. by an ontological and not merely 'moral' or psychological necessity, that *whoever does not love the brother whom he 'sees,' also cannot love God whom he does not see, and that one can love God whom one does not see only by loving one's visible brother*" (247; emphasis added).

17. Rahner, *The Church and the Sacraments*, 22; cf. Rahner, "Personal and Sacramental Piety," 121.

18. See Rahner, "The Word and the Eucharist," in *TI,* 4:253–286, at 279, and "Personal and Sacramental Piety," 114 ff.

19. Rahner, "On the Theology of Worship," 147 ff., "Considerations," 169 ff, and "How to Receive a Sacrament and Mean It," 74–76.

20. Skelley adds a warning: "'Secular history' is simply a concept which is necessary to maintain the gratuity of grace. The reality is that the history of salvation is coextensive with the whole history of the human race. But the history of salvation and the history of the world are not identical. The history of the world is not only a history of salvation; it is also a history of guilt and sin. Furthermore, the presence of God's saving communication is hidden in ordinary history because everyday historical events do not give any unequivocal indications of the salvation (or damnation) taking place within them. The dynamic process of God's gracious self-communication and our response taking place throughout the routine course of human life is usually hidden and ambiguous" ("The Liturgy of the World and the Liturgy of the Church: Karl Rahner's Idea of Worship," *Worship* 63 [1989]: 112–132, at 122).

21. Rahner, *The Church and the Sacraments,* 17–23. Rahner links the latter point to concepts of sacraments' being "instituted by Christ" and functioning *ex opere operato.* He says that our certainty of a sacrament's authenticity and efficacy is not confirmed simply by biblical proof texts or mechanical exactitude in administration. Rather, "[a] fundamental act of the Church in an individual's regard, in situations that are decisive for him, an act which truly involves the nature of the Church as the historical, eschatological presence of redemptive grace, is *ipso facto* a sacrament." (41).

22. Rahner, "How to Receive a Sacrament and Mean It," 76, and "On the Theology of Worship," 148.

23. NCCB, "A Theological and Pastoral Colloquium," 13–14.

24. Skelley, "Liturgy of the World," 125. He elaborates, "This means that, for Rahner, the world and its history are the primary and original form of liturgy. The liturgy of the world is not just *a* liturgy, in the sense of it being one of a variety of possible examples of liturgy. It is not merely a particular realization of a universal idea of liturgy, nor is it liturgy in an analogous sense of the term. The liturgy of the world is the most basic and complete form that liturgy takes; it provides the original content for the notion of liturgy. . . . The dynamic process of God's self-communication and our acceptance of it, *as this process is experienced in daily life,* is the original experience of liturgy. Every type of explicit worship is a symbolic manifestation of this original form of worship, the liturgy of the world" (emphasis added).

25. Rahner, "Considerations," 175. Recalling Vatican II's *Constitution on Divine Liturgy,* Rahner remarks that it is somewhat simplistic to say that the Church's

liturgy is the "source and summit" of our lives. Here Rahner describes a person with a healthily integrated spiritual life, embracing his preferred model of grace: "Such a person sees the Mass as only a tiny sign of the Mass of the world, but he does not see it as unimportant. On the one hand, he can regard it as the 'summit and source' of his life only in a very qualified sense. 'Summit,' yes, but he leaves it up to God which moment, sacred or profane, will be the decisive moment in which he finally succeeds in giving himself to God. 'Source,' yes, but he knows that it flows from the real source, the transcendent saving God and unique saving death of the Lord, and he needs but to open his heart in faith, hope, and love for the water of eternal life to well up everywhere from the depths of his existence" ("How to Receive a Sacrament and Mean It," 76).

26. Gallagher, "Family as Sacrament," 7.

27. Ibid., 10. In his analysis of recent magisterial statements on family, Donald Miller notes John Paul II's sense of the "primordial sacramentality" of creation, the world, the human body, and natural marriage, which are visible sign of God's love for His people (as contrasted to sacramental marriage, which is also a sign of Christ's love for the Church) (*Concepts of Family Life in Modern Catholic Theology*, 103, 150, 154, 164 ff., 184). Miller then comments on the U.S. bishops' discussion in *A Family Perspective in Church and Society*, where the bishops explore how family can be understood both as a *natural* institution (arising from our social instincts) and as *domestic church*.

> The two realities are the same family; one aspect builds on the other. . . . Just as the baptized couple sacramentalizes God's covenantal love *and* Christ's love for the Church in one marital union, so a Christian family sacramentalizes, in an analogous sense, the social aspect of humankind *and* the ecclesial nature of the Church in one familial community. The goods of society *and* those of the Church are found and expressed in the interaction and interdependence of family life. Thus, the family is the basic cell of society and the Christian family is also a domestic church. . . .
>
> Just as natural and Christian marriage make present the covenantal relationships between God and creation/Jesus and the Church, so the Christian family makes present the Church and gives it specific cultural and historical expression. (163–164)

Miller clarifies that the term "sacrament" in this context is used in the same sense as in *Lumen Gentium* #1 to describe the Church as a "general sacrament" (164 n. 137). Though Miller does not link this understanding of sacrament with Rahner's theology, the shared interpretation is obvious.

28. See Michael Himes and Kenneth Himes, *Fullness of Faith* (New York: Paulist Press, 1993), 82–83: "The moments when we encounter, usually with a shock, the depth of ultimacy of our acts, whether good or evil, agapaic or selfish, are sacramental encounters. Sacraments are experiences which uncover for us the presence of the radical mystery of God's self-gift which is the ground of every experience.... Sacraments are not intrusions into the secular world; they are points at which the depth of the secular is uncovered and revealed as grounded in grace. Accordingly, any true and just estimation of the secular world is dependent on an appreciation of sacramentality. If one does not have an openness to the sacramental depth of one's everyday actions and choices, one's relationships with others, and the places and things with which one comes into contact on a daily basis, then one fundamentally misunderstands who one is and what the world is like."

29. Mary Perkins, *Beginning at Home* (Collegeville, MN: Liturgical Press, 1955), 65.

30. Ibid., 107.

31. Ibid., 107–108.

32. Miller says, "[T]he family's role as the basic foundation of and locus for the formation of civil and ecclesial community emerges clearly as social service or ministry when viewed in light of the family's baptismal call to holiness and the parents' call to marital sacramentalization.... [T]he everyday tasks of marital and family life become acts of ministry, evangelization, and liturgy when perceived from the perspective of faith" (*Concepts of Family Life*, 184).

33. Finley, *Christian Families in the Real World*, 76, 80 (emphasis added).

34. Boyer, *A Way in the World*, 76–77: "It is the bland and repetitious part of life at the center that seems its greatest defect; the reality of a life of care often seems as far from spirituality as possible. It is true that it is the greatest burden of this life, but it is *not* true that it is far from spirituality. Spirituality is what draws a person closer to God, which means that it is also what draws a person closer to his or her own humanness, since it is in that that God's will is expressed in each of our lives.... Spirituality reveals how close God's truth is to us. It does this not simply by stating the truth, but by slowly drawing it into our lives. After all, something is not accepted as true simply with a nod of the head or even by a public profession. It is accepted as true only when its truth enters a person's very being. This may happen slowly, and it may not come easily. It is in the rigors of spirituality that truth is born, because it is there that it becomes not just another piece of the mind's furniture but something with blood and bone. In the spirituality of the family those rigors are found in the living out of the sacrament of the routine, that is, the slow discovery that the routine *is* a sacrament, the discovery of what is one of the most profound truths it is possible to know, the truth of the sacredness of the ordinary."

35. Ibid., 84–85: "The insight that brings full awareness very seldom follows immediately upon first hearing. Most often the hearing is followed by a long secondary stage, that of discipline. Here the truth that there is something sacred in every act is recognized, but not felt. It is when a person has given assent to this truth but still day after day goes by and all that he or she does seems just as mundane as ever. The alarm goes off in the pale light of morning and another day of work lies ahead. The dishes are piled by the sink, to be washed once again. The child cries and the telephone rings, the floor must be washed—where, one asks, is the sacred in any of this? This is where the discipline of the sacrament of the routine is revealed. To recognize the fact that there is something sacred in the ordinary is only to plant a seed. The seed must be allowed to grow. It must be tended so that little by little it can develop into the full, living reality. And like a seed which, once planted, lies buried for weeks, months, or even years with nothing visible, this truth, once planted in the consciousness, will appear invisible to the heart, a truth not yet really true since it is without life. But if tended long enough, it will begin to show itself. . . . For some people such awareness seems to grow of itself, a wildflower that takes root in their hearts. Others have to tend more carefully. I know of one man who, as soon as he wakes in the morning, says to himself, 'This is the day the Lord has made, I will rejoice and be glad.' He continues to say this whenever there is a lull in the day or he feels a need to renew his strength. At first it was often little more than rote repetition, but gradually every time he said it to himself he began to see how true it was. 'Today *is* the day the Lord has made,' he would think. 'I *will* rejoice and be glad.' It became a certainty that lingered in his consciousness long after the prayer had been said."

36. Finley, *Christian Families in the Real World*, 79–80.

37. Mitch Finley and Kathy Finley elaborate: "By reflecting on their own best moments with their children parents learn more about how God 'feels' and 'acts' in relationship to them. When parents stand back and let the toddler learn to walk by falling and getting up to try again, they learn that this is how God is with them, too. . . . Even the most ordinary behavior of a child can teach parents more about the meaning of Jesus' words that we must become like a child if we would enter the kingdom of heaven. Words of Martin Luther illustrate in depth some words from the Sermon on the Mount: 'Do as your children do. They go to bed at night and sleep without worries. They don't care when they will get soup or bread tomorrow; they know that Father and Mother will take care of it.' Parents are very effectively evangelized by their children, if they are open to this. They can gain many insights into the meaning of the old adage, 'Act as if you had faith and faith will be given to you'" (*Christian Families in the Real World*, 134–135).

For more on children as models of faith and religious educators of their parents, see Perkins, *Mind the Baby*; Michael True, *Ordinary People: Family Life and*

Global Values (Maryknoll, NY: Orbis Books, 1991), 63; Ed Willock, "Marriage for Keeps," in Ward, *Be Not Solicitous,* 230–231; Carol Lakey Hess, "Family Spirituality," *Union Theological Seminary Review* 5 (Spring 1992): 81–107, at 103–105; and Bunge, *The Child in Christian Thought,* esp. chap. 1.

38. The Finleys offer examples: "The two year-old is fascinated with an insect as it crawls up the side of a tree. The on-the-ball parent may simply include in his or her sharing of the child's excitement a comment about how wonderful our good God must be to be able to make such a big tree and such a tiny bug. The ten year-old is awestruck by a spectacular lightning storm or is anxious about his or her own parents' marriage upon hearing of the divorce of a schoolmate's parents. These are opportunities for 'God-talk,' natural times when the sacred can be acknowledged and invoked in genuine, non-pietistic ways—ways that simply include the sphere of the sacred in conversation" (*Christian Families in the Real World,* 132).

39. True, *Ordinary People,* 62–66.

TEN. FURTHER CONSIDERATION OF DOMESTIC CHURCH IN LIGHT OF SACRAMENTAL ECCLESIOLOGY

1. Rahner, *The Church and the Sacraments,* 111–112.

2. See especially works by Foley, Knieps-Port le Roi, Peelman, Provencher, Lincoln, Haughton, Heaney-Hunter, Thomas, Boelen, Kilcourse, Falardeau, and Örsy in the bibliography.

3. Richard Lennen, *The Ecclesiology of Karl Rahner* (Oxford: Clarendon Press, 1995), 216.

4. Rahner, "Sacramental Basis," 65–66.

5. Lennen, *Ecclesiology of Karl Rahner,* 229–238.

6. A situation where this premise might be overridden is where the shortage of priests and geographical isolation of some Christian families combine to make regular celebration of the Eucharist impossible.

7. Rahner, "Sacramental Basis," 60; cf. 55, 58, 65. See also Rahner, "The Christian among Unbelieving Relations," in *TI,* vol. 2 (Baltimore, MD: Helicon Press, 1963), 355–372, and "Notes on the Lay Apostolate," in *TI,* 2:319–352. "Such a lay apostolate is obligatory for the Christian. It flows from his Christian being and from the duty and strength of that supernatural love of neighbor which commands and enables the Christian not merely to regard others as neighbors in the worldly sphere but also in the realm of salvation. Although such a love of neighbor embraces all men, in the sense that it does not exclude anyone a priori and in principle from its proximity, it has a certain gradation by its very nature as a real-

istically Christian and not abstractly idealistic virtue: it begins nearest home, with the family, etc.; it favors those belonging to the household of the faith; in brief, its radiating power is permitted to remain rooted in its "domicile," it is not sent-forth. This is not only its limitation but also its strength: it is an apostolate in the concreteness of the familiar milieu, heart to heart, in the reality of earthly life, in the concreteness of everyday happenings and not abstract theory, by real living example and not in doctrinal, general norms, in demonstration of the power of grace within the prosaic context of everyday life" ("Notes on the Lay Apostolate," 340).

8. Rahner, "Sacramental Basis," 53–54. In "Notes on the Lay Apostolate," Rahner argues that the line separating laity and clergy is not so neat as often imagined. "[T]he hierarchical apostolate is the apostolic mission constituting the office in virtue of which the apostle is *sent out*; the lay apostolate . . . [is] the apostolate of man *in* his original place-in-the-world" (338). In practical life, however, "the transition from one of these apostolates to the other is quite fluid," because many lay people take on various (unordained) ministries in the Church. Rahner recommends that these ministries be formally recognized so that the lay apostolate can be valued for its own sake, not judged according to whether or not lay persons take on hierarchical tasks.

9. Rahner, "Sacramental Basis," 62.

10. James McGinnis and Kathleen McGinnis, "The Family as Domestic Church," in *One Hundred Years of Catholic Social Thought*, ed. John A. Coleman (Maryknoll, NY: Orbis Books, 1991), 120–134, at 125, 129 ff.

11. Boyer, *A Way in the World*, 64–70.

12. Ibid., 24–25: "Living human life in the context of family produces an understanding that discovers in every change the element that never changes. This truth is at the heart of ritual. Rites of the human seasons have come to be called 'rites of passage' because they occur at points of change in human life: birth, puberty, marriage, death. But although they mark points of transition, transition itself is not the subject of the ritual, but those elements within the change that do not change. . . . And it is interesting that the great liturgies meant to mark the incidences in human history when the divine burst through and shattered the rhythm of family life do so with symbols basic to the family [e.g., the Passover and Eucharistic meals]—and so by means of the family itself affirm each instance's eternal significance. . . . This then is the great gift of the spirituality of the family and the covenant of parenthood in particular—direct participation in the cycles of eternity and the opportunity to see within the processes of individual love the working of a greater love."

13. Edwards, "The Open Table: Theological Reflections on the Family," *Australasian Catholic Record* 22, no. 3 (July 1995): 327–339, at 331 ff.; Parella, "Towards

a Spirituality of the Family," 132ff.; Miller, *Concepts of Family Life in Modern Catholic Theology,* 63, 68, 119–120, 123, 152–154, 171; Häring, "The Christian Family as a Community for Salvation," 146–158; Fotiou, "Water into Wine," 103.

14. For instance, values of justice and equality can be embodied in equitable allocation of household chores, in patronizing businesses run by minorities, in choosing to live, worship, or attend school in multiethnic neighborhoods, in selecting children's books that show persons who may seem different having the same life experiences as anyone else. Values of peace and nonviolence are embodied in fair disciplinary practices, in treating strangers with courtesy even when they block traffic or slow down a grocery-store line, in avoiding gratuitously violent toys, television, and music, and in praying as a family for peaceful resolutions to the violence that appears on the daily news. Values of stewardship and community can be made real in a simple lifestyle that avoids luxuries and uses excess time or money to help those in need. Families who habitually exchange household tools or children's clothes with neighbors, who enjoy and care for public parks and libraries instead of purchasing private means of entertainment, who make time to chat with the quirky aunt or the new kid at school, or invite them home to visit likewise train themselves to overcome individualistic tendencies. Parents who make a point to acknowledge and reciprocate favors and gifts, who remark on God's small blessings in their lives, who apologize to their children when they lose their temper and train their children to do the same, who voice the family's need for God's help and forgiveness help instill in themselves and their children a healthy sense of humility and gratitude.

Mary Perkins adds an important clarification: "Obviously, this is a habit of mind to be established, not a puritanical check-list. We and the children need things that are just for fun, need to do things just for fun without always consciously adverting to ultimate significances. But such significances do need to be in the back of our minds, to have been thought out at some time or another, or the fun will cease to be fun and become distraction and escapism" (*Beginning at Home: The Challenge of Christian* Parenthood [Collegeville, MN: Liturgical Press, 1955], 54).

15. See especially the chapter entitled "Ten Years Later" in the 1990 revised edition of the McGinnises' *Parenting for Peace and Justice,* in which the authors assess the impact that years of faith-based lifestyle choices have had on their teenage children.

16. Most important are Rahner's "Church of Sinners" and "The Sinful Church in the Decrees of Vatican II," in *TI,* vol. 6 (Baltimore: Helicon Press, 1969), 253–269, 270–294.

17. Rahner's use of the mother/child image partially undermines his stated principle that the Church is not an entity separate from the lives of its members.

Still, it is fair to say that from the perspective of individual believers, the larger community, which stretches back to the time of Christ, has a parental quality, both in "begetting" the individual and in serving as an authority in the believers' religious maturation.

18. See Rahner, *Foundations of Christian Faith*, 389–390.

19. Rahner, "The Church of Sinners," 261–262, 268; cf. Lennen, *Ecclesiology of Karl Rahner*, 28–29.

20. Rahner, "Marriage as a Sacrament," 210–211; cf. 203.

21. Ibid., 203, 211.

22. Ibid., 211. See also Rahner, "The Church of Sinners," 263. At this point, the link Rahner has made between domestic church and local church seems to break down. How large a local community is necessary to have "the fullness of Church in a particular locale"? If, according to Rahner's sacramental ecclesiology, the Church is coextensive with the lives of her members, what is it about the Church as a whole (contrasted to a sacramental marriage) that guarantees that, on balance, it will be an effective sign of Christ? Is it sheer size? This is suggested in "The Church of Sinners": "The Church is also really so holy in so many of her members, and this holiness can be ascertained even empirically. . . . In a way which is not at all self-evident but extraordinary, she really has been in all ages the mother of saints." (262).

23. Parrella, "Towards a Spirituality of the Family," 138.

24. Leckey, *The Ordinary Way*, 120. Rahner was convinced that though the Church is not ideal, it is the one to which our savior has permanently united himself. When faced with the Church's all too obvious failings, a properly Christian response is twofold. First, we should not abandon the Church in pursuit of another ideal. Rather, we should remember that our own sins contribute to the sinfulness of the Church and compromise Christ's presence in the world. Second, we should take a second look at the Church, so as not to miss the daily miracles of holiness God works in her despite her finitude ("The Church of Sinners," 265–268). Rahner's allowance of a difference between the indefectibility of the Church as a whole and that of individual marriages leaves room for detachment from one's spouse or family in extreme circumstances that threaten the health of one's body or soul.

25. Skelley, *The Liturgy of the World*, 80–82. See also Rahner, "The Church of Sinners," 263–265; Wright, "A Way That You Know Not" and "Transfiguration," chaps. 5 and 9 in *Sacred Dwelling*, Finley, "Spirituality and the Single Parent," chap. 7 in *Christian Families in the Real World;* "Our Child Is Mentally Defective," 111–115, in Ward, *Be Not Solicitous;* and Harvey Egan, "Mysticism in Daily Life," *Studies in Formative Spritiuality* 10, no. 1 (February 1989): 7–26, at 11ff.

26. Perkins, *Beginning at Home*, 5–7; see parallel discussion at 39–140 on marriage, and sex particularly, as a foreshadowing of eternal happiness in love: "He

made the image, the foreshadowing as crude, as humorously incongruous with the Reality which it signifies, as His Wisdom deemed necessary to keep us from mistaking the means for the end. A rightly ordered sense of humor about sex and marriage is, therefore, a proper reaction to the whole range of Reality."

ELEVEN. DOMESTIC CHURCH: THE PRIMARY SCHOOL OF VIRTUE

1. To clarify definitions, I see formation in virtue as one component, but probably the most complex and important component, of religious education—which should also include familiarity with doctrines, scriptural and other narratives, heroes, customary worship, and organizational history of one's tradition.

2. *Gaudium et Spes* #52.

3. *Familiaris Consortio* #42.

4. *Familiaris Consortio* #2.

5. *Familiaris Consortio* #40.

6. *Familiaris Consortio* #36. Most magisterial texts on family life focus on parental formation of children, but family life is equally influential in religious formation of adults. An example will be provided at the end of this chapter. Any household can make lifestyle commitments that cultivate virtue in its members—whether it is a two-parent family with teenagers, a divorced woman with custody of her grandchildren, a group of young adults living together in a Jesuit Volunteer Corps community, or an empty-nester couple taking care of an elderly parent. Cultivating virtue is a lifelong enterprise, and it is never too early, or too late, to start, for virtue is formed by practice and maintained by practice. Because cultivating virtue means habituating the intellect, will, and passions into harmony, it seems to me that practice will have the most lasting influence on character if it engages people on an everyday basis, among persons with whom they are most physically and emotionally invested. This being said, the situation of a parent or parents with children at home is especially important to moral educators. In order not to cultivate bad habits (vices) that later need to be unlearned, it is best to start from the beginning and raise children in an environment that consistently preaches and practices its model of the good life.

7. *Familiaris Consortio* #38.

8. These include faith, hope, charity, and by extension the various moral and intellectual virtues informed by charity. Together these are called *supernatural* virtues.

9. *Lumen Gentium* #41.

10. "Healthy Family Life," *The Pope Speaks* 41, no. 1 (1996): 42–45, at 45; cf. *Familiaris Consortio* #43.

11. For the exceptional approach, see Kathleen Chesto, *Family-Centered Intergenerational Religious Education* (Kansas City, MO: Sheed & Ward, 1988).

12. See Frank Proctor, "Teaching Faith in the Family: A Historical Overview," *Religious Education* 91, no. 1 (Winter 1996): 40–54. For a critique of neglect of families as religious educators in theory and in practice, with positive attention to domestic church, see Thompson, *Family: The Forming Center;* Kehrwald, "A Family Sensitivity in Parish Ministry"; and Karen Sue Smith and Sarah Randag, "Please Pass Down the Faith," *U.S. Catholic* 63, no. 11 (November 1998): 17–21.

13. Even the work of Craig Dykstra, who intends his approach to Christian education to be grounded on visional or character ethics, needs to be approached with caution in this respect. His description of the "before" and "after" experience that churches should hope to elicit is appropriate for some converts to Christianity, but not for many who, in the words of Horace Bushnell, "grow up Christian and never know themselves as being otherwise" (see chap. 1). Dykstra writes, "In Christ, self-preoccupation begins to disappear in a way in which it never could without the presence of Christ. As a result, people feel much less burdened, able to think more clearly, and able to do things they could not do before. Christians find that they are living a different life, because they have a new point of reference that brings everything else into focus. They recognize this new life as something they have been given in their experience with Christ, and know it is not something they have or could have achieved by themselves. . . . The impact on the moral life of these experiences is that, in being freed from the burden of establishing and sustaining the self over against others, we are freed to live for others. We are able to see our loved ones in a new light. Because affection, anger, or indifference can no longer ultimately engulf or destroy us, we are free to see our loved ones more as they really are. This enables us to serve them, care for them, bear pain and suffering with them, open ourselves and give ourselves to them, without fearing that in doing so we might be used in such a way that we will be destroyed. The same is true for our relations to our neighbors and peers. Because we know we are already established and sustained by that which is indestructible, we are no longer under compulsion to hurt others in order to keep from being hurt, or to better others in order to place ourselves above them" (*Vision and Character: A Christian Educator's Alternative to Kohlberg* [New York: Paulist Press, 1981], 117–119).

14. For scholarly introductions, see William Spohn, S.J., "The Return of Virtue Ethics," *Theological Studies* 53 (1992): 60–75; and Lee Yearley, "Recent Work on Virtue," *Religious Studies Review* 16, no. 1 (January 1992): 1–9. For introductions more accessible to beginning students, see James Keenan, S.J., *Virtues for Ordinary Christians* (Franklin, WI: Sheed & Ward, 1996); and Bill Dodds and Michael Dodds, O.P., *The Seeker's Guide to Seven Life-Changing Virtues* (Chicago: Loyola Press, 1999).

15. See Thomas Aquinas, *Summa Theologica*, 3 vols, trans. Fathers of the English Dominican Province (New York: Benzinger Brothers, 1947)—hereafter *ST; Treatise on the Virtues*, trans. John A. Oesterle, (Notre Dame, IN: University of Notre Dame Press, 1966); and *On the Virtues in General*, trans. John Patrick Reid, O.P. (Providence, RI: Providence College Press, 1951).

16. *Catechism of the Catholic Church* ## 1803–1845.

17. Aquinas, *ST* I-II, 63.1–2. The Aristotelian principle Aquinas adopts is "Not by nature nor contrary to nature do the virtues come to be in us; rather, we are adapted by nature to receive them and are perfected by habit" (see Aristotle, *Nicomachean Ethics*, trans. Martin Ostwald [New York: MacMillan Publishing, 1962], 1103a25).

18. On this point, see Keenan, *Virtues for Ordinary Christians*, 3–25; and Dodds and Dodds, *Seeker's Guide*, 1–8.

19. On links between religious formation and learning of language, both of which entail formation of perception, see Dean Martin, "Learning to Become a Christian," *Religious Education* 82, no. 1 (Winter 1987): 94–114, and Michael Warren, "Religious Formation in the Context of Social Formation," *Religious Education* 82, no. 4 (Fall 1987): 515–528. Related, of course, is recent virtue ethicists' attention to community, each with its "narratives" or "stories" to make sense of reality, as the setting in which anyone learns what virtue is.

20. Though I have not encountered this element in Aquinas, Aristotle in *Nicomachean Ethics* comments repeatedly that *praise* is the mark of virtue (see 1101b10–1102a1, 1103a10, 1105b30–1106a10). In order for praise to actually function as a mark of virtue—that is, for a person to learn when to praise others, how to recognize good role models, and how to judge his or her own behavior as virtuous—words and rituals of praise must become associated with virtuous behavior. Repetition in varied circumstances will enable learners to develop an inductive understanding of what "praiseworthiness" (aka goodness or virtue) means, in general and as particularly appropriate for them.

Along with praise for good behavior, mentors must also let learners know when they ought to feel *ashamed* for improper behavior. Aquinas, like Aristotle, views sorrow or shame as a mark of persons who have a basic grasp of what goodness is, even if they sometimes do not act upon it (*ST* II-II, 156.3). Obviously such learners would not feel shame and sorrow in appropriate settings if they had not been taught to do so, through words and rituals. While no one enjoys feeling shame, it is a method of reprimand more civilized than others, such as corporal punishment. It is fitting in a program of character development that aims for independent, prudential thinking and self-motivated desire for goodness, rather than blind conformity to a set of rules, or calculated pursuit of rewards and avoidance of punishment.

21. Because of the persuading power of the emotions, family stories may have a special impact in achieving these goals. My children have many favorites. To promote the virtue of temperance, we might tell the story about the time Daddy stayed up too late with his friends and drank too much beer. The next morning, he woke up to find that his mother had "on the spur of the moment" arranged for him to take six of his youngest nieces and nephews to the zoo—on a sultry summer day in New Orleans! To teach our children gratitude, my husband and I use memorable personal stories to remind them of things they take for granted. "Did you know that when growing up I didn't have a microwave? Or a computer? Or a Gameboy? Or air conditioning (in New Orleans!)? I slept in a double bed with my two brothers—the only way we could fit was for me to sleep between them with my head opposite theirs. We all smelled feet all night! When we rode in the family station wagon, my spot was the little space between the second and third seats. Once I rode all the way from New Orleans to Colorado and back stuck in that crack!" Amazed, our kids chime in, "Did you have a refrigerator? Were TVs invented back then?" To encourage our children in forgiveness and peacemaking, we might tell the story about the time Mom and her sister (Aunt Mary) had a fight over a bottle of sunscreen. Mom wanted to take the sunscreen on a trip to Mexico with her parish youth group, but Aunt Mary wanted to have the suncreen at home to work on her tan. Mom got to take the bottle of sunscreen to Mexico, but Aunt Mary had the last word by secretly coating all the pants zippers in her sister's suitcase with Superglue. Mom was stuck the entire week in Mexico unable to wear any pants other than a pair of green overalls. "Why were you fighting about a bottle of sunscreen?" my children ask. I remind them of similar arguments they've had and ask them whether the issue of dispute was really important or whether the bickering really benefited anyone. Usually my kids get the point, at least temporarily.

22. This point is in keeping with Aquinas's fondness of organizing phenomena into consistent categories. In his catalogue of virtues, Aristotle suggests creating an agreed-upon name or description, for otherwise "nameless virtues" will aid in recognizing behaviors that fall into these categories and in recognizing situations where they are called upon (*Nicomachean Ethics* 1125b17, 1127a14 ff). This point helps us understand how revelation, and community traditions that interpret it (aka "narratives"), serve as crucial ingredients needed to steer humans' natural desire to be good (or, in Rahner's terms, their unthematic transcendent striving) to help cultivate supernatural virtue.

23. James Fowler notes that the strong, but neglected, strand in Christianity which considers that the heart of Christian *paideia* focuses on forming a distinct set of Christian *emotions or affections* "takes on fresh dimensions as we learn more about the bi-hemispheric functioning of the human brain" ("A Gradual

Introduction to the Faith," in *The Transmission of the Faith to the Next Genera-tion*, ed. Norbert Greinacher and Virgil Elizondo, Concilium Series, vol. 174 [Edinburgh: T & T Clark, 1984], 47–53, at 51). For a discussion of moral forma-tion via family life, in conversation with behavioral sciences and with particular attention to emotional formation, see Barbara Redmond, *Domestic Church: Pri-mary Agent of Moral Development* (Ph.D. diss., Boston College, 1998), and Ti-mothy O'Connell, *Making Disciples: A Handbook of Christian Moral Formation* (New York: Crossroad, 1998).

24. Here "love" includes a mixture of motivations, such as trust, desire for companionship, desire for praise and reward from a particular person, fear of scorn and punishment, etc.

25. Charity is said to "inform" all intellectual and moral virtues (e.g., wis-dom, patience, generosity, courage, justice), so that the goal of each sort of good habit is perceived in relation to our final end, that is, our relationship with God (*ST* I-II, 58.3; II-II, 44.1). Specific virtues become varied expressions of love for God via love of neighbor.

26. See Stephen Pope, *The Evolution of Altruism and the Ordering of Love* (Washington, DC: Georgetown University Press, 1994).

27. Aquinas, *ST* II-II, 25.1; II-II, 26.7.

28. Prudence, like charity, is said to inform other virtues such as patience, generosity, courage, or justice. Prudence is the skill of interpreting general values in particular circumstances. For a discussion of how prudence is refined through balancing responsibilities of self-care, care for special relations such as family members (fidelity), and care for the common good (justice), see James Keenan, "Proposing Cardinal Virtues," *Theological Studies* 56, no. 4 (1995): 709–729, also his *Virtues for Ordinary Christians*, part 3. For detailed study of the virtue of pru-dence in relationship to family life, see Marilyn Martone, *The Virtue of Prudence in Context* (Ph.D. diss., Fordham University, 1995).

29. Rather than "Christian virtue," Aquinas prefers the expression "perfect virtue." He considers virtues of pagans "imperfect" or "virtues in a restricted sense" (*ST* I-II, 65.2).

30. Aquinas, *ST* I-II, 55.4. Thus, James Keenan observes that "[i]n the medieval view, they [the infused virtues] were infused as suddenly as St. Catherine of Siena 'learned' Latin-that is, overnight" ("How Catholic Are the Virtues?" *America* 76, no. 20 [June 7, 1997]: 16–22, at 17). He continues, "Today, we may describe the infused virtues with a little more appreciation of time and human exigency." Our interest in domestic church as a "school of virtue" calls for just such an ap-preciation. Aquinas's categories of causality, natural/supernatural orders, and acquired/infused virtues have been examined in a vast amount of scholarship that cannot be explored here. But some warnings are in order. If natural and super-

natural virtue are defined primarily with reference to acquisition and infusion, or the statement, "which God works in us without us," then these terms may

- imply a magical understanding of the effects of baptism and penance,
- call into question the physiological and psychological integrity of adult converts to Christianity, who often seem to approach baptism with charity and correlated virtues already established,
- suggest humans and God act independently as causes of two separate sets of virtues (one for secular life and one for religious life), or
- suggest that good works of Christians are moved by the Spirit and grace, while good works of everyone else in the world are not.

Any such interpretation of virtue would be out of step with contemporary Catholic ecclesiology and sacramental theology. The third item bespeaks a compartmentalizing of sacred and secular life that is particularly at odds with the understanding of domestic church I am advocating.

31. Yet, Aquinas painstakingly distinguishes *disposing* from *causing*, as indicated by the phrase, "God works in us without us." He examines the proposal that God might enlist human activity as a secondary cause of these virtues, but rejects the idea and suggests that God in fact has opted for an infusion method in order to manifest his power (*ST* I-II, 51.4; 63.3). The term *increase*, as contrasted to possible alternatives like *gradual infusion*, is in keeping with Thomas's understanding of sanctifying grace, which as a *second nature* cannot be given incompletely or partially. As he sees it, one either *has* or *does not have* sanctifying grace, charity, and correlated virtues.

32. See especially Boyer, *A Way in the World*, chapters on the "sacrament of care" and the "sacrament of the routine"; Gallagher, "Family as Sacrament"; Roberts, "The Family as Domestic Church: Contemporary Implications."

33. See *Catechism of the Catholic Church* ## 1265–1266. The *Summa Theologica* does not have a section devoted specifically to ecclesiology, and certainly not to domestic church. As discussed previously in chapter 9, Rahner considered that Aquinas's sacramental theology was incomplete without the context of a developed ecclesiology. The same is true for Aquinas's treatment of the virtues. Aquinas gives every indication that sanctifying grace and its effects, including charity and correlated virtues, are normally dependent on the sacrament of water baptism (*ST* III, 65.4; cf. 61.1, ad. 2; 69.4, 6). Exceptional cases of "baptism by blood" and "baptism of the Spirit" have their meaning in relation to the normal case (*ST* III, 66.11). John Patrick Reid's editorial notes to *On the Virtues in General* review different theological opinions on the doctrine of virtue infused at baptism, especially in the case of infants, which circulated in Aquinas's day and shortly thereafter (159–160).

34. Aquinas, *ST* III, 68.9.

35. Despite his remarks about the order of charity, and despite the fact that he describes charity as friendship with God, Aquinas says charity differs from human love relationships: "The Philosopher [Aristotle] says, in reference to friendship (*Ethic.* viii.5) that *want of intercourse,* i.e., the neglect to call upon or speak with one's friends, *has destroyed many a friendship.* Now this is because the safe-keeping of a thing depends on its cause, and the cause of human virtue is a human act, so that when human acts cease, the virtue acquired thereby decreases and at last ceases altogether. Yet this does not occur to charity, because it is not the result of human acts, but is caused by God alone" (*ST* II-II, 24.10).

36. Aquinas, *ST* III, 68.9, ad. 2.

37. Aquinas, *ST* III, 62.1; 64.1–3. Contemporary theologians may prefer the expression "mediating cause."

38. See parallels in *Catechism of the Catholic Church* ## 1253–1255. The *Catechism* adds nuances that complement my proposals. Whether it be infants or adults who are being baptized, faith is said to require a community of believers and to develop beyond baptism. At the same time, there is a remnant of Aquinas's distinction between "disposing" and "causing" and of his idea of God "working in us without us" to infuse the supernatural virtues. Section 1254 reads, "*Preparation* for baptism leads only to the *threshold* of new life. Baptism is the *source* of that new life in Christ from which the entire Christian life springs forth" (emphasis added).

39. See *Familiaris Consortio* #68.

40. Rahner and those influenced by him will remind us that sacraments such as baptism and reconciliation are *not simply acts of God, but also human acts.* This point seems absent in Aquinas's explanation of supernatural virtues being infused by God "working in us without us." Bernard Cooke in *Sacraments and Sacramentality* (Mystic, CT: Twenty-Third Publications, 1983), especially in chapters 1–4, speaks of the function of religion, ritual, symbols, and sacraments as they help humans individually and communally to construct a "hermeneutic of experience" or a distinctive interpretation of the meaning of life.

41. *Familiaris Consortio* #48: "Thus in the case of baptized people, the family, called together by word and sacrament as Church of the home, is both teacher and mother, the same as the worldwide Church."

Brennan Hill and Marie Hill provide a helpful illustration: "We have scared many parents off by telling them that they are "primary religious educators." . . . What should be clarified is that parents nurture the faith more through living and sharing than through formal instruction. . . . [M]uch of what they consider everyday living is in fact genuine ministry and catechesis. For instance, parents should know that their unconditional personal acceptance of their children is all-important and integrally linked to catechesis. . . . Needless to say, it is difficult for a person with a poor self-image to accept the unconditional love of God" ("The Family as a Center of Ministry," in *Family Ministry*, ed. Gloria Durka and Joanmarie Smith [Minneapolis, MN: Winston Press, 1980], 203–226, at 212–213).

42. Chapters 9 and 10, above, described sacramental perspective as an outgrowth of faith and as intrinsically connected with embodiment or activity. Aquinas similarly holds that faith "precedes" charity (or, charity presupposes faith), and faith is imperfect without charity and its works (*ST* I-II, 62.4; 65.5).

43. See Paul Waddell, *The Primacy of Love: An Introduction to the Ethics of Thomas Aquinas* (New York: Paulist Press, 1992), esp. chap. 4.

TWELVE. DOMESTIC CHURCH: A MISSING LINK IN THE CONSISTENT LIFE ETHIC

1. Wright, *Sacred Dwelling*, 148–149.
2. See the web site http://www.ipj-ppj.org.
3. See the web site http://www.catholicworker.org. Mark and Louise Zwick are especially well-known spokespersons for the Catholic Worker movement today. Their group, Casa Juan Diego, in Houston, Texas, can be reached at www.cjd.org.
4. See Duane Elgin, *Voluntary Simplicity* (New York: Quill, 1993), Joe Dominguez and Vicki Robin, *Your Money or Your Life* (New York: Penguin, 1993); Barbara DeGrote Sorensen, *Tis a Gift to Be Simple* (Minneapolis: Augsburg, 1992); Goldian Vandenbroeck, *Less is More* (Rochester, VT: Inner Traditions, 1996). Of course, this movement has historical parallels in vowed religious communities under the name "voluntary poverty."
5. See especially David Thomas, "Home Fires: Theological Reflections on the Family," in *The Changing Family*, ed. Stanley Saxton et al. (Chicago: Loyola University Press, 1984), 15–22, at 19–21; Finley, *Christian Families in the Real World*, chap. 10; and Leonard Doohan, *Laity's Mission in the Local Church*, 87–89. These authors explore the evangelizing and prophetic mission of domestic churches as specifications of local and universal church. Thomas writes, "Evangelization, catechesis, worship, and ministry will all have their family expressions, but because of the earthly character of family life, they will be rather secular in appearance" (17).
6. Because countercultural choices are involved, these authors find their witness a struggle. Those who are parents of teens and adult children are aware that their children may not adopt their convictions and lifestyle. However, they remain hopeful and in retrospect seem convinced that their lifestyle choices have

impacted their children's consciences in a way no other teaching method could. Michael True remarks, "[I]t has made our conversations about peace and justice concrete. If they don't quite understand or agree with our practice, they do seem to get the message that we are serious about our criticisms of militarism, materialism, and capitalism. This does not mean that they have quit complaining about our old car, used furniture, and hand-me-down clothes. And I haven't either" (Michael True, *Homemade Social Justice* [Chicago: Fides/Claretian Books, 1982], 93). Cf. McGinnis and McGinnis, *Parenting for Peace and Justice*, chap. 8; Jan Johnson, *Growing Compassionate Kids: Helping Kids See beyond Their Backyard* (Nashville: Upper Room Books, 2001).

 7. Wright, *Sacred Dwelling*, 160.

 8. McGinnis and McGinnis, "Family as Domestic Church," 129; cf. True, *Homemade Social Justice*, chap. 5.

 9. McGinnis and McGinnis, "Family as Domestic Church," 129–132.

 10. McGinnis and McGinnis, "Family as Domestic Church"; Miller, *Concepts of Family Life in Modern Catholic Theology;* Cahill, *Family: A Christian Social Perspective;* Martin, "Family as Domestic Church"; Hinze, "Catholic: Family Unity and Diversity in the Body of Christ"; Roberts, "Family as Domestic Church"; Doohan, "Family," in *Laity's Mission in the Local Church;* and "The Church as Family," in *The Lay-Centered Church;* all cited above. See also Rubio, "Does Family Conflict with Community?", 597–617.

 11. McGinnis and McGinnis, "Family as Domestic Church," 125.

 12. Ibid.

 13. Ibid.

 14. There is one notable exception—almost every student of mine presumes that Christians should resist cultural preoccupation with promiscuous sex.

 15. Rubio, "Does Family Conflict with Community?", 601.

 16. Though he is perhaps the best-known spokesperson for the consistent life ethic, neither Bernardin nor Catholicism has a monopoly on the expression or the approach. For an evangelical Christian parallel, see Ronald Sider, "Abortion Is Not the Only Issue," *Christianity Today*, July 14, 1989, 27–38. For helpful overviews, see the video *The Seamless Garment* (Kansas City, MO: Seamless Garment Network, 1989) and the two-volume video series *A Consistent Ethic of Life: Is Consensus Possible?* (Princeton, NJ: Films for the Humanities and Sciences, 2001). The Seamless Garment Network (http://:www.seamless-garment.org) is an umbrella association of scores of organizations that aim to protect human life "from womb to tomb" and further the quality of human life as well.

 17. An essay relating a Rahnerian understanding of grace, sacramentality, and sacred/secular realms to the consistent life ethic is Kenneth Himes and Michael

Himes, "Grace and a Consistent Ethic of Life," in *Fullness of Faith,* 74–103. An essay on the consistent life ethic in connection with both Aquinas's theory of virtue and family nurturance is Marilyn Martone, "What Families Can Teach," *America,* April 1, 1995, 15–19.

18. Two collections of Bernardin's works are Joseph Cardinal Bernardin et al., *Consistent Ethic of Life,* ed. Thomas Fuechtmann (Kansas City, MO: Sheed & Ward, 1988)—hereafter *CEL;* and *A Moral Vision for America,* ed. John Langan, (Washington, DC: Georgetown University Press, 1998).

19. See, for instance, Bernardin, "Gannon Lecture," in *CEL,* 9–10.

20. See, for example, Bernardin, "The Consistent Ethic of Life and Health Care Systems," in *CEL,* 51.

21. Martone, "What Families Can Teach."

22. In addition to Richard McCormick's "The Consistent Ethic of Life: Is There A Historically Soft Underbelly?" in the *CEL* collection (96–122), see Christine Gudorf, "To Make a Seamless Garment, Use a Single Piece of Cloth," *Conscience* 17, no. 3 (Autumn 1996): 10–21.

23. James Gustafson, "The Consistent Ethic of Life: A Protestant Perspective," in *CEL,* 196–208; Lisa Sowle Cahill, "Response to James Gustafson," in *CEL,* 210–217; John Connery, "A Seamless Garment in a Sinful World," *America* 151 (1984): 5–11.

24. On this point see John Finnis, "The Consistent Ethic: A Philosophical Critique," in *CEL,* 140–181, at 150.

25. Aquinas, *ST* I-II, 65.1; 61.4, ad. 1.

26. For a related discussion see Cathleen Kaveny, "The Limits of Ordinary Virtue: The Limits of Law in Implementing *Evangelium Vitae,*" in *Choosing Life: A Dialogue on* Evangelium Vitae, ed. Kevin Wildes and Alan Mitchell (Washington, DC: Georgetown University Press, 1997), 132–149.

27. Bernardin, "Address: Consistent Ethic of Life Conference," in *CEL,* 88.

28. Bernardin observed that the content of the consistent life ethic could be supported by both philosophical reflection on the dignity of the human person, as well as Western political philosophy's insistence that certain inalienable rights are due to all humans precisely because they are human. He also observed that at a more or less conscious, experiential level, each of us relies on the premise that others respect our life ("Address at Seattle University," in *CEL,* 26).

29. Bernardin, "Euthanasia: Ethical and Legal Challenge," *Origins* 18, no. 4 (May 1988): 52–57, at 54.

30. Ibid.

31. Bernardin, "The Face of Poverty Today," in *CEL,* 38; cf. his remarks on the human family in "The Challenge and Witness of Catholic Health Care," in *CEL,* 67, and "The Death Penalty in Our Time," in *CEL,* 61, 63.

32. McGinnis and McGinnis, *Parenting for Peace and Justice*, 2.

33. Jack Nelson-Pallmeyer, *Families Valued: Parenting and Politics for the Good of All Children* (New York: Friendship Press, 1996), 250. For similar sentiments see Johnson, *Growing Compassionate Kids*, chap. 13.

34. Bernardin, "The Catholic Moral Vision in the United States," in Langan, *A Moral Vision for America*, 155.

35. Bernardin, "Address: Consistent Life Ethic Conference," in *CEL*, 88.

36. See Bernardin, "The Consistent Ethic of Life: Stage Two," in *CEL*, 255.

37. McGinnis and McGinnis, *Parenting for Peace and Justice*, 3.

38. Bernardin, "The Consistent Ethic of Life and Health Care Systems," in *CEL*, 57.

39. Himes and Himes, *Fullness of Faith*, 81–85, 88. Speaking to the relationship between sacramentality and the consistent life ethic, the Himes brothers explain, "Viewed from one perspective, and correctly so viewed, every event is secular; viewed with equal correctness from another perspective, every event is sacred. . . . Thus every act bears within it ultimate issues, although, of course, we as individuals and members of communities are not always attentive to the dimensions of ultimacy in our deeds" (81–82).

40. Speaking of the Christian family as a "small church within the larger church," Stavros Fotiou says that each family should become an "icon of Trinitarian communion, a way to find unity in diversity." This may sound quite abstract and otherworldly, but what Fotiou has in mind is that Christian families will teach people (both *ad intra* and *ad extra*) to see and appreciate the sacramental, transcendent dimensions of so-called secular affairs: "The family thus becomes a place where being would have priority over having, where inner fulfillment would be more important than competing for power, and where science and technology would serve life, not death. Its members thus transform, with the wine of Cana, every aspect of human life: they transform politics into ministry, economy into philanthropy, work into creation, science into love of beauty. In this modern world of autoeroticism and consumption, this world of ignorance of others and destruction of relationships, the adventure of marriage as a sacrament of love and freedom, as the starting point for the transformation of the entire world, is the church's call to every potential disciple of Christ" ("Water into Wine," 103–104).

41. Bernardin, "Linkage and the Logic of the Abortion Debate," in *CEL*, 21.

42. One example Bernardin cites frequently is civil rights legislation: "The fact that a spontaneous consensus is lacking at a given moment does not prohibit its being created. When he was told that the law could not legislate morality, Dr. Martin Luther King, Jr. used to say that the law could not make people love their neighbors, but it could stop their lynching them. Law and public policy can

also be instruments of shaping a public consensus, they are not simply the product of consensus" ("Address: Consistent Ethic of Life Conference," in *CEL*, 92–93).

43. Bernardin, "Religion and Politics: The Future Agenda," *Origins* 14 (1984): 321–328, at 326.

44. Among other ways, this interest was expressed in Bernardin's invitation to the Catholic Theological Society of America in 1993 for study of the idea (see chap. 1). Also significant is John Paul II's link of domestic church with the theme of a "Gospel of Life," (e.g., *Evangelium Vitae* #92), a theme Bernardin acknowledges as consonant with his own thought (e.g., "The Catholic Moral Vision in the United States," 155).

45. See Bernardin, "The Catholic Moral Vision in the United States," 152.

46. See, for instance, "The Role of the Religious Leader in the Development of Public Policy," in Langan, A Moral Vision for America, 26–36; see also commentary by Frans Jozef van Beeck, John Finnis, and Bryan Hehir in *CEL*.

47. Bernardin's remarks at the 1987 Consistent Ethic Symposium indicated dissatisfaction with the way discussion of the life ethic was being steered: "The debates over moral methodology and concrete moral imperatives [are] draining vital energy from the lives of individual believers and from the Church as a whole. And at times, I myself become frustrated because I do not see a way in which we can move beyond this debate" (*CEL*, 251).

48. Bernardin, "Wade Lecture," in *CEL*, 17–18, and "Address to National Right to Life Convention," in *CEL*, 20.

49. John Carr, "Natural Allies: Partnership between Social Justice and Family Ministries," in *Using a Family Perspective in Catholic Social Justice and Family Ministries,* ed. Patricia Voydanoff and Thomas Martin, (Lewiston: Edwin Mellen Press, 1994), 99–141, at 101–102.

50. Bear in mind that *Gaudium et Spes* #43 named the "dichotomy between professed faith and practice of our daily lives" as "one of the most serious errors of our age."

51. Rubio, "Does Family Conflict with Community?", 600–601.

52. Ibid., 611.

53. Ibid.

54. Martone, "What Families Can Teach," 15. Martone might have given more attention to the fact that some persons fail to recognize that life has value, to live in relationship, and so forth because of mixed messages or outright vicious habits conveyed in their families. With these facts in mind, the impact of family life on a consistent life ethic becomes all the more clear.

55. Rubio recounts evening meals in her childhood home, which were an occasion for family members to discuss their public service outside the home (her father's work in legal services for the poor, Girl Scouts, volunteer work for parish

and local community, etc.). She says, "My father's work did not account for all that our family stood for, but it did play a major role in forming our ideas about who we were as a small Christian community. My example is undoubtedly elitist; few have the privilege that my father enjoys of doing this kind of intellectually challenging and morally invigorating work. Still, there are many people who see work as something more than individualistic pursuit of self-fulfillment or monetary gain. Teachers, health-care workers, social workers, business people, day-care providers, government workers, and many others choose their work because of their social commitment. Perhaps not many of these workers think of their work as part of their family's social mission, but they could. Surely their work defines them in significant ways and influences their families in ways no less important" (605).

56. For instance, Michael True writes, "[I]s there any work more difficult than the juggling act performed by most mothers and some fathers on an ordinary morning around the breakfast table: feeding a baby perhaps only recently weaned to table food, while answering the ten-a-minute questions of the ordinary 3-year-old, in the midst of settling a quarrel between two 10-year-olds (your own and a troublesome neighbor's)—all at the same time. How many people are flexible or intelligent enough, really, to keep three dialogues going, at three different stages of development, among those children? Yet family teaching and learning about peace and justice takes place here.

"These things may seem very distant from the problems of teaching social justice, but I think they are not, and it is important to mention them, in passing, before going on to the more rational concerns parents face. These irrational considerations arise because of the nature of the family as a community. Here children have their first experience with how people react to one another: how love is expressed, how conflicts are resolved, how decisions are made and how work is allocated. There is no set formula for handling any of these matters, no best way for everyone. And what is done will vary greatly, depending on the needs and gifts and personalities of different people. But if peace and justice are to have some priority in a community of people, some attention must be given to the way in which these questions are addressed" (*Homemade Social Justice*, 12–13).

57. Martone, "What Families Can Teach," 15–16.

58. Ibid., 16–17. These words, which Marilyn Martone published in 1995, are especially poignant in light of her family's continuing life story, for in February 1998 her daughter Michelle suffered severe brain trauma in a freak auto accident. The result was a coma lasting several months and many ongoing disabilities. Ever since then Marilyn's family has been tested in fidelity and courage as they struggled amidst numerous obstacles to assist Michelle in her recovery. For some of the insights learned through this experience, see Martone's "Making Health Care

Decisions without a Prognosis: Life in a Brain Trauma Unit," *Annual of the Society of Christian Ethics* 20 (2000): 309–327.

59. McGinnis and McGinnis, "Family as Domestic Church," 125–126.

60. "The type of knowledge that parents use is a form of practical reasoning that does not offer the absolute certitude we have been trained to expect from decisions that have to do with life issues. As to acting morally, we have often been given lists of acts that we were told should never be done. . . . If we followed the rules, we were able to feel fairly certain that we had acted rightly. For instance, if we did not use artificial contraception, did not abort, did not actively kill our terminally ill family members, we could be fairly certain that we were life-sustainers" (Martone, "What Families Can Teach," 17).

61. Martone, "What Families Can Teach," 18–19. Cf. "Making Health Care Decisions without a Prognosis," 311–315.

62. Bernardin, "The Consistent Ethic of Life and Health Care Systems," in *CEL*, 57.

63. Miller, *Concepts of Family Life in Modern Catholic Theology*, esp. chaps. 1–2.

64. Doohan, *Laity's Mission in the Local Church*, 88. He offers this illustration: "A family's commitment to simplicity of life and a sharing with the poor can speak much more forcefully than the witness of priests or religious. For the latter, it is always difficult for people to distinguish between personal poverty and institutional wealth, and even when priests or religious live simply, neighbors continue to identify them with wealthy churches or institutions. Nowadays, the public witness to evangelical simplicity and poverty is more clearly appreciated in family life, where the witness is corporate, long-range, and lived in insecurity."

65. "A consistent ethic does not say everyone in the Church must do all things, but it does say that as individuals and groups pursue one issue, whether it is opposing abortion or capital punishment, the *way* we oppose one threat should be related to support for a systemic vision of life. It is not necessary or possible for every person to engage in each issue, but it is both possible and necessary for the Church as a whole to cultivate conscious explicit connection among the several issues. And it is very necessary for preserving a systemic vision that individuals and groups who seek to witness to life at one point of the spectrum of life not be seen as insensitive or even opposed to other moral claims on the overall spectrum of life. . . . No one is called to do everything, but each of us can do something" ("Continuing the Dialogue," in *CEL*, 15). Again, "Does this mean that everyone must do everything? No! There are limits of time, energy, and competency. There is a shape to individual vocation. People must specialize, groups must focus their energies. The consistent ethic does not deny this. But is does say something to the Church: It calls us to a wider witness to life than we sometimes manifest in our separate activities. The consistent ethic challenges bishops to

shape a comprehensive social agenda. It challenges priests and religious to teach the tradition with the breadth it deserves. And it challenges Catholics as citizens to go beyond the divided witness to life which is too much the pattern of politics and culture in our society" ("Address at Seattle University," in *CEL*, 83).

66. McGinnis and McGinnis, "Family as Domestic Church," 129; Bernardin, "Wade Lecture," in *CEL*, 17; Bernardin, "Linkage and the Logic of the Abortion Debate," 25. See also Michael True, *Ordinary People: Family Life and Global Values* (Maryknoll, NY: Orbis Books, 1991), 125.

67. Bernardin, "The Consistent Ethic of Life: Stage Two," in *CEL*, 254.

Conclusion

1. For instance, William Spohn, "The Return of Virtue Ethics," *Theological Studies* 53 (1992): 60–75, at 63 ff; David Haddorf, "Can Character Ethics Have Moral Rules and Principles? Christian Doctrine and Comprehensive Moral Theory," *Horizons* 23, no. 1 (1996): 48–71. On the other hand, Bernardin's life ethic could be viewed as a repackaging of the distinctive "works of charity" that were very much a part of Aquinas's virtue theory. Works of charity are summarized by the two great commandments, love of God and of neighbor, because the neighbor is loved by God (*ST* II-II, 25.1; 27.8). These are further specified as interior acts of peace and joy, as well as exterior acts of fraternal correction, and as spiritual and corporal works of mercy (*ST* II-II, 28–33).

SELECT BIBLIOGRAPHY

MAGISTERIAL STATEMENTS

Vatican II. *Lumen Gentium* #11; *Apostolicam Actuositatem* #11; *Gaudium et Spes* #48.
Catechism of the Catholic Church. Rome, Libreria Editrice Vaticana, 1994. ## 1656–58, 1666.
Paul VI. *Evangelii Nuntiandi* (1975), #71.
John Paul II. *Catechesi Tradendae* (1979), #68.
———. *Christifideles Laici* (1988), #62.
———. *Evangelium Vitae* (1995), #92.
———. *Familiaris Consortio*(1981), ## 21, 38, 48, 49, 51–54, 59, 61, 65, 86.
———. *Letter to Families* (1994), ## 3, 5, 13, 15, 16, 19.

Collections of John Paul II's speeches on family:
    O'Byrne, Seamus. *The Family: Domestic Church.* Athlone, Ireland: St. Paul Publications, 1984.
    John Paul II, *Christian Family in the Teachings of John Paul II.* Homebush, Australia: St. Paul Publications, 1990.

Synod of Bishops (1980). "Message to Christian Families." *Origins* 10, no. 21 (1980): 321–323.

National Conference of Catholic Bishops, Committee on Marriage and Family. *A Family Perspective in Church and Society* (1988). Tenth-anniversary edition, 1998.
    ———. *Follow the Way of Love.* Washington, DC: United States Catholic Conference, 1994.
    ———. "A Theological and Pastoral Colloquium: The Christian Family, a Domestic Church" (summary report of colloquium held at Notre Dame, IN, June 15–16, 1992).

Pontifical Council for the Family. *Family, Marriage, and 'De Facto' Unions.* Washington, DC: United States Catholic Conference, 2001.

Books and Articles

Ahr, Peter. "The Internal Dynamics of the Sacrament of Marriage." In *Working Papers on the Theology of Marriage,* ed. James McHugh, 12–19. Washington, DC: USCC Family Life Bureau, 1967.

Alessio, Luis and Hector Muñoz. *Marriage and Family: The Domestic Church.* Trans. Aloysius Owmen. Staten Island, NY: Alba House, 1982.

Anderson, Ray, and Dennis Guernsey. *On Being Family.* Grand Rapids, MI: William B. Eerdmans, 1985.

Aubert, Jean-Marie. "La famille cellule d'église." *Divinitas* 26, no. 3 (October 1982): 305–314.

Banks, Robert. *Paul's Idea of Community: The Early House Churches in Their Historical Setting.* Grand Rapids, MI: William B. Eerdmans, 1980.

Bendroth, Margaret. "Horace Bushnell's *Christian Nurture.*" In *The Child in Christian Thought,* ed. Marcia Bunge, 350–364. Grand Rapids, MI: William B. Eerdmans, 2001.

Boatz, Margaret Ryan. "The Domestic Church Today." *Liturgy* 7, no. 3 (1988): 53–59.

Boelen, Bernard. "Church Renewal and the Christian Family." *Studies in Formative Spirituality* 2, no. 3 (November 1981): 359–369.

Bourg, Florence Caffrey. *Christian Families as Domestic Churches: Insights from Theologies of Sacramentality, Virtue, and the Consistent Ethic of Life.* Ph.D. diss., Boston College, 1998 .

———. "Domestic Church: A New Frontier in Ecclesiology." *Horizons* 29, no. 1 (Spring 2002): 42–63.

———. "Domestic Church: A Survey of Literature." *INTAMS Review* 7, no. 2 (Fall 2001): 182–191.

———. "Domestic Churches: Sociological Challenge and Theological Imperative." In *Theology and the Social Sciences,* ed. Michael Barnes, 259–276. Annual Publication of the College Theology Society, vol. 46. Maryknoll, NY: Orbis Books, 2001.

———. "Family as a 'Missing Link' in Bernardin's Consistent Life Ethic." *Josephinum Journal of Theology* 8, no. 2 (Summer/Fall 2001): 3–26.

———. "The Family Home as the Place of Religious Formation." In *Religious Education of Boys and Girls,* ed. Lisa Sowle Cahill and Werner Jeanrond, 9–16. Concilium Series, vol. 4. London: SCM Press, 2002.

Bowman, Thea, ed. *Families: Black and Catholic, Catholic and Black.* Washington, DC: United States Catholic Conference, 1985.

Boyer, Ernest. *A Way in the World: Family Life as a Spiritual Discipline.* San Francisco: Harper & Row, 1988.

Brakman, Sarah Vaughan. "Responsibilities within the Family." In *Vision and Values: Ethical Viewpoints in Catholic Tradition,* ed. Judith Dwyer, 129–147. Washington, DC: Georgetown University Press, 1999.

Branick, Vincent. *The House Church in the Writings of Paul.* Wilmington, DE: Michael Glazier, 1989.

Brennan, Patrick. "The Domestic Church and a Family Perspective." In *Re-imagining the Parish: Base Communities, Adulthood, and Family Conscious-ness.* 115–120. New York: Crossroad, 1990.

Bushnell, Horace. *Christian Nurture.* Cleveland, OH: Pilgrim Press, 1994.

Cahill, Lisa Sowle. "Las familias Ofrecen una vía para transformar la sociedad." *Diakonia* 20, no. 79 (July–September 1996): 75–85.

———. "Families Offer Way to Transform Society." *National Catholic Reporter,* March 8, 1996.

———. *Family: A Christian Social Perspective.* Minneapolis, MN: Fortress Press, 2000.

———. *Sex, Gender, and Christian Ethics.* Cambridge: Cambridge University Press, 1996.

———. "Sex, Gender, and the Common Good: Family." In *Religion, Ethics, and the Common Good,* ed. James Donahue and Theresa Moser, 145–167. Annual Publication of the College Theology Society, vol. 41. Mystic, CT: Twenty-Third Publications, 1996.

Caldecott, Stratford. "The Family at the Heart of a Culture of Life." *Communio* 23, no. 1 (Spring 1996): 89–100.

Carretto, Carlo. *Famiglia, piccola chiesa.* Rome: Editrice a.v.e., 1971.

Chesto, Kathleen O'Connell. *Family-Centered Intergenerational Religious Edu-cation.* Kansas City, MO: Sheed & Ward, 1988.

Clerici, Luigi. "The Church as Family: African Church Communities as Fami-lies of Jesus and God: A Biblical and Ecclesiological Reflection." *African Chris-tian Studies* 11, no. 2 (June 1995): 27–45.

Didimizio, Daniel, and Jacqueline Haessly. "Spiritual Formation and Family Life." *Studies in Formative Spirituality* 2, no. 3 (November 1981): 371–381.

Doohan, Leonard. "The Church as Family," In *The Lay-Centered Church: The-ology and Spirituality.* Minneapolis, MN: Winston Press, 1984.

———. *Laity's Mission in the Local Church.* San Francisco: Harper & Row, 1986.

Dulles, Avery. *The Splendor of Faith: The Theological Vision of John Paul II.* New York: Crossroad, 1999.

Edwards, Denis. "The Open Table: Theological Reflections on the Family." *Aus-tralasian Catholic Record* 22, no. 3 (July 1995): 327–339.

Elliott, J. H. "Philemon and House-Churches," *Bible Today* 22 (1984): 145–150.

Eugene, Toinette. "African American Family Life: An Agenda for Ministry within the Catholic Church." *New Theology Review* 5, no. 2 (1992): 33–47.

———. "Lifting as We Climb: Womanist Theorizing about Religion and the Family." In *Religion, Feminism, and the Family,* ed. Anne Carr and Mary Stewart van Leeuwen, 330–343. Louisville, KY: Westminster/John Knox Press, 1996.

Evdokimov, Paul. "Ecclesia domestica." *Anneau d'Or,* no. 107 (1962): 353–362.

———. *The Sacrament of Love: The Nuptial Mystery in the Light of the Orthodox Tradition,* trans. Anthony Gythiel and Victoria Steadman, 121–123. Crestwood, NY: St. Vladimir's Seminary Press, 1985.

———. "The Theology of Marriage." In *Marriage and Christian Tradition,* with George Crespy and Christian Duquoc, trans. Agnes Cunningham, 67–104. Techny, IL: Divine Word Publications, 1968.

Everett, William Johnson. *Blessed Be the Bond: Christian Perspectives on Marriage and Family.* Philadelphia, Fortress Press, 1985.

Fahey, Michael. "The Christian Family as Domestic Church at Vatican II." In *The Family,* ed. Lisa Sowle Cahill and Dietmar Mieth, 85–92. Concilium Series, vol. 4, 1995. London: SCM Press, Maryknoll, NY: Orbis Books, 1995.

Falardeau, Ernest. "The Church, the Eucharist, and the Family." *One in Christ* 33, no. 1 (1997): 20–30.

———. "The Eucharist and the Domestic Church." *Emmanuel* 102, no. 9 (November 1996): 538–541.

———. "Eucharist and Family: Essential to Communion." *Church* 11, no. 4 (Winter 1995): 19–22.

———. "The Family as Communion." *Emmanuel* 102, no. 8 (October 1996): 89–92.

———. "Mutual Recognition of Baptism and the Pastoral Care of Interchurch Marriages." *Journal of Ecumenical Studies* 28, no. 1 (Winter 1991): 63–73.

Filson, F. V. "The Significance of the Early House Churches." *Journal of Biblical Literature* 68 (1939): 105–112.

Finley, Mitch. "A Family Ecclesiology." *America* 149 (July 30, 1983): 50.

Finley, Mitch, and Kathy Finley. *Christian Families in the Real World: Reflections on a Spirituality for the Domestic Church.* Chicago: Thomas More Press, 1984.

Foley, Gerald. *Family-Centered Church: A New Parish Model.* Kansas City, MO: Sheed & Ward, 1995.

Foley, Mary Ann. "Toward an Ecclesiology of the Domestic Church." *Église et Théologie* 27 (1996): 351–373.

Fotiou, Stavros. "Water into Wine, and Eros into Agape: Marriage in the Orthodox Church," In *Celebrating Christian Marriage.* ed. Adrian Thatcher, 89–104. Edinburgh and New York: T & T Clark, 2001.

Freund, John, and Joanne Heaney-Hunter. *Sacramental Marriage and the Difference It Makes.* New York: Pueblo Publishing, 1984.

Gallagher, Maureen. "Family as Sacrament." In *The Changing Family,* 5–13. Chicago: Loyola University Press, 1984.

Grisez, Germain. "The Christian Family as Fulfillment of Sacramental Marriage." *Studies in Christian Ethics* 9, no. 1 (1996): 23–33.

Grootaers, Jan, and Joseph Selling, eds. *The 1980 Synod of Bishops: "On the Role of the Family."* Leuven, Belgium: Bibliotheca Ephemeridum Theologicarum Lovaniensium LXIV, 1983.

Guroian, Vigen. "The Ecclesial Family: John Chrysostom on Parenthood and Children." In *The Child in Christian Thought,* ed. Marcia Bunge, 61–77. Grand Rapids, MI: William B. Eerdmans, 2001.

———. "An Ethic of Marriage and Family." In *Incarnate Love: Essays in Orthodox Ethics.* Notre Dame, IN: University of Notre Dame Press, 1987.

———. "Family and Christian Virtue: Reflections on the Ecclesial Vision of John Chrysostom." In *Ethics after Christendom: Toward an Ecclesial Ethic,* 133–154. Grand Rapids, MI: William B. Eerdmans, 1994.

Häring, Bernard. "The Christian Family as a Community for Salvation." In *Man before God: Toward a Theology of Man,* 146–158. New York, P. J. Kenedy & Sons, 1966.

Haughton, Rosemary. In *The Knife Edge of Experience.* London: Darton, Longman & Todd, 1972. "Experience of Family."

———. *Problems of Christian Marriage.* New York: Paulist Press/Deus Books, 1968.

Hays, Edward. *Prayers for the Domestic Church: A Handbook for Worship in the Home.* Easton, KS: Forest of Peace Books, 1979.

Heaney-Hunter, Joanne. "The Domestic Church: Guiding Beliefs and Daily Practices." In *Christian Marriage and Family: Contemporary Theological and Pastoral Perspectives,* ed. Michael Lawler and William Roberts, 59–78. Collegeville, MN: Liturgical Press, 1996.

———. "The Domestic Church Proclaims the Gospel of Life." *Living Light* (Fall 1995): 27–38.

———. "The RCIA: Model for Marriage Preparation?" *Living Light* (Spring 1991): 209–217.

Herman Hendrickx, "The 'House Church' in Paul's Letters." *Theology Annual* 12 (1990–1991).

Hill, Brennan. "Reformulating the Sacramental Theology of Marriage," in *Christian Marriage and Family: Contemporary Theological and Pastoral Perspectives,* ed. Michael Lawler and William Roberts, 3–21. Collegeville, MN: Liturgical Press, 1996.

Hill, Marie, and Brennan Hill. "The Family as a Center of Ministry." In *Family Ministry*, ed. Gloria Durka and Joanmarie Smith, 202–226. Minneapolis, MN: Winston Press, 1980.

Hinze, Christine Firer. "Catholic: Family Unity and Diversity within the Body of Christ." In *Faith Traditions and the Family*, ed. Phyllis Airhart and Margaret Lamberts Bendroth, 53–72. Louisville, KY: Westminster/John Knox Press, 1996.

Hitchcock, Helen Hull. "Remodeling the 'Domestic Church.'" *Crisis* 11 (April 1993): 9–10.

Jantsch, Catherine. "Domestic Church: A Great Place to Start." *National Catholic Reporter* 22, no. 14 (September 12, 1986).

Kelly, Thomas. "The Sacramentality of Marriage as Primary Model of Discipleship." *INTAMS Review* 7, no. 1 (Spring 2001): 13–25.

Kilcourse, George. *Double Belonging: Interchurch Families and Christian Unity.* New York, Paulist Press, 1992.

———. "Interchurch Families: Living Ecumenically." *Church* 8, no. 3 (Fall 1992): 20–23.

Klauck, Hans-Josef. "Die Hausgemeinde als Lebensform im Urchristentum." *Münchener Theologische Zeitschrift* 32, no. 1 (1981): 1–15.

Knieps-Port le Roi, Thomas. "Marriage and the Church: Reflections on an Underrated Relationship." In *Celebrating Christian Marriage*. ed. Adrian Thatcher, 105–118. Edinburgh: T & T Clark, 2001.

Konerman, Gregory J. "The Family as Domestic Church." In *Church Divinity*, ed. John Morgan, 58–67. Bristol, IN: Wyndham Hall Press, 1991.

Langan, Thomas. "Bolstering the Domestic Church." *Communio* 9, no. 2 (1982): 100–109.

Lange, Josef. "Familie, Familiengruppe und Kirchliche Gemeinde: Fakten, Trends und Perspektiven." In *Wandel der Familie—Zukunft der Familie*, ed. Volker Eid and Laszlo Vaskovics, 242–262. Mainz, Germany: Mathias-Grünewald-Verlag, 1982.

Lawler, Michael. *Family: American and Christian.* Chicago, Loyola Press, 1998.

———. "Towards a Theology of Christian Family." *INTAMS Review* 8, no. 2 (Spring 2002): 55–73.

Lawler, Michael, and Gail Risch. "Covenant Generativity: Toward a Theology of Christian Family." *Horizons* 26, no. 1 (Spring 1999): 7–30.

Leckey, Dolores. *The Ordinary Way: A Family Spirituality.* New York: Crossroad Publishing, 1982.

Lincoln, Timothy. "Ecclesiology, Marriage, and Historical Consciousness: The Domestic Church as an Ecumenical Opportunity." *New Theology Review* 8, no. 1 (February 1995): 58–68.

Lodi, E. "Famiglia: Chiesa domestica nella tradizione patristica." *Rivpatlit* 18 (1980): 221ff.

Lwaminda, P. "The African Synod and the Family." *African Christian Studies* 11, no. 2 (June 1995): 46–53.

Mackin, Theodore. *The Marital Sacrament.* Mahwah, NJ: Paulist Press, 1989.

Martin, Thomas. "The Family as Domestic Church: Why There Is a Family Perspective on Social Issues." In *Using a Family Perspective in Catholic Social Justice and Family Ministries,* ed. Patricia Voyandoff and Thomas Martin, 19–38. Roman Catholic Studies, no. 6. Lewiston, NY: Edwin Mellen Press (1994).

Martos, Joseph. "The Evolving Ideal of the Family in Catholic Tradition." In *The Ideal in the World's Religions: Essays on the Person, Family, Society, and Environment,* ed. Robert Carter and Sheldon Isenberg, 233–251. St. Paul, MN: Paragon House, 1997.

Mastroianni, Ennio. "Christian Family as Domestic Church: A Brief Theological Inquiry." Preparatory paper for NCCB Committee on Marriage and Family's colloquium on domestic church, held at Notre Dame, IN, June 15–16, 1992.

May, Patricia, and William May. "The Family as a Saved and Saving Community: A Specific and Original Ecclesial Role," with a response by Timothy O'Donnell and Catherine O'Donnell. In *The Church at the Service of the Family,* ed. Anthony Mastroeni, Proceedings from the Sixteenth Convention of the Fellowship of Catholic Scholars. Orange, CA: 1993.

May, William. "The Christian Family: A Domestic Church." In *Marriage: The Rock on Which the Family Is Built,* 101–119. San Francisco: Ignatius Press, 1995.

McDonough, Patricia. "Dying and Rising with Christ." *Catholic Telegraph* vol. 168, no. 44 (November 5, 1999).

McGinnis, James, and Kathleen McGinnis. "Family as Domestic Church." In *One Hundred Years of Catholic Social Thought,* ed. John A. Coleman, 120–134. Maryknoll, NY: Orbis Books, 1991.

Mette, Norbert. "Die Familie als Kirche im Kleinen." In *Wandel der Familie— Zukunft der Familie,* ed. Volker Eid and Laszlo Vaskovics, 263–283. Mainz, Germany: Mathias-Grünewald-Verlag, 1982.

———. "The Family in the Teaching of the Magisterium." In *The Family,* ed. Lisa Sowle Cahill and Dietmar Mieth, 74–84. Concilium Series, vol. 4. London: SCM Press; Maryknoll, NY: Orbis Books, 1995.

Meyendorff, John. *Marriage: An Orthodox Perspective.* Crestwood, NY: St. Vladimir's Seminary Press, 1984.

Miller, Donald, O.F.M. *Concepts of Family Life in Modern Catholic Theology from Vatican II through Christifideles Laici.* San Francisco, Catholic Scholars Press, 1996.

Mulligan, Mary. "Family: Become What You Are." *New Theology Review* 5, no. 2 (May 1992): 6–19.

O'Loughlin, Frank. "Theology of the Family." *Compass* 29 (Spring 1995): 33–40.

Örsy, Ladislas, S.J. "Faith, Sacrament, Contract, and Christian Marriage: Disputed Questions." *Theological Studies* 43, no. 3 (September 1982): 379–398.

———. "Interchurch Families and the Eucharist." *Doctrine and Life* 47, no. 1 (January 1997): 10–13.

———. "Interchurch Families and Reception of the Eucharist." *America* 175, no. 10 (October 12, 1996): 18–19.

Osiek, Carolyn, and David Balch. *Families in the New Testament World: Households and House Churches.* Louisville, KY: Westminster/John Knox Press, 1997.

Owan, Kris. "African Marriage and Family Patterns: Towards Inculturative Evangelization." *African Christian Studies* 11, no. 3 (September 1995): 3–22.

Parrella, Frederick. "Towards a Spirituality of the Family." *Communio* 9, no. 2 (Summer 1982): 127–141.

Peelman, Achiel, O.M.I. "La famille comme réalité ecclésiale." *Église et Théologie* 12 (1981): 95–114.

Perkins, Mary. *Beginning at Home: The Challenge of Christian Parenthood.* Collegeville, MN: Liturgical Press, 1955.

Pollard, John. "Leaders in the Domestic Church." *Momentum* 20 (April 1989): 19–21.

Potvin, Thomas. "La famille: Église domestique." *Prêtre et Pasteur* 83 (1980): 311–322.

Provencher, Normand, O.M.I. "The Family as Domestic Church" (condensed version). *Theology Digest* 30 (September 1982): 149–152.

———. "Vers une théologie de la famille: L'église domestique." *Église et Théologie* 12 (1981): 9–34.

Rahner, Karl. *The Church and the Sacraments.* New York, Herder & Herder, 1963.

———. *Foundations of Christian Faith.* New York Seabury Press, 1978.

———. "Marriage as a Sacrament." In *Theological Investigations,* 10: 199–221. New York: Seabury Press, 1977.

———. "The Sacramental Basis for the Role of the Layman in the Church." In *Theological Investigations,* 8: 51–74. New York: Seabury Press, 1977.

Raiser, Konrad. "Interchurch Marriages Shape an Ecumenical Space," *INTAMS Review* 6, no. 2 (Autumn 2000): 173–174.

Raja, R. J. "Structures of Mortar and Stone May Give Place to Family Gatherings and Domestic Church." *National Catholic Reporter* 21, no. 17 (November 30, 1984).

Redmond, Barbara Deveney. *The Domestic Church, Primary Agent of Moral Development.* Ph.D. diss., Boston College, Institute for Religious Education and Pastoral Ministry, 1998.

Roberts, J. Deotis. *Roots of a Black Future: Family and Church*. Philadelphia: Westminster Press, 1980.

Roberts, William. "The Family as Domestic Church: Contemporary Implications." In *Christian Marriage and Family: Contemporary Theological and Pastoral Perspectives*, ed. Michael Lawler and William Roberts, 79–90. Collegeville, MN: Liturgical Press, 1996.

———. "Theology of Christian Marriage." In *Alternative Futures for Worship: Christian Marriage*, ed. Bernard Cooke, 47–63. Collegeville, MN: Liturgical Press, 1987.

Rossi, Albert. "Pastors of the Domestic Church." *Liguorian* 82 (April 1994): 18–19.

Rubio, Julie Hanlon. "Does Family Conflict with Community?" *Theological Studies* vol. 58 (December 1997): 597–617.

Ruiz, M. R. "La familia como iglesia domestica." *Studium* 18 (1978): 321–332.

Smith, Karen Sue, and Sarah Randag. "Please Pass Down the Faith." *U.S. Catholic* 63, no. 11 (November 1998): 17–21.

Stackhouse, Max. *Covenant and Commitments: Faith, Family, and Economic Life*. Louisville, KY: Westminster/John Knox Press, 1997.

Stebbins, H. Lyman. *The Priesthood of the Laity in the Domestic Church*. Fairhaven, MA: National Enthronement Center, 1978.

Thomas, David. "Family Comes of Age in the Catholic Church." *Journal of Family Ministry* 12, no. 2 (Summer 1998): 38–51.

———. "Home Fires: Theological Reflections on the Family." In *The Changing Family*, ed. Stanley Saxton et al., 15–22.Chicago: Loyola University Press, 1984.

Thompson, Marjorie. *Family, The Forming Center*. Nashville, TN: Upper Room Books, 1989.

Trujillo, Alfonso. "The Family at the Center of New Evangelization." In *The Church at the Service of the Family*, ed. Anthony Mastroeni, 3–21. Steubenville, OH: Franciscan University Press, 1993. Proceedings of the Sixteenth Convention of the Fellowship of Catholic Scholars, Orange, CA, 1993.

Wagua, Prisca. "Pastoral Care for Incomplete Families: A Forgotten Ministry in Africa." *African Ecclesiastical Review* 38, no. 2 (April 1996): 114–124.

Whitehead, K. D. *Marriage and the Common Good. Proceedings of the Twenty-Second Convention of the Fellowship of Catholic Scholars*, Deerfield, IL, September 24–26, 1999. South Bend, IN: St. Augustine's Press, 2001.

Witte, John. *From Sacrament to Contract: Marriage, Religion, and Law in the Western Tradition*. Louisville, KY: Westminster/John Knox Press, 1997.

Wright, Wendy. *Sacred Dwelling: A Spirituality of Family Life*. New York: Crossroad, 1989.

INDEX

adoption, 81, 92

Aquinas, Thomas, Saint, 20, 74, 97, 99, 120, 125, 127–130, 132, 143, 144, 154, 157

annulment, 71

Augustine, Saint, 10, 27, 57

Baltimore Catechism, 6, 7, 41

baptism, 4, 11, 13, 27–29, 36, 42, 44, 58, 66, 69–86, 112, 117, 128, 130, 131, 134

Bernardin, Joseph Cardinal, 21, 141–149, 151, 154–157

Bible
  Acts, 10
  Colossians, 8, 9
  1 Corinthians, 8, 9
  Ephesians, 9, 10, 11, 77
  family imagery, 9, 65, 114
  family/married life in biblical times, 9, 87–88
  house churches discussed, 9, 84, 113
  household conversions, 10
  Isaiah, 65
  John, Gospel of, 133
  1 John, 128
  Leviticus, 88
  Mark, Gospel of, 88
  Matthew, Gospel of, 10, 75, 88, 128
  Philemon, 9
  Proverbs, 88
  Romans, 9
  Son of Songs, 88
  2 Timothy, 9

birth control, 14, 25, 149, 158

bishops, 17, 19, 26, 32, 35, 89, 94, 110, 113, 147–149, 155
  compared to head of household, 10, 12, 27
  1980 Synod of Bishops, 13

catechesis, 17, 40, 43, 44, 75, 109, 114, 122

Catechism of the Catholic Church, 13, 72, 125, 129

celibacy, 7, 18, 19, 37, 50

charity, 35, 59, 120, 127–129, 132, 133, 135, 146, 149, 154

child/childhood, 5, 6, 8, 9, 11, 17, 24, 36, 43–48, 54, 55, 61, 62, 67, 69, 71, 72, 76–79, 81–86, 88–93, 104–108, 114, 119, 120, 122–123, 127, 129, 130, 133, 135, 137, 138, 149, 152
  adult children, 47, 65, 75, 81, 89, 106
  childless families, 77, 81
  children of God, 49, 79, 92

Chrysostom, John, Saint, 10, 27, 76

Church
  as body of Christ, 1, 18, 23, 25, 26, 95, 112
  Church Universal, 21, 26, 27, 31, 32, 33, 34, 36, 42, 77, 83, 84, 85
  domestic church as sacrament, 102, 108, 113
  as family, 12, 13, 15, 44, 116
  local church, 13, 27, 28, 32, 33, 34, 35, 110, 115, 116
  as mother, 73, 116, 132
  as sacrament, 21, 26, 32, 33, 35, 95, 97, 99–101, 107, 111, 117, 121, 130

FLORENCE CAFFREY BOURG is assistant professor in the Department of Religious and Pastoral Studies at the College of Mount Saint Joseph in Cincinnati, Ohio.